A PASSION FOR THE TRUE AND JUST

A Passion for the True and Just

Felix and Lucy Kramer Cohen and the Indian New Deal

ALICE BECK KEHOE

THE UNIVERSITY OF
ARIZONA PRESS

TUCSON

The University of Arizona Press
www.uapress.arizona.edu

Printed in the United States of America
21   20   19   18   17   16   7   6   5   4   3   2

ISBN-13: 978-0-8165-3093-9 (cloth)
ISBN-13: 978-0-8165-3290-2 (paper)

Cover design by Lori Lieber Graphic Design, Inc.
Cover photos: (front) Lucy and Felix with unidentified Indian friends, ca. 1937; (back left) Felix and Lucy hiking in the forest, photos courtesy of the Felix S. and Lucy Kramer Cohen Photograph Collection; (back right) Secretary of Interior Harold Ickes with delegates of the Confederated Tribes of the Flathead Indian Reservation (Montana), photo courtesy of Library of Congress.

The phrase "A passion for the true and just" is attributed to John Collier, 1953, and appears in *Indian Affairs and the Indian Reorganization Act: The Twenty Year Record*, ed. William H. Kelly. Tucson: University of Arizona Press, 1954. The full quotation appears on the dedication page to this volume.

Library of Congress Cataloging-in-Publication Data
Kehoe, Alice Beck, 1934–
 A passion for the true and just : Felix and Lucy Kramer Cohen and the Indian New Deal / Alice Beck Kehoe.
    p. cm.
 Includes bibliographical references and index.
 ISBN 978-0-8165-3093-9 (hardback)
 1. Cohen, Felix S., 1907–1953. 2. Cohen, Lucy Kramer, 1907–2007. 3. Indians of North America—Government relations—1934– 4. Indians of North America—Legal status, laws, etc. 5. New Deal, 1933–1939. 6. Commandments (Judaism) 7. Antisemitism—United States—History—20th century. 8. United States. Indian Reorganization Act. 9. United States. Bureau of Indian Affairs—Officials and employees—Biography. 10. United States—Politics and government—1933–1945. I. Title.
 E93.K24 2014
 323.1197—dc23

                        2013039495

♾ This paper meets the requirements of ANSI/NISO Z39.48-1992 (Permanence of Paper).

"An interest in the Indian can be symbolical of, or instrumental toward, interest of far greater scope. Felix Cohen had a world wide passion for the true and the just."
— *John Collier, December 1953, dedicating the symposium to Felix Cohen, who had died less than three months earlier*

Contents

Illustrations

Figures

Acknowledgments

Years after reading Ken Philp's publication of the 1983 symposium on the Indian Reorganization Act, I looked at it again and noticed that Mrs. Felix Cohen had been a student of Franz Boas. John Collier, the famous Commissioner of Indian Affairs promoting the 1934 Indian Reorganization Act, had stated in his autobiography that anthropologists had not contributed to the preparation of the radical landmark act. Historians seemed to take him at his word. Did Mrs. Cohen have no influence on her husband's work drafting and implementing the act? What had happened to Lucy Kramer Cohen, a Barnard graduate (like me) and a student of Boas?

Seeking information on this woman, I was able, thanks to a suggestion from the late anthropologist Mel Ember, to contact her daughters and through them, her niece Nancy Kramer Bickel. Bickel was preparing a DVD on her aunt's life, using family records and a video interview she had filmed in 2000. Bickel called her film A *Twentieth Century Woman*, for Lucy Kramer, 1907–2007, was very much a modern American woman taking advantage of slowly developing opportunities. Bickel's unstinting generosity, abetted by her cousins Gene Cohen Tweraser and Karen Cohen Holmes, in sharing her material and discussing our subject illuminated the Indian New Deal from a perspective quite different from collections of official documents and formal memos. Access to Lucy's papers deposited in 2010 in Yale's Beinecke Library confirmed my suspicions that she had played a significant role in the Indian New Deal, and that contrary to Collier's statement, Boas had influenced it through his students.

Not only had *cherchez la femme* broadened the horizon of the Indian New Deal, I was seeing Felix Cohen in a new light. He made me think of my own father, Roman Beck, 1904–1992, a Jewish lawyer educated in New York who had taken a position in Roosevelt's New Deal, with the National Labor Relations Board. I knew the liberal Social Democrat secular patriotic Jewish Americans of my parents' and the Cohens' circles. On my bookshelf is my dad's copy of Felix Frankfurter's autobiography. Of course my father and his lawyer friends did not match Felix Cohen's extraordinary brilliance (nor his height), and my mother accepted a bourgeois homemaker role that would not satisfy Lucy Kramer (to be fair to my mother, her family had not permitted her to attend college, while Lucy's family pushed her to enroll in Barnard). The more I read about the Cohens, and the more critically I read the Indian Reorganization Act, the *Handbook of Federal Indian Law*, and Cohen's many papers, the more I sensed that Jewish culture of his and my parents' generation. They accepted Rabbi Hillel's admonition, that basic mitzvah, that we must do what we can to help our fellow humans. In that they were, and knew themselves to be, Jewish. It matters.

Following Felix Cohen's life from his privileged boyhood as the son of a leading philosopher to his first real job as Assistant Solicitor at the Department of the Interior, thanks to one of his father's pupils, and his introduction to Indian people as Collier campaigned to get his radical act accepted, clarified Cohen's work. The Indian Reorganization Act was gutted to its bare skeleton before it passed Congress, and what did pass was Collier's main goal, revocation of dispossessing Indians of their land. Cohen's idea of an Indian court system was thrown out. Collier had no intention of surrendering any real power over his bureau's wards. He accepted limited municipality-like local government on reservations, with his bureau holding veto power over local acts.[1] I think working with tribes to implement this formal step toward limited governance opened Cohen's eyes to Indian reality, while his adroit legal mind let him and his boss Nathan Margold push envelopes to the utmost.

As I thought out these insights, I benefited very substantially from assistance and discussions with Nancy Bickel and her cousins Gene Cohen Tweraser and Karen Cohen Holmes, Dalia Tsuk, Cohen's legal-scholar biographer, and Mark Thiel, archivist at my own university, Marquette. Mark was trained by Fr. Francis Paul Prucha, professor of history at Marquette and principal historian of US Indian policies. Fr. Prucha's always gracious and generous friendship has been a privilege. Nancy O. Lurie, distinguished anthropologist, is the other senior scholar here in Milwaukee able and kindly willing to answer and expand upon my queries. David Reed Miller, Arthur J. Ray, and John Strong are ethnohistorian colleagues who have sharpened my understanding for years.

To my disappointment, I could find no one still alive on the Montana Blackfeet Reservation who knew their legal counsel from 1949 to 1953, Felix Cohen. Although even George Pambrun's daughter didn't recall Felix Cohen being spoken of, the decades I've been visiting the rez have materially contributed to this study. Being there, in Indian Country, is critical to comprehending US Indian policies, seeing what happens to my friends' projects and lives. I was very fortunate in happening, in my first job out of Barnard, to land on the territory of the Amskapi Pikuni, the Blackfeet Nation, and be able to know so many there, from *inawa'sioskitsip*—"leader-hearted"—national figures including Earl Old Person, Darrell Robes Kipp, and the late Elouise Cobell, to more local leaders including Carol Tatsey Murray, John Murray, Dr. Dorothy Still Smoking, Linda Matt Juneau, Dr. Rosalyn La Pier, David Dragonfly, Fred and Ramona DesRosier and their family, Lea Whitford and her colleagues on the Blackfeet Community College faculty, Darrell Norman, and perhaps most significantly, my collaborator on the history of the Amskapi Pikuni," Stewart E. Miller. Stew, like Felix Cohen, was a thoroughly admirable man who died much too young. *Oki*, my Pikuni friends.

Finally, this book was made possible by a stipend from Yale's Beinecke Library, in November 2010, to research Lucy Kramer Cohen's papers. The collegiality of the history and anthropological archaeology departments made the month very pleasant, and it was gratifying to be invited to present this research on the Cohens at the 2011 Lamar Conference, hosted by Yale's history department.

Alice Kehoe
Milwaukee, Wisconsin
June 2013

A PASSION FOR THE TRUE AND JUST

Introduction

A T-shirt sold on Indian reservations is emblazoned "Battling Terrorism Since 1492." It could as well be sold in synagogues: Columbus sailed out of Palos harbor in the wake of the last of the ships transporting Spain's Jews into exile, and their confiscated wealth financed his voyage (Roth [1932] 1966:271–72; Uchmany 2001:187). Jews and American Indians share a history of persecution from Christian nations. That, and the Jewish mitzvah—obligation—to help the less fortunate led several American Jews to work toward, and then within, the Indian New Deal. Their role has not been emphasized in histories of this major shift in US Indian policy. It is the argument of this book that the blatant anti-Semitism of the 1930s downplayed the critical contributions of these men and one woman.

Focusing on Felix Cohen, a brilliant legal scholar who wrote the legislation of the Indian New Deal, and his anthropologist wife, Lucy Kramer, this book brings forward their involvement and contextualizes it. Although America in the 1930s accepted open discrimination against Jews, Franklin Roosevelt insisted on recruiting the best men, and even women, to his New Deal. The story of the Indian New Deal reflects revolutions not only in the status of American Indians but also of American Jews. Beyond the Indian New Deal, Cohen's construction of the concept of inherent sovereignty for America's "domestic dependent nations" became part of the foundation of the international movement for indigenous rights, culminating in the 2007 United Nations Declaration on the Rights of Indigenous People (Wiessner 2008:1145, n. 26).

Because I am an anthropologist, I see actors in history constrained or empowered by the cultures in which they live. My experience as an Ashkenazi Jewish American whose parents were contemporaries of the Cohens—my father a lawyer employed in the New Deal (National Labor Relations Board), and my ethnographic fieldwork with American First Nations including the Montana Blackfeet for whom Cohen had been legal counsel—informs my reading of historical documents. Looking at the formal public presentation of the Indian New Deal in 1934, I see that what was meant to be a startling reversal of federal Indian policy reflected a decade of change set in motion after World War I. International yearning for a peaceful and just world was epitomized by Woodrow Wilson's call for a "general association of nations . . . formed on the basis of covenants designed to create mutual guarantees of the political independence and territorial integrity of States, large and small equally" (Wilson 1918).

Three constituencies in the United States overlapped around 1930: the hegemonic Protestant Christians, Ashkenazi immigrants' children rapidly rising into middle-class acceptability, and American First Nations regaining population after their late nineteenth-century nadir. All three were buffeted by the Great Depression economic breakdown. The Indian New Deal is more than a narrative of crusading John Collier persuading Congress to pass his bill endorsed by Senator Burton Wheeler and Representative Edgar Howard. It is part of American cultural history. Its three protagonists are Collier, from Southern and Puritan aristocracies; Felix Cohen and his wife Lucy, New York–born children of Social Democrat Jews from eastern Europe; and Harold Ickes, astute Chicago politician working for Midwest Progressive principles at the top of Roosevelt's administration. The three men formed a troika, each critical to the success of the Indian New Deal.

Chapter 1 introduces the background to the 1934 Indian New Deal. Its predecessors ranged from Thomas Jefferson, who as president worked up a plan to dispossess Indians by luring them into debt and taking land as payment, through President, formerly General, Grant's "Peace Policy" of final military conquests, to the turn-of-the-century Dawes Act which divided reservations up into small farms and sold off "surplus" land. After that nadir of contempt for Indians, a rebound of Indian population in the twentieth century, coupled with Indians' admirable service in World War I, brought US citizenship to American-born Indians and growing realization that Christianizing-and-civilizing policies had been harsh failures. President Hoover's acceptance of the Meriam Report in 1928 was the beginning of the shift carried through in the Roosevelt administration. Already in 1923, the socially well-connected John Collier had organized the American Indian Defense Association to mobilize liberal Americans to free Indians from stringent federal control. A decade later, Collier became Commissioner of Indian Affairs in the New Deal. His rival for the position, Harold Ickes, had caught Roosevelt's ear and gained a higher appointment, Secretary of Interior, the department in which Indian Affairs is located.

Chapter 2 details the Indian Reorganization Act (IRA) of 1934, also termed the Wheeler-Howard Act after its congressional sponsors. This landmark legislation reversed the policy of dispossessing Indians of tribal lands, and it presented a road to economic sustenance on reservations through chartering tribal councils as business corporations. What the IRA did not do was end wardship status of Indian tribes. Felix Cohen's father had published a classic article distinguishing property from sovereignty (see chapter 5). Felix's first year with the Office of Indian Affairs opened his eyes to the fundamental problem of how far Indian nations' sovereignty might extend.

Chapter 3 sets the scene for Felix Cohen's activities during the 1930s. For the first time in US history, the election of Franklin Roosevelt brought Jews into the top levels of the executive branch. In the desperate circumstances of the Great Depression, Roosevelt would not countenance passing over highly qualified personnel because they were Jews. Brokering the breakthrough was Felix Cohen's namesake, Harvard law professor Felix Frankfurter. Anti-Semitism had been taken for granted. Now brilliant young Jews such as Nathan Margold and Felix Cohen, eager to work for social justice, were given significant opportunities.

Chapter 4 tells the stories of Felix Cohen and Lucy Kramer, their background and recruitment to the Office of Indian Affairs, and their work there. As the story moves into 1936, the Nazi threat to Jews spurred Morris Cohen to organize prominent American Jews, including Franz Boas, to try to save those in Germany. One proposal was to bring Jewish families to colonize Alaska. Secretary of Interior Ickes favored that means of developing Alaska and assigned Felix Cohen to work it up into a bill for Congress. It didn't pass.

Chapter 5 moves into Felix Cohen's triumph, the *Handbook of Federal Indian Law*. His biographer, Dalia Tsuk, titled Cohen the "architect of justice," appropriately conveying how he built a legal edifice to support First Nations' rights. Underlying his edifice is Franz Boas's teaching of historical particularism and cultural relativism, anthropological principles justifying First Nations' claims to sovereignty over their own people. Ignoring Indians' adult competencies, the United States and Canada had applied "coercive tutelage" to the American nations they overcame, teaching them that assimilation to Anglo society was their only path to survival. In the year of Felix Cohen's untimely death, 1953, Congress passed Public Law 280, which intended to terminate Indians' special status, shifting federal responsibilities under treaties to the states.

Chapter 6 concerns the third of Cohen's trilogy of works meant to establish justice for American Indians, the Indian Claims Commission Act. Cast in a standard adversarial Anglo legal framework and prepared to make only monetary awards, not land, for successful claims, the commission could not resolve the deep grievances impelling most of the claims. Margold, Cohen, and Ickes had died by the time the commission was fully activated. Its principal achievement was to change historiography dealing with American First Nations. Calling upon many anthropologists to research and testify, cases brought in a range of data not usually collected or consulted by historians. A new discipline, ethnohistory, developed to employ this breadth of material.

Chapter 7 leaves the Indian New Deal to fill in the background of anti-Semitism endured by Felix and Lucy Cohen and their friends. I argue that what has been omitted from histories of the Indian New Deal is Margold and the Cohens' commitment to Social Democrat "revolution through the ballot box" and the intellectualism inculcated by their Ashkenazi immigrant families. Felix's father, Morris Raphael Cohen, called his generation's emigration an epic quest. Their children's professional success and safe middle-class life was their goal achieved, yet even these children were segregated in housing, in recreation, in employment, and under quotas in schools.

Chapter 8 delves into conflicts let loose by the IRA's push for tribal constitutions and business charters. Worry that these were a foreign culture's instruments and that Congress would not appropriate enough money for lengthy in-depth studies of existing First Nations' governance traditions provoked Collier to curtail such studies in favor of quickly written model constitutions. Felix and Lucy Cohen's experiences visiting Indian reservations after the IRA passed awakened Felix to the continued paternalism in the Office of Indian Affairs.

Chapter 9 looks at the years following Felix Cohen's resignation from the Department of the Interior, when he worked for a law firm that allowed him to develop a practice in Washington focusing on Indian claims. His friend and former colleague Ted Haas was involved at this time in a landmark Supreme Court case, *Tee-Hit-Ton Indians v. United States*, in which the majority justices decided against the Indians, stating "every

American schoolboy knows that the savage tribes of this continent" lost their lands by "conquerors' will." "Every American schoolboy" had more force, for this 1955 Court, than Cohen's *Handbook of Federal Indian Law.*

Chapter 10 concerns the concept of sovereignty, central to First Nations' assertion of rights under their treaties. Felix's father, Morris, had published a landmark legal discussion distinguishing sovereignty from the power of property owners in Anglo law. This chapter illustrates, with a description of the Montana Blackfeet, how limited Indian sovereignty was under the Office of Indian Affairs. Felix Cohen was legal counsel to the Blackfeet during his last few years. After his death, another Jewish American born in 1907, Sol Tax, began what he termed "Action Anthropology," working with Indians in the roles of resource person and advocate. Tax organized the 1961 American Indian Chicago Conference, similar to Collier's 1934 congresses except that instead of selling a top-down program to the delegates, Tax facilitated discussions among them, leading to their formal declaration of Indian goals. The Chicago Conference admitted participants from federally unrecognized Indian nations, groups denied by Collier. The chapter closes with the issue of who are Indians—not only the issue of percentage of "Indian blood," or performing native culture, but the fundamental issue raised by historian Roger Echo-Hawk, member of the Pawnee Nation: if race is a sociopolitical construct, not biological fact, then Echo-Hawk can reject being "Indian." His nation is a confederacy of the Chaui, Pitahawirata, Skidi, and Kitkehahki, called "Pawnee Indians" only in the nineteenth century when confronted by the encroaching United States.

Chapter 11 situates the Cohens' "passion for the true and the just" that Collier eulogized for Felix, against the mid-twentieth-century *scientistic*— not scientific—search for universal laws of human behavior that could be used to control citizens. Against this naïve and antidemocratic goal, Felix developed principles of legal realism to make laws and jurisprudence relate to social conditions and human needs. Morris' and Felix's work toward legal realism reflects the Judaic obligation to act morally, that is, to resist and correct injustice and to use one's talents to help others. Their view rejects legal ideals of elegant rhetoric and cold logic admired by some of America's intellectual Brahmins.

Chapter 12 concludes the book by reviewing the issue of sovereignty. "Settler sovereignty," subsumed under "settler colonialism," developed in the nineteenth century in former Anglo colonies from settlers' recognition of two sovereignties, indigenous and theirs, each with jurisdiction only over its own members. As indigenous people were dispossessed of their land, settlers demanded sovereignty over everyone in a territory. Against this realpolitik, Cohen's *Handbook* upholds his argument that treaties still stand in law, recognizing Indian nations' inherent sovereignty. The chapter also notes that racism remains active around Indian reservations today.

Some readers may be puzzled by my anthropological style. Congruent with our technique of participant observation, anthropologists use the discourse "method of apt illustration" (Gluckman 1961:7) to forward an argument. In this mode, general statements are supported by, and vivified with, cases observed in the field. Superficially, the discourse may appear to be rambling anecdotes, at least to students accustomed to syllogistic presentations. Case law is the better comparison, and not by accident, for the anthropologist who articulated our method of apt illustration, Max Gluckman, came from a legal background and taught his students to assemble their ethnographic data in terms of extended cases.

In this book, I draw upon my decades of research and participant observation with American First Nations. Readers can obtain more information and background from my textbook *North American Indians: A Comprehensive Account* (Kehoe 2006b). Overall, the present book juxtaposes two histories seldom merged, that of the Indian New Deal and that of Jews in twentieth-century America. It should not be surprising to find overlap between these histories of peoples persecuted since 1492.

Note: It may be slightly confusing that sometimes the agency within the Department of the Interior responsible for Indians is called the Office of Indian Affairs, sometimes the Bureau of Indian Affairs; the title shifted.

CHAPTER ONE

The Indian New Deal

The Indian New Deal in Franklin Roosevelt's administration was an extraordinary about-face in US policy, a radical acknowledgment of injustice and historical untruths. Credit for this critical shift is conventionally given to Roosevelt's commissioner of Indian Affairs, the crusading John Collier. Collier spoke passionately about Indians' rights to preserve their cultures and practice their religions. As commissioner, he implemented moves to shift Indian children from English-language boarding schools into local day schools with indigenous-language primers, to create elected tribal business councils for managing reservation economies, and to restore Indian land to the tribes. John Collier was the effective spokesman for the Indian New Deal and the administrator for its policies. He was not the power behind the Indian New Deal, nor its architect: Harold Ickes was the former, and Felix Cohen was the latter.

Collier the Crusader fits a conventional scenario, one man's courageous fight against entrenched oppression. In the 1930s America wasn't ready to see a Jewish man in a crusader's cape. *Time* magazine ran an article in May 1934 detailing how few Jews served in Roosevelt's administration, mostly as "bright young legalites to do spade work for the Brain Trust" ("National Affairs" 1934). Harold Ickes hired them, going so far as to name one, Nathan Margold, Solicitor for the Department of the Interior, and Margold hired another, Felix Cohen, as an assistant solicitor in Interior. Ickes was too astute a politician to appear in a crusader's cape. He termed himself a "curmudgeon," deflecting attention away from his deep commitment to Progressive principles. Felix Cohen and his anthropologist wife

9

Figure 1.1. Secretary of Interior Harold Ickes handing the first constitution issued under the Indian Reorganization Act to delegates of the Confederated Tribes of the Flathead Indian Reservation (Montana). Photo from Library of Congress.

Figure 1.2. Nathan Margold. Image provided by Worth Mentioning Public Relations (William Margold).

Figure 1.3. Felix Cohen. Photo courtesy of the Felix S. and Lucy Kramer Cohen
Photograph Collection.

and collaborator, Lucy Kramer, were further to the left: they were card-carrying members of the Socialist Party of the USA.[1] Critics of the Indian New Deal charged that it was trying to "make Reds of the red men." There was substance to the charge.

Behind the Cohens' allegiance to socialism lies the European Social Democrat movement, popular among Ashkenazi Jews. The movement was socialist, not Bolshevik, fitting well into Talmudic principles attributed to the great sage Rabbi Hillel: "If I am not for myself, then who will be for me? And if I am only for myself, then what am I? And if not now, when?" and, "That which is hateful to you, do not do to your neighbor. That is the whole Torah."[2] These profound injunctions can be considered a mitzvah, that is, a commandment, to work for social justice. It is in this sense that Felix Cohen's work on the Indian New Deal may be seen as a mitzvah.

Harold Ickes, descended from Protestant American families that settled in western Pennsylvania in the eighteenth century, came to a similar moral imperative from Presbyterian strictures heightened by childhood poverty and his struggle for a college education at the University of Chicago. Cohen described Ickes as he observed him "during the past 10 years of rough and tumble political work under a boss [Ickes] who has never allowed the slightest glimmer of high idealism to appear in any speech and who has, nevertheless, done more good things than any less curmudgeonly member of the President's Cabinet."[3]

These two men of such different backgrounds and lives, one a tall athletic intellectual from immigrant Jewish parents settled in New York City, the other a short Chicago politician embroiled in a tumultuous marriage to an heiress, shared a drive to emancipate America's "domestic dependent nations" from its harsh yoke.[4] Neither man, in contrast to Collier, entertained a romantic notion of Indians as nature's pure primitives. It was a crying need for justice that sustained them, justice that their legal skills could bring within reach.

In this book, I describe each member of Interior's triumvirate, Ickes, Collier, and Felix Cohen, the history of federal Indian policy and of the First Nations governed by it, and the Indian New Deal. I pay attention to the indirect influence of Franz Boas through his student Lucy Kramer Cohen. Her substantial unrecompensed work on the Indian Reorganization Act of 1934 and the *Handbook of Federal Indian Law* can now be documented in her personal papers, archived after a life spanning not quite a century. The conventional story of the Indian New Deal featuring Collier has the mythic proportions of a crusader's quest. Adding an appreciation of the Chicago curmudgeon's consummate political skill and the

Cohens' Jewish liberal principles turns a red-and-white picture into a richly colored tapestry. My anthropological training prompts me to delineate cultural patterns seldom explicitly voiced in documents, what Pierre Bourdieu (1977:78) termed *habitus*, a society's conception of reality expressed through its language and metaphors. Anti-Semitism in the 1930s affected acknowledgment of Jews' roles in the Indian New Deal while it spurred those Americanized Jews to embrace a modern secular life. Their habitus nevertheless incorporated ethos and discourse patterns experienced growing up in immigrant Ashkenazi families. Intersecting with Collier's privileged WASP romanticism and Ickes's Progressive principles, Felix Cohen and his supervisor at Interior, Nathan Margold, carried liberal Jewish Social Democrat ideals into the crafting of the Indian New Deal.

The Indian Old Deal

Franklin Roosevelt's promise to give America a "New Deal" excited a wide range of reformers. Among them were citizens urging respect for American Indians. Although Indians had been given citizenship in 1924, largely in recognition of their valor in World War I, they still were considered wards of the federal government. Chief Justice John Marshall had declared in 1831, in *Cherokee Nation v. Georgia*, that with the United States, Indians had a relationship "perhaps unlike that of any other two people in existence," for they were "domestic dependent nations" whose members were as "a ward to his guardian" (quoted in Prucha 1986:76). Marshall's trio of Supreme Court decisions, *Johnson v. McIntosh* (1823), *Cherokee Nation v. Georgia* (1831), and *Worcester v. Georgia* (1832), ironically protected First Nations against rapacious states while establishing the foundation for their subordination to federal domination.

Initially, the United States inherited and continued the British practice of negotiating treaties with Indian nations. Until after the Civil War, there was no real alternative; Indian nations could and did fight wars along their frontiers and massacre trespassing whites. Once a treaty was signed, clauses that Indians usually believed to give usufruct rights to US citizens were generally interpreted by the federal government to have ceded possession of territory. A surprising number of treaties completed in the field were never ratified by the US Congress, with no notification to the Indian signatories that the treaty was therefore invalid. Congress finally declared, in 1871, that it no longer would entertain treaties with the by-then emasculated Indian nations.

When the Civil War ended, the federal government commanded one of the largest and best-equipped armies in history. President Grant, its field commander during the war, used it for his "Peace Policy," a simple one that called for military conquest of all surviving American Indian nations, and when they were defeated, then there would be peace.[5] In line with deploying his army, Grant built forts in contested territories and appointed military officers as agents to the Indians. Deviation from obedience to the government's agents would be punished with "all needed severity" (Prucha 1986:153, quoting Grant's secretary of the interior). Openly promoting a policy of Christianization, Grant's administration apportioned the Indian reservations among Christian mission enterprises, supporting their schools designed to Christianize the Indians. This was expected to save the federal government money, as the Christian churches were to share costs. The result was chronically underfunded Indian schools, where children's labor was called upon to maintain facilities and provide food.

Negotiating treaties had an ugly underbelly. Thomas Jefferson, like fellow Virginia plantation owners such as George Washington, was acutely aware that appropriating Indian lands was the easiest path to wealth, not so much by developing agribusinesses upon them as by land speculation, buying huge tracts cheaply and selling plots in them to homesteaders. The United States followed British precedent in claiming preemption right to Indian lands. That is, the government and the government alone could buy Indians' land; no private person or state might do so. Preemption rests upon the Doctrine of Discovery in international law, the right to land accruing to the nation (via its agent such as Columbus) that first discovers territory not inhabited by a Christian citizenry. The British Crown thereby claimed all of North America north of Spanish conquests. It is still so recognized in Canada, while after the American Revolution the US federal government took over claims for what became US territory. By selling tracts of ceded Indian lands, the government obtained money sufficient to repay all its Revolutionary War debts and then the bank loans for the Louisiana Purchase (Miller 2008:96). Transactions on such a scale favored dealing with speculators interested in brokering thousands of acres, rather than selling subsistence plots to individual farmers. Until the 1920s, the United States considered taking over land from Indians to be its obligation to its citizens.

Where should the Indians go? George Washington and Thomas Jefferson saw clearly that they should retreat ever westward. Britain had attempted to halt colonists at the crest of the Appalachians, a boundary that would protect Britain's fur trade. Americans had challenged that boundary and, as an independent United States, intended to take over the lush valleys of the Midwest. With the Louisiana Purchase, even the Mississippi River would not constrain colonists. Jefferson formulated US Indian policy in 1803, during his first term as president: the United States would take Indian land, by treaty cession or purchase, or in payment for debts incurred in the federal government's trading posts in Indian territory. Indians would move west beyond colonization settlement. Assimilation into Euro-American society was supposed to be an alternative to removal, but Indian nations that did adopt "civilized" clothing, farming, and commerce (notably the Southeast's "Five Civilized Tribes"—Cherokee, Choctaw, Chickasaw, Creek, and Seminole) became business competitors as well as landowners, targets for removal along with so-called savage nations.

Indian Affairs was administered through the War Department until 1849, when President Polk created a Department of the Interior to direct agencies dealing with land usage and patents. Transferring Indian Affairs to that new department seemed sensible in the year after the United States' conquest of Mexican territories brought it across the continent to the Pacific. It is telling that the United States had a Department of State beginning in 1789 to deal with foreign nations, with Jefferson its first Secretary of State. Logically, because Indian Affairs managed "dependent nations" allied through treaties, the bureau should have been under the State Department. Keeping it in the War Department and then, with international recognition of US territory completed from sea to sea, placing it within Interior mutely signified the government's attitude toward First Nations. They were enemies to be conquered until the balance of military power, backed by Western international law, weighed decisively against them. Once the United States reached its Manifest Destiny (a Mexican War slogan), its nearly illimitable lands and all resources therein should be administered by a Department of the Interior.

Practically, not much changed in 1849. Military officers on the internal frontiers acted as Indian agents throughout the nineteenth century. After the post–Civil War final defeats of Indian nations, reservation agencies became dumping grounds for incompetent, frequently alcoholic or drug-addicted, army officers, "always called 'the Major,'" Clark Wissler ([1938] 1971:13) reported. "His duty was to keep these Indians from alarming settlers by wandering abroad, and to feed, clothe, and house them upon an inadequate budget" (23).

Along with the military paterfamilias on the reservations, Indians were forced to accept missionaries and farming instructors. In 1850, after the Department of the Interior was established, its commissioner of Indian Affairs announced that the Indian must be

> controlled and finally compelled by sheer necessity to resort to agricultural labor or starve. . . . It is only under such circumstances that his haughty pride can be subdued. . . . There should be assigned to each tribe . . . a country . . . of limited extent and well-defined boundaries, within which all, with occasional exception, should be compelled constantly to remain until such time as their general improvement and good conduct may supersede the necessity of such restrictions. (quoted in Prucha 1986:112–13)

A few years later, the next commissioner of Indian Affairs changed the usual terms of treaties to allow money stipulated to be paid to the territory-ceding Indians to be applied to "their moral improvement and education" and for tools, farm development, and whatever "will be calculated to advance them in civilization" (Prucha 1986:115). Thus Indian nations were excluded from the US capitalist money economy. Annuities agreed to in the treaties were applied to salaries, buildings, and supplies given to Euro-American agents.

"Kill the Indian and save the child" was the most heartrending aspect of US policy toward Indians. Children as young as four or five were literally torn from weeping mothers' arms, piled into wagons, taken to boarding schools, their clothing stripped, hair cut, bodies scrubbed, put into uniforms, and set to manual labor and domestic chores. Native languages and religious practices were sternly forbidden. Some boarding schools were on reservations where parents might visit one day a month, while the ideal was to keep Indian children away from their families until adulthood. Toward this end, many schools were off the reservation, even a thousand or more miles distant, and during school holidays the children were placed with Euro-American families as farm or household help. In this way, Indian children might become strangers to their people, ignorant of their language, beliefs, customs, and history. Racism in the dominant society prevented these young people from assimilating as had been desired. They perforce returned to their reservations to try to earn a living by their manual skills. Their long years in the boarding schools had provided minimal academic education, inadequate for entrance into colleges, West Point, or engineering. Despite the clear ability of a few Indians who achieved professional status, such as Dr. Charles Eastman (a Dakota) or Brigadier Gen-

eral Ely Parker (a Seneca Iroquois on General Grant's Civil War headquarter staff and then commissioner of Indian Affairs during Grant's
presidency), the myth persisted that Indians were a lower race needing to
evolve through a peasant farming stage before their descendants might be
capable of academic learning.

Allotment of reservation lands was the culminating outrage of the
United States against its "domestic dependent nations." Jefferson held
out to his compatriots the ideal of the "yeoman farmer," supposedly the
backbone of Anglo-Saxon (English) society. Yeomen were smallholders
operating their farms with the labor of their families and servants. Their
enterprise provided household subsistence plus surplus or goods sold for
cash. Yeoman farmers were literate without aspiring to advanced learning. For Jefferson, a nation built upon such a citizenry close to nature,
owning land and tools to support families, able to read newspapers and
political tracts, would be a true republic. Not that Jefferson himself was
a yeoman; he was an aristocrat recklessly spending far more than his
plantation slaves could produce. America preferred the ideology of an
agrarian republic rather than frank acknowledgment of ruthless land
speculators and factories employing thousands of young women at low
wages. Agrarian ideology promoted ending the "Indian problem" by allotting reservation lands to their residents as small farms. No other way
of shoving Indians into the next evolutionary stage could be offered,
because the 1862 Homestead Act applied only to US citizens, and few
Indians were citizens prior to Congress granting them citizenship in
1924.

Settling Indian couples and their children onto their own little farms
instead of continuing a communal life was expected to motivate them to
work hard to improve their farms, paralleling the enterprise of citizen
homesteaders.[6] For Indians' ultimate good, Congress in 1887 passed the
Dawes General Allotment Act (named after a senator) enabling the federal
government to survey reservations into 160-acre quarter sections, the same
as a basic homestead under the 1862 Homestead Act, and allot them to
individual Indians as patents good for twenty-five years. At the end of that
time, an Indian would be given fee simple title to his or her allotment and
would receive citizenship. During the twenty-five years of the patent, the
Indian agent had power over it because the land was still in trust. Agents'
power over an allotment could be extended beyond the twenty-five years if
the agent said the Indian was not yet competent to hold fee simple (independent ownership).

Incredible as it may seem, no provision was made in the Dawes Act for allotting land to Indians not yet born when reservations were surveyed. In consequence, allotments were divided up among the original family's heirs, generation after generation, leaving no one with sufficient land to work with. Furthermore, agents during the twenty-five-year patent period and longer customarily leased allotments to non-Indians—ranchers, miners, oil drillers. Lease fees were often below market levels, and the money went through the Bureau of Indian Affairs into the federal government's General Treasury. Indian allotment holders received little, were not furnished financial statements, could not object to the leaser, and tended to be told to pay taxes on land they got nothing from. Worst of all, after a survey created 160-acre plots for every enrolled Indian of the survey date, unallotted reservation land was declared surplus to be sold to non-Indians. A decade after passage of the Dawes Act, half of Indian lands had been sold off.

The Dawes Act was implemented beginning in the 1890s, with many reservations not allotted until a decade or more into the twentieth century, since allotment required not only land survey and plotting but also establishing a tribal roll through census documenting residents' degree of tribal parentage. Twenty-five years after a reservation was allotted, the time when fee simple titles should have been obtained, could be the 1920s or early 1930s. Indians were then already citizens, a significant number were army veterans, and most spoke English. That generation could see the blatant mismanagement of reservations brought to a head when allottees, if still alive, were supposed to get title. In parallel, that generation of non-Indian "friends of the Indian" organizations saw the mistake of their predecessors who had believed that allotment in severalty would benefit Indian families. The 1920s commissioner of Indian Affairs engaged the independent, Rockefeller-financed Institute for Government Research to study the condition of American Indians and recommend improvements. Lewis Meriam, leader of the project, completed the report, *The Problem of Indian Administration*, in 1928. Meriam's staff urged professional planning in the Office of Indian Affairs, as well as more money for programs to upgrade education, health care, and economic development on reservations. President Hoover responded positively to the Meriam Report, increasing Indian Affairs appropriations in the 1930 federal budget. Schools, both boarding schools and the now-recommended day schools on reservations, were given more funds, reducing the drudgery children had performed to grow food and maintain premises, and efforts were made to attract better medical care providers. What was not addressed was the glaring mess of allotments and leases.

The Indian New Deal

Geronimo and his Apache band were captured and imprisoned in 1886, the last "hostiles" from the Indian Wars. A year later came the Dawes Act, as if the door had slammed shut on First Nations' independence and ways of life. For Plains nations, the essential substance—bison—had disappeared by 1883, slaughtered by the millions to ship hides for machinery belts (Taylor 2007). Factories hummed in the East and in Europe while Indian people were reduced to eating handout rations of salt pork and maggoty flour, much the worse for months of freighting and warehousing. Beef cattle were sometimes purchased from colonist ranchers for reservation people, to be driven long distances, perhaps held up for months by early snow as happened to a herd bought for Montana Blackfeet, who starved by the hundreds during the winter of 1883–1884. All over Indian Country, dispossession from resources led to malnourishment, increasing vulnerability to tuberculosis, diphtheria, whooping cough, measles, and other diseases. Efforts to build up farming and ranching encountered setback after setback, from drought or frost to fluctuating markets for livestock and wool and the ineptitude or corruption of many agents.

The 1928 Meriam Report confirmed the failure of the United States' long-standing policy of removal or assimilation. A central issue and rallying point during the 1920s was the proscription of Indian religious practices. Christianizing heathens had been a legitimating mission for European invasions for a thousand years, from medieval Crusades, through Columbus's and Cortés's commissions, to Grant's Peace Policy. Southwestern Pueblos presented a peculiar case because they had been forcibly converted to Catholicism by Spanish friars in the seventeenth century. Their revolt of 1680 drove the Christian priests out of their pueblos for a dozen years, until they were brutally reconquered by Spanish forces. From then on, most Pueblo people practiced both Catholic and Pueblo rituals. When the federal government forbade native dances, the Bureau of Catholic Indian Missions protested that their Pueblo congregations had been Christian for four hundred years. Adding to the confusing claims were groups of Euro-American artists and writers believing they witnessed pure primitive spirituality and/or the primitive origins of art in Pueblo dance spectacles. Santa Fe and Taos were New Mexican centers for these "pilgrims," with Taos providing a picturesque adobe pueblo adjoining the villa of wealthy Mabel Dodge, who took for her fourth husband a Taos man, Tony Lujan. In her adobe mansion, Mrs. Luhan (she anglicized Tony's surname so her guests would pronounce it correctly) introduced literary lions such as novelist D. H. Lawrence and fellow socialites such as Harold Ickes's wife Anna Wilmarth to red-hued rocks and colorful natives.

Tony Lujan learned American politics in his wife's salon, using her contacts and funds to work toward effectively organizing all Pueblos to challenge Bureau of Indian Affairs policies. Among Mabel's guests was John Collier, son of the mayor of Atlanta, Georgia, who had produced a world's fair–type city exposition that brought in costumed Indians. From that boyhood vision of Indians, John Collier remained convinced that the Indian race preserved the spirituality he hungered for. Along with camping, canoeing, and hiking in wilderness, Collier wanted to work with underdogs. Initially, immigrants were the ones he helped through settlement houses in New York and then California. Visiting the Luhans at Taos, Collier was entranced by the pueblo's dances and Catholic ceremonies. Suppressing these, he felt, would kill the last American remnants of true religion.

Senator Bursum of New Mexico had galvanized the Pueblo Indians and their friends in 1922 by a bill in Congress to resolve disputes between Pueblos and Americans over land claimed by both. The Pueblo Indians' titles were based on Spanish grants that had been continued when Mexico became independent. Under the 1848 Treaty of Guadalupe Hidalgo, Mexican citizens including Pueblos retained their lands in what became New Mexico. Pueblos technically were not "Indians" for the US government in this matter of land grants. In 1913, the US Supreme Court ruled that Pueblos were Indians under federal law. Now their land grants were in effect reservations. If a pueblo had sold some of its original Spanish grant to a non-Indian, was that sale invalidated by the law that Indians could sell only to the US government? Bursum's bill forced the Pueblos to defend their title, not easy when their grants went back two centuries or more. John Collier led protests by white friends-of-the-Indians organizations, creating in 1923 the American Indian Defense Association, with himself as executive secretary.

Congress responded to the outcry against Bursum's bill by passing in 1924 the Pueblo Lands Act with power to examine the land grants and decide which claims were valid. Collier then turned to defense of Indian dances and rituals, his American Indian Defense Association publishing a pamphlet, *The Indian and Religious Freedom*. The year 1924 was propitious in that the United States had just decreed all Indians born in the nation as citizens. For the first time, members of American First Nations could demand rights under the First Amendment to the Constitution:

"Congress shall make no law respecting an establishment of religion, or prohibiting the free exercise thereof."

One effect of the enlightened policy to provide day schools on reservations so that Indian children could remain with their families was to make it easier for reservation superintendents to insist that all children attend school. In 1924, that catalyzed crises at Taos and Zuni when Pueblo leaders were forbidden to take selected boys out of school to be placed in religious training for priestly roles. After their indigenous education, they could resume Western schooling, the Pueblo officials promised. Giving precedence to native religions was precisely contrary to the "civilizing" aim of government schooling, which still equated civilization with Christianity. John Collier in 1924 had just won his fight to retain Pueblo lands through the Pueblo Lands Act. Fighting the destruction of Pueblo religions through eliminating traditional priesthood training should now be the focus of his crusade to preserve the societies he fervently admired. On his side he had the artists and writers sharing his romantic view of Indians, and anthropologists and archaeologists familiar with southwestern First Nations. Against him were missionaries, their churches, the Bureau of Indian Affairs, most Americans, and a number of Pueblo people, mostly educated at boarding schools, who accepted the conflation of civilization, Christianity, and Western culture.

Collier's principal ally in the American Indian Defense Association was Stella Atwood, a Californian active in the General Federation of Women's Clubs. Atwood had created an Indian Welfare Committee in 1916 within the Southern California Federation of Women's Clubs, raised concern over World War I Indian veterans' problems, persuaded (with Nakoda writer Gertrude Bonnin [Zitkala Sa]) the General Federation of Women's Clubs to move her committee to the national level, and in 1922, received a private donation to hire John Collier as researcher for the Indian Welfare Committee. From that and groups of artists, anthropologists, and well-to-do eastern liberals, in 1923, Collier created his American Indian Defense Association. Mrs. Atwood continued rallying the considerable political power of two million organized, mostly middle-class American women who had themselves won the right to vote only in 1920. Picturesque Pueblo women walking with beautiful painted water jars on their heads became icons of natural femininity. Almost always nameless in popular photos, they were described as modest, dignified, devoted to home and family. Newly enfranchised American women could help these people suffering injustices from the same men who had opposed female suffrage.

Like Harriet Beecher Stowe epitomizing the evil of American slavery in *Uncle Tom's Cabin* (1852), a Euro-American woman, Helen Hunt Jackson, had in *Century of Dishonor* (1881) and *Ramona* (1884) dramatically exposed genocidal injustice suffered by American Indians. When Jackson published, it seemed natural that concerned readers should support the recently organized Women's National Indian Association, led by a minister's widow. Its first goal was "covenant-keeping with tribes to which solemn pledges had been given, and that no treaty should be abrogated or broken without the free consent of the Indian tribe named in it." Apparently without seeing any contradiction, the founder, Amelia Quinton, listed as a further goal to pressure the federal government to "grant a legal status to Indians, the protection of law, lands in severalty, and education" (1894:71). Poignantly, a turn-of-the-century woman devoted to teaching in Indian schools, Mary Dissette, wrote to a politician, "I wish I could help the cause [protecting Oklahoma Indian nations] but as a woman has no political status, and is classed with the Indians she is helping to raise to the dignity of citizens, I am helpless" (Dissette 1906, quoted in Jacobs 1999:24).

A generation later, dignified at last, Euro-American women dedicated to helping Pueblo Indians no longer were inspired by Christian evangelism—quite the contrary. Mabel Dodge Luhan, her friend the writer Mary Austin, and anthropologist Elsie Clews Parsons flamboyantly rejected Christian sexual morality, Christian theology, and women's subordination. Proto–New Agers, they wanted it all, orgasms and spiritual ecstasy, although only Mabel Dodge found it all in one Pueblo man. While Parsons, trained in sociology and an associate of anthropologist Franz Boas, meticulously recorded Pueblo religions to preserve their details, and Luhan led a variety of influential guests to appreciate Pueblo ways of life, Austin popularized them in romantic stories. These women, and their associate John Collier, have been categorized by cultural historians as part of the "antimodern movement" (Lears 1981).

Where Pre-Raphaelites in Europe embraced a medieval past of shining knights and lovely damsels (and no pigs rooting in garbage-strewn streets, no peasant wet nurses for well-born infants, no laborers with no clothes but what they had on), American antimodernists could take the train to New Mexico and see villages that looked like archaeologists' depictions of humankind's Neolithic stage. The resemblance was set up by archaeologists using ethnographic analogy to interpret sites and artifacts; for example, if pottery in a site was handmade without a wheel, then the potters might have lived in mud-hut villages like New Mexican pueblos. Mabel Dodge came literally closest to capturing that antimodern life in her adobe mansion, even as Tony Lujan's Taos wife, Candelaria, and children lived within the Pueblo community next door. Coming to Taos from New York City, John Collier saw what he had been seeking, homes blended into the colors of nature, woods and wildflowers and a pure stream—the beauty he had craved through wilderness camping now combined with human warmth. Pueblos were much more gratifying than the immigrants in New York settlement houses, simple-looking and not ambitious to get rich. Collier could be the Parsifal redeeming ancient purity.

Energetic, passionate, impatient, often irascible though sometimes charming, John Collier was the American Indian Defense Association. He worked full time lobbying politicians and cultivating allies, hardly the usual duties of a research assistant, the position he held for Atwood's committee. His political activities became the charge by which his conservative opponents in New Mexico, groups favoring assimilation and/or individualization of Indians, attacked him and persuaded the president of the General Federation of Women's Clubs to terminate his employment in 1924 and pressured Stella Atwood to restrain her committee. Collier then had to hustle to raise funds from wealthy patrons himself, mostly in California, to get a salary and operating money. Diatribes against the commissioner of Indian Affairs, Charles Burke, kept up the issues of Pueblo religious freedom and then of royalties for leased mineral and oil exploitation, in spite of Burke's good-faith efforts to avoid confrontations, moderate imposition of compulsory schooling, and channel shares of royalties paid to states into roads and similar public works on reservations. For the next eight years, Collier relentlessly damned Burke's ameliorative policy and the multiple inadequacies of the Office of Indian Affairs. His "propaganda," as his dramatic charges were often termed, goaded the Secretary of the Interior to commission the Meriam Report and to replace Commissioner Burke with a Quaker, Charles Rhoads, engaged to follow the recommendations of Meriam's group. Good intentions notwithstanding, Rhoads's reforms failed to grapple with the deep flaws of US Indian policy.

Early in 1924, Collier had prepared, as part of his campaign against the Bursum bill, a speech, "The Impending Destruction of the Pueblos—the Oldest Democracy in the World." En route to the East Coast to speak against Bursum, Collier and the delegation of Pueblo Indians he led stayed briefly in Chicago, hosted by several families who were friends of his sister there. One of the homes was that of Harold and Anna Wilmarth Ickes. The "Oldest Democracy" speech, filled with cries against wrongs suffered by Indians, greatly moved Ickes. His years of watching and struggling against the decline of the Progressive Party had not dimmed his fervor, even though, in contrast to Collier, Ickes was highly self-disciplined and political in the sense of maneuvering out of the public eye. Ickes also had seen pueblos, spoken with Tony Lujan, and understood the poverty under the picturesque. As a lawyer, he knew that propaganda is not sufficient to overturn legislated rules; shrewd strategies must be devised. As a Chicagoan, he was suspicious of wealthy East Coast and California patrons. As a self-made man, he distrusted Collier, son of privilege in Ickes's eyes. For these reasons, Harold Ickes refused to sit on the board of the American Indian Defense Association, virtually a one-man show of Collier's passion, but his interest in combating injustices against Indians did not abate.

Franklin Roosevelt's New Deal, boldly proclaimed in a time of unprecedented economic crisis, beckoned both Collier and Ickes. Roosevelt would select an entirely new team for the executive branch, down to such relatively minor functionaries as commissioner of Indian Affairs, and John Collier was surely the most prominent candidate for that post. Harold Ickes's candidacy for the same post was, in keeping with the man's complicated persona as famously self-styled "curmudgeon," not so straightforward. His desire to help Indians obtain justice, their rights, and economic relief was real and deep—in his autobiography, he mentions that in college he "specialized in anthropology, ethnology, and folk psychology" (Ickes 1943:263). His understanding of politics was also deep and astute. It seems that it was primarily Anna Wilmarth Ickes who triggered her husband's bid for Indian Affairs (Watkins 1990:271). From her retreat in New Mexico near Gallup, she worked to alleviate Indians' suffering; in 1931 she told her friend Margaret Dreier Robins, leader of the Women's Trade Union League, that Indian women were undernourished and without any foods suitable for weaned babies; that Rhoades's administration had provided "a little more food a day and better food" to schoolchildren; that Indians could earn money marketing beans they raised if only a machine for washing beans could be purchased; and finally, "at the other end of my list" of desired assistance, an elderly medicine man needed a buffalo tail for a clan ritual, but the director of the Lincoln Park Zoo in Chicago would not cut off a tail from a dead bison because then the hide would be less valuable (quoted in Watkins 1990:271). Anna, who was herself campaigning for reelection to the Illinois legislature, objected to Harold organizing old-line Progressives for Franklin Roosevelt's Midwest election campaign. Harold told her that he would apply to be commissioner of Indian Affairs if Roosevelt were elected. Anna saw that to be a possible means toward winning the struggle to aid the Indians she saw as so destitute.

Collier did his best to undermine his rival's chance to be commissioner, urging Ickes to try for assistant secretary of the Interior rather than the lower position of commissioner. That appealed to Ickes—then the thought came to him of asking his senator friends to suggest him to Roosevelt, not for assistant secretary, but for the cabinet post, Secretary of Interior. When Roosevelt won, he offered that job to the very senators Ickes had spoken to. They refused. Roosevelt wanted to bring Progressives into his administration, despite the decline of that party. Ickes (among others) was mentioned as a longtime Progressive. Time was running out for Roosevelt to fill all the positions he had to appoint. Ickes was recommended by a Chicago fellow campaigner. Roosevelt called Ickes in for a personal interview and late in February 1933 offered Ickes the appointment. That left the position of commissioner of Indian Affairs for John Collier. It made Harold Ickes John Collier's boss. Ickes knew he could rely on Collier to put himself on the side of Indians: that is, to truly reverse US policy that Indians had to go when whites wanted their land. However abrasive Collier might be, he wouldn't flinch before opposition. Ickes could work on the multitudinous other issues and problems of the Department of the Interior while Collier championed Indian reform.

Could justice at last prevail for America's First Nations? Anthropologist Clark Wissler wasn't optimistic. "No doubt we shall go on bungling Indian affairs for the simple reason that the problems presented are of no particular economic and social importance to the nation at large" (Wissler [1938] 1971:19).

CHAPTER TWO

The Indian Reorganization Act

To give Indians a New Deal, Harold Ickes and John Collier needed to prepare legislation for Congress and to prepare a battle plan to get it through Congress. Ickes's Solicitor for the Department of the Interior, Nathan Margold, knew a young lawyer, son of the respected City College of New York philosophy professor Morris Cohen, who could draft the legislation. Felix Cohen had no experience with Indians, but Margold was looking for legal skill, a quick mind, and a strong desire to work for social justice. Margold knew, too, that Cohen's wife, Lucy Kramer, was an anthropologist familiar with Indians through Franz Boas's program at Columbia University. A couple of other young lawyers were hired along with Cohen for the project.

The strategy devised within the Department of the Interior to revolutionize US policy toward First Nations was to enlist a senator and a congressman from western states to sponsor a bill in the form of a proposed act of Congress. Harold Ickes knew very well that because Congress has the power to regulate Indian affairs, decided in 1823 by Chief Justice John Marshall in *Johnson v. M'Intosh*, any lasting change in policy needed congressional legislation. He knew also that issues of Indian affairs were likely to more directly affect western states. Ickes chose Burton Wheeler, senator from Montana, and Edgar Howard, congressman from Nebraska.

Burton K. Wheeler affiliated with the Progressive Party a year after he came into office as senator from Montana in 1923. He had left his native Massachusetts to earn a law degree at the University of Michigan and continued westward to find employment, settling in Butte, Montana. Admiring populist champion William Jennings Bryan, Wheeler won election to the Montana legislature in 1905. Six years later, Butte elected a Socialist mayor and city council. Wheeler championed labor — Butte was notorious for the dangers miners faced in its huge copper mine — and then, as a district attorney during World War I, refused to indict antiwar protesters. In 1924, he was on the national ballot as Progressive Party vice presidential candidate with Robert La Follette Sr., senator from Wisconsin, running for president. The Progressives carried Wisconsin and garnered several million votes from western states, against Calvin Coolidge's Republican majority. Like Bryan a generation earlier, Wheeler fought for farmers and labor against powerful industrial and railroad interests. Supporting Franklin Roosevelt in his bid for the presidency, Wheeler was disappointed that the New Deal president deviated from older populist principles, and in 1936 broke with Roosevelt over his design to add younger men, men of his own choice, to the Supreme Court to counteract the six justices over seventy years of age. In 1934, however, Wheeler still was considered liberal.

Edgar Howard, representative from Nebraska, entered Congress the same year as Wheeler, 1923, although he would lose the 1934 election, leaving Washington at the beginning of 1935. His selection to cosponsor the Indian Reorganization Act (IRA) accrued from his chairmanship of the House Committee on Indian Affairs, as Wheeler did for the Senate's parallel committee. The House committee was willing to continue the reversal of Indian education policy initiated by Commissioner Rhoads in 1931 when he authorized shifting Indian children from boarding schools to local schools. In April 1934, Congress passed the Johnson-O'Malley Act, permitting the Department of the Interior to contract with states to provide education, medical, and welfare programs to Indians. This measure brought up the issue of payment for services, since states cannot tax reservation Indians. Johnson-O'Malley was in a sense feel-good legislation and, like many such, it passed easily because it elided the hard question of from where and from whom, does the money come? Howard's and Wheeler's committees had to face the issue in debating the proposed IRA. The IRA raised other red flags for the committees, too: ending allotments found favor (maybe it would be easier for whites to buy reservation land) but not the goal of increasing tribal lands in common trust; mineral rights were hotly argued; and the section for creating tribal courts administering their own laws smacked of revolution. Neither House nor Senate committee favored the IRA as it was written when submitted.

The Johnson-O'Malley and Wheeler-Howard Acts

Why should Johnson-O'Malley have sailed through Congress while Wheeler-Howard met resistance? A critical difference was that Johnson-O'Malley lay within the states' rights agenda, whereas Wheeler-Howard, truly innovative and revolutionary in its original draft, was about the federal government relinquishing some of its power over its anomalous domestic dependent nations. Such a major challenge to the United States' long-standing Jeffersonian principle of assimilation or elimination came bundled with the unsettling notion that communalism might be good. America was built by capitalism; capitalism had apparently failed to save America from the 1930s Great Depression; alternative politics such as communism and socialism seized their opportunity (Soyer 2012). Conservative congressmen resisted surrendering the country to capitalism's enemies. Word circulated that John Collier had published, in 1922, an article extolling Pueblo communities as "The Red Atlantis." He must be a Red. That Atlantis is a myth apparently didn't signify.

Comparing the Johnson-O'Malley and Wheeler-Howard acts illuminates both the trend toward recognizing the Indian entitlements that they capped, and the socialist concept in the IRA reflecting Collier's and the Cohens' idealistic visions. Burton Wheeler wasn't duped. His Senate Committee on Indian Affairs and Howard's House committee rejected pages and pages of the voluminous IRA bill, paring it down to a document ending allotment of Indian lands, allowing but not requiring consolidation of tribal members' land into tribal trust, and recommending that tribes set up and incorporate representative elected tribal business councils. The Office of Indian Affairs (OIA) and Secretary of the Interior retained power over tribal councils' actions. Harold Ickes's realistic realignment of federal Indian policy passed, with Collier's and the Cohens' visionary models deleted. Wheeler himself so disliked the bill he sent up that he attempted in 1937 to get it repealed, an effort no doubt tied in with his marked disappointment with Roosevelt, particularly over the president's bright idea of overcoming Supreme Court opposition by adding new, liberal justices to the Nine Old Men on the bench. Failing to garner enough support to repeal the 1934 act with his name, Wheeler and his fellow congressmen busied themselves with bigger New Deal issues—the Farm Credit Administration, Tennessee Valley Authority, Securities Act, Wagner Act (National Labor Relations Act), Social Security, Federal Food, Drug and Cosmetic Act—a long list of legislation affecting all Americans, not just a few hundred thousand Indians.

Johnson-O'Malley was the culmination of a decade-and-a-half shift from the guiding belief that Christian schooling would civilize Indian children. First came Congress's 1924 acceptance that the Fourteenth Amendment to the Constitution, "All persons born or naturalized in the United States, and subject to the jurisdiction thereof, are citizens of the United States and of the State wherein they reside," should apply to Indians, albeit with modification of state jurisdiction. Citizenship threw into relief that prohibiting Indian religious observances and forcing Indians to attend Christian churches are unconstitutional. Indian education suffered from underfunding, with the churches expecting the federal government to support Indian children in the boarding schools and the government supposing the churches would pay since these were missions. Addressing this problem, Senator Hiram Johnson of California, a Progressive and close friend of Harold Ickes, proposed, unsuccessfully, in 1926 that states, specifically California which he represented, should assist in providing education and medical services for Indians. In 1929, President Hoover responded to the revelations and recommendations of the Meriam Report by requesting that Congress appropriate a little over a million dollars for the undernourished, ill-clothed children in Indian boarding schools. Opposed by the chairman of the House Appropriations Subcommittee, Hoover's request was slashed to a mere quarter of a million. Two years later, the Secretary of the Interior did allocate the amount requested, out of his department's budget. The 1920s was also a decade of zealous explorations for mineral wealth, colliding with Indians' anxieties over despoiling their lands and their experiences of failure to be paid due royalties. These several issues fueled Collier's American Indian Defense Association.

Hoover's commissioners of Indian Affairs, Charles Rhoads and Henry Scattergood, a pair of Quakers who worked as a team, surprisingly and correctly identified the "highly paternalistic administration" as the core of "the Indian problem." They hired W. Carson Ryan Jr., a professor of education from liberal Swarthmore College who had served on Meriam's team, to reform Indian education. In line with John Dewey's theory of schooling advocating children learning through activities, Indian children would practice vocational skills suited to rural families. How did this differ from the previous farm and domestic work in the boarding schools? It relieved children of the heaviest drudgery. John Collier thought well enough of this Progressive educator to keep him in his post as director of Indian education in the OIA after Collier became commissioner. This indicates very well the continuity between the Hoover administration's policies and the Indian New Deal in what may be termed "humanitarian issues."

Besides ameliorating the lot of Indian children in schools, Hoover's commissioners managed to relieve Indians of their burden of debt for large irrigation construction projects on reservations, many of them impracticable but often kept going because they were the few wage-paying jobs available for reservation men. The commissioners' recommendation for an Indian claims commission fell on deaf ears, and their urging that tribes be allowed more control over their reservations—less paternalism—similarly met resistance in Congress. Hoover's Indian policy, built from the Meriam Report, was the actual beginning of the Indian New Deal.

From this background it is evident that the Johnson-O'Malley Act was the culmination of liberal reform of federal Indian policy. In a nutshell, it eased the jurisdictional restriction against states dealing with their Indian peoples. The act stated "that the Secretary of the Interior is hereby authorized, in his discretion, to enter into a contract or contracts with any State or Territory having legal authority so to do, for the education, medical attention, agricultural assistance, and social welfare . . . of Indians in such State or Territory . . . and to expend under such contract or contracts moneys appropriated by Congress [for these purposes]" (US Statutes at Large, 48:596).

One exception was made, at the insistence of Oklahoma's Senator Elmer Thomas, chair of the Senate's Indian Affairs Committee, to exclude the Indians of the state of Oklahoma. Senator Thomas repeated the exclusion of his state's Indians from the Wheeler-Howard Act (the IRA) as well. He argued that Oklahoma's Indian people were civilized, in contrast to "Far Western" tribes, so in his opinion did not need federal special legislation.[1] Thomas's equivalent in the House, Representative Will Rogers (not to be confused with the part-Cherokee entertainer of the same name), agreed with him. Eventually, Congress passed a special bill, the Thomas-Rogers 1936 Oklahoma Indian Welfare Act, giving Oklahoma Indians most, but not all, of the earlier bills' provisions.

The IRA came to Wheeler and Howard as a fifty-two-page document proposing four major reforms:

1. Indian lands: repeal of the Allotment Act and restoring lands to tribal ownership.
2. Indian self-government: tribes could form chartered corporations, with constitutions and bylaws, and Congress would provide a revolving credit fund for Indian economic development.
3. Special education for Indians: Indian cultures would be encouraged through support for arts, crafts, traditional activities, and teaching in

schools attended by Indian children, and scholarships would be given to Indian students for college or vocational training.

4. Court of Indian Affairs: creating a Court of Indian Affairs to deal with matters on reservations and where an Indian was a party in a legal case (such as probate).

In addition, the bill asked that Indians be given preference for OIA employment, exempt from federal civil service rules.

Every portion of the bill was attacked. "Progress" toward assimilation into the US citizenry would be set back and "progressive" Indians would be penalized. Representative Howard's House committee decided the bill was so impossible that they rewrote it into a succinct document repealing allotment, permitting chartered business corporations but not the original bill's equivalent of municipalities for local self-government, ordering the Department of the Interior to extend its environmental protection to Indian lands and keeping Indians' right to make claims against the United States. Promotion of Indian cultures and the proposed Court of Indian Affairs were eliminated from the bill. Prompted by Secretary Ickes and Secretary of Agriculture Henry Wallace, President Roosevelt spoke for the bill in one of his radio broadcasts to the public, urging acceptance of our "Indian wards' . . . freedom [and] . . . the right to continue to exist" (quoted in Prucha 1986:323). The president wrote formally to Representative Howard,

> My interest has been attracted to your bill, H.R. 7902, because of the virile American principles on which it is based. Opportunities for self determination for the Indians in handling their property by providing modern corporate management, participation in local government, a more liberal education system through day schools and advanced health measures are provided in the bill.
>
> Adequate provision is made for his training in the management and protection of his property, and the conservation of his health during the period that must intervene before the Indian may be intrusted with the complete management of his own affairs. In offering the Indian these natural rights of man we will more nearly discharge guardianship that has destroyed initiative and the liberty to develop his own culture. Sincerely yours, Franklin D. Roosevelt, President (Deloria 2002:296–97)

Passed by Congress in June 1934, the Indian Reorganization Act was "to conserve and develop Indian lands and resources; to extend to Indians the right to form business and other organizations; to establish a credit system for Indians; to grant certain rights of home rule to Indians; to provide for vocational education for Indians; and for other purposes" (preamble, Pub. L. 73–383). John Collier managed to persuade Congress a year later to pass an Indian Arts and Crafts Act creating an Indian Arts and Crafts Board to supervise making and marketing of Indian artists' work, thereby restoring, as it were, one of the deleted sections of the original Wheeler-Howard bill. Collier also implemented the IRA by bringing New Deal agencies including the Civilian Conservation Corps, the Public Works Administration, Works Progress Administration (WPA), the Soil Conservation Service, and the Forest Service onto Indian reservations. The commissioner needed to maximize such interaction because Congress expressed its dislike of the IRA by cutting OIA appropriations from nearly $53 million for 1934, before the act was passed, to less than $38 million in 1937.

The IRA accomplished its political purpose, to move American Indians further—but far from completely—out of wardship. Harold Ickes's commitment to social justice for Indians was inaugurated. To Collier and Felix Cohen, the assistant solicitor who drafted the original bill, the senators and representatives had gutted their bill, cutting out the sections that could facilitate model social democratic communities. Cohen had opened the draft of the bill with a revolutionary statement, "That it is hereby declared to be the policy of Congress to grant to those Indians living under Federal tutelage and control the freedom to organize for the purposes of local self-government and economic enterprise, to the end that civil liberty, political responsibility, and economic independence shall be achieved among the Indian peoples of the United States" (quoted in Deloria and Lytle 1984:67).

Intending to grant Indians "civil liberty" was unprecedented, and although Collier accepted the line, no doubt thinking of freedom for Pueblo Indians to practice their own religions, Cohen would have drafted the line for the larger purpose of ensuring Indians' rights as citizens—a major element in the *Handbook of the Federal Indian Law* he would write next.

In the fight to push Congress to pass the bill, Collier took an unprecedented step, traveling around the country to speak on behalf of the bill in open meetings with its principal stakeholders, members of First Nations. These congresses, as he called them, not only brought Indians into the political action but really were examples of the principle of social democracy. On the other hand, like the IRA itself, the meetings did not give power to the Indian nations. Collier and Ickes could not fully reject considering First Nations as wards.

Collier's Indian Congresses

The first of Collier's meetings to discuss the proposed IRA, the Great Plains Congress, was held in the Rapid City, South Dakota, Indian School, March 2–5, 1934 (figure 2.1). Two hundred Indians from forty tribes attended. Collier was accompanied by Walker Woehlke, one of the Bureau's field representatives, Interior Department assistant solicitors Melvin Siegel and Felix Cohen, and two OIA land policies specialists, James Stewart and Ward Shepard. Assistant Commissioner William Zimmerman took part on the last day. Interpreters translated speeches and remarks into Sioux and Mandan, a service Shoshone and Blackfeet delegates said

Figure 2.1. John Collier with Talks Different and August Moccasin, March 3, 1934, at Rapid City Indian Congress. Mr. Moccasin was from Fort Belknap Reservation, Montana, home to Assiniboine (Nakoda) and Gros Ventre (Aaniiih) nations. Photo probably taken by Felix Cohen. Photo courtesy of the Felix S. and Lucy Kramer Cohen Photograph Collection.

they did not require. Transcripts of all that was said were typed up daily, mimeographed, sent to Washington, and distributed to the delegates' tribes.

Opening the congress, Collier admitted to "terrifying facts" regarding Indian poverty in the United States, remarking that in contrast, America's neighbors, Canada and Mexico, were increasing "Indian wealth" in their countries. (He was referring to the Cárdenas administration in Mexico expropriating estates to form *ejidos*, communal land for peasant villages. The wealth of Indians in Canada was not increasing.) The commissioner stated,

> I believe that the Indians would be in agreement with us in saying that the answer to the evils of the past and the present is not to abolish the guardianship and responsibility of the Federal Government but to change it so that it will build up the property of the Indians instead of taking it away. Build up the life, the health and the liberty of the Indians instead of taking them away. . . . The present Secretary of the Interior, Secretary Ickes, and the present Commissioner, myself, hold the position that we do hold because we are expected to bring about changes and reforms in the Federal guardianship until the change becomes good instead of bad. Both . . . have stood for one thing above all which was, that it was the duty of the Indians themselves to determine what their own life shall be. It is for the Indians themselves to determine what laws Congress shall pass for them. (quoted in Deloria 2002:27)

If the Indian delegates caught the blatant contradiction in the last two sentences, they did not protest.

Next, Collier said, "I talk first about your property" (quoted in Deloria 2002:28). A cynical observer might be reminded of John Locke, the seventeenth-century English political writer whose treatises made private property the foundation of civil society. Collier expounded on the drastic diminution of Indian land in the United States since the 1887 Dawes General Allotment Act, concluding that loss of Indian lands must stop, that land must be restored to tribes and to landless Indians, and declared, "say what we like about the bad results of allotment, we say plenty, but allotment has created individual valid property rights in individuals. That fact is there and has to be dealt with" (29). Here was the crux of Indian opposition to the Wheeler-Howard Act. Indian people did not want to lose their allotments. They felt (and still feel) strongly tied to the parcel chosen by their family. They did not want their allotments merged into a commune.

Collier told the delegates, "from one of the Pacific Northwest reservations comes in a telegram: 'We don't want socialism or communism'" (30).

Collier mentioned a "telegram which I hold in my hands from somebody up at Fort Peck [a Montana reservation] who protests that nothing must be done to destroy the treaty rights of the Indians, so nothing must be passed on [by Congress]" (quoted in Deloria 2002:35). A woman delegate had asked "whether we [Collier and Ickes] wanted them [Indians] to secede from our Government. . . . [What] is being laid before you is intended to bring it about so that the Indians will not want to secede from the Government and won't need to" (41). Amos One Road, a college-educated Sisseton Lakota who had collaborated with anthropologist Alanson Skinner, brought up the issue of treaties. Describing an 1867 treaty with his people, the Sisseton, he pointed out that they had signed a clause giving an allotment—in effect a homestead—to "the man who fences and plows two or three acres . . . different from the Dawes Act." One Road concluded, "if this Bill becomes true this is the last and greatest treaty that will be made and it will terminate all previous treaties" (75). Other speakers during that afternoon of the third day similarly referred to treaties that had promised them substantial land, only to have those promises abrogated. Collier did not seem to comprehend the import of these questions during that first congress. By the last two, he responded. In Muskogee, Oklahoma, Ned Blackfox, Principal Chief of the Cherokee Nation, brought in copies of Cherokee treaties of 1828, 1833, and 1835, asking through an interpreter how specific provisions in these treaties would be affected by the proposed bill. To the Muskogee meeting, Collier stated, "The Wheeler-Howard Bill does re-create the heart of the old treaties. It is the way in which your tribal life, insofar as it fits into the modern world, can be reborn and it will be given full recognition. This legislation does not abrogate any treaty or diminish any treaty but it will not establish some of your most precious rights, pledged to you by treaties, then taken away in violation" (316).

At Hayward, Wisconsin, Walter Woehlke, the OIA field representative chairing the meeting, told the delegates that the commissioner and his staff had inserted new language into the bill that "specifically states that no part of this bill shall be construed to impair, to diminish, or to do away with any right or claim that any Indian has against the United States Government on the basis of old treaties." He added, "Nothing in this bill would have affected these treaties anyway" (quoted in Deloria 2002:372).

A footnote to the congresses was put into the transcript of the last day of the four-day Plains congress by session chairman Henry Roe Cloud, a

Winnebago educator with a master's degree from Yale. He recorded this note: "Honorable Commissioner of Indian Affairs, Mr. Collier—Not one Indian woman had a voice in this Indian council and may I submit in writing—this new plan is our only salvation. Let's all join in and accept the new Bill and make the best of our advantages." Roe Cloud commented, "She said more in that one line than all the speeches put together. This is a member of the Pine Ridge Sioux delegation. She does not give her name" (quoted in Deloria 2002:97).

All the congresses revealed that tribal Indians could be articulate and skilled and persistent in argument. Many complained that the legislation put before them was confusing without far more time to read, analyze, and discuss it. As Canadian anthropologist Noel Dyck comments, "the cumulative experience of members of reserve communities with the institutions of both Canadian [and American] and western society is far broader than most [non-Indians] ever imagine" (1991:5).

Revolution or Evolution?

It was revolutionary for the top staff of the OIA to travel around the country to meet en masse with hundreds of their raison d'être. Collier was obsessed with seizing the momentum of Roosevelt's New Deal, fearing, rightly, that radical programs would soon become vulnerable to campaigns by entrenched conservatives. He told the Five Civilized Tribes at Muskogee, Oklahoma,

> President Roosevelt came in and appointed an extraordinarily strong man for Secretary of the Interior—Secretary Ickes, a man of great power to the Government, great force of character and mind—and I do not think there has ever been a Secretary of the Interior who cares about the Indian problem as he does. His interest goes back many years of time as a citizen. In addition, another man came into the cabinet under President Roosevelt—Secretary Wallace. Many of you may not know this, but Secretary Wallace has a burning interest in the Indian matter. It is one of the deepest things in his life. This interest in Indians is almost a religion with him and he has a great deal of wisdom about the Indian race and its needs. So we have two powerful men in the cabinet, two dominant men of the cabinet who want to do the right thing. . . . Now it is a remarkable set-up that we have, with a President more popular than any president in our lifetime, with almost irresistible driving force, and

with Congress itself all ready to go the limit in behalf of the Indians, and with a Cabinet actively friendly to the Indians. . . . [This is] the time when the Indian can get anything within reason. Nobody can tell how long that situation is going to last. . . . If you wait too long then want [the legislation], the time may have passed and the opportunity gone. (quoted in Deloria 2002:316)

Given the decade of attacks upon the Bureau of Indian Affairs, the appointment of the Meriam Committee and acceptance of its damning report, and Hoover's encouragement of reform, it might seem that by 1934 the tide had already turned in Indian affairs. Johnson-O'Malley's easy passage, during the same months as Collier's congresses, would indicate that. Collier never alluded to the Johnson-O'Malley bill at the Indian congresses. Listeners could infer that significant improvements in education, medical services, and welfare, as well as land protection, were dependent on the Wheeler-Howard bill. To put Collier's sense of urgency in context, 1934 was still the depth of the Great Depression. Nearly everyone in America was hard hit economically. Unemployed masses marched on Washington. Collier manipulated to the utmost to pull New Deal emergency measures onto reservations. To fulfill his duty to help Indians, he needed the crucial heart of Wheeler-Howard, restoration of tribal land bases. Allotment was played out by the 1930s but the provision in the Dawes Act for allotments to go into fee patent after twenty-five years, although the time was extended for another ten years in the 1930s, still threatened almost complete dissolution of Indian country. American Indians were not only the poorest of the poor in Depression America, they were handicapped more than any other group of Americans by a century of laws and regulations promulgated under the wardship model. That Collier and Ickes did not seek to repudiate wardship shows the persistence of the American—one could say Anglo, as it characterized Canadian Indian policy also—legitimating myth of the Indian as child of nature in a wilderness.

Felix Cohen attended the Indian congresses with Collier. He was called upon to explain the section proposing a Court of Indian Affairs and legal angles of other sections of the bill, a task shared with his fellow assistant solicitor, Melvin Siegel. Cohen told the Navajo Tribal Council at its special session at Fort Defiance, Arizona, March 12–13, 1934,

Friends: This is a very peculiar bill, and many people have misunderstood it. Most laws that deal with Indians say that the Indians must do

this or that. This law does not give a single command to any Indian insofar as the self-government part of the law is concerned. If this law of
self-government is passed by Congress and your people don't want to
take advantage of it, you can leave the law written on the paper and it
will have no life. This law, when it passes Congress, is only the beginning of things. . . . [If you take charters,] in the end, the Indian Office
will no longer be a Bureau that governs your people, because you will
be doing the governing yourselves. Rather, the Indian Office will be an
adviser to you. The Indian Bureau will be like the Weather Bureau [giv-
ing] farmers good advice, and sometimes it gives them bad advice, but it
does not compel them to take the advice. . . . But this future will not
come tomorrow. It will take some time before your people will be ready
and willing to run the various functions and services that the United
States Government is now running for you. This bill merely lays down
a new road. (quoted in Deloria 2002:152–53)

At this point in his education about First Nations, Cohen accepted the
wardship model. In his speech to the Navajo council, he said that if they
accepted a charter it "will be like a contract between your people and the
United States Government. And in this charter, or contract, the United
States Government will guarantee to you many powers which you have
not had before" (quoted in Deloria 2002:152). When he wrote his great
Handbook of Federal Indian Law a few years later, Cohen saw that Indian
tribes party to treaties with the United States did not need charters or contracts to obtain local government. In that work, he stated, "Reference to
the so-called 'plenary' power of Congress over the Indians, or more quali-
fiedly, over 'Indian tribes' or 'tribal Indians,' becomes so frequent in recent
cases that it may seem captious to point out that there is excellent authority
for the view that Congress has no constitutional power over Indians except
what is conferred by the commerce clause and other clauses of the Constitution" (Cohen 1942:90). He cites Justice Marshall's opinion in *Worcester
v. Georgia*, 1832, that Indians "are not limited by any restrictions on their
free actions" (Cohen 1942:90).

Cohen's *Handbook* is the radical break in US dealings with the First
Nations within its borders. The Indian Reorganization Act's section ending land allotment and restoring tribal lands is legal under the commerce
clause, which indeed was written to comprehend disposal of Indian lands.
The sections offering limited self-government and business corporation
structure overstep the Constitution as Marshall interpreted it, while the
proposal for a federal court of Indian affairs is merely an instrument to

fulfill the commerce clause. It took extraordinary jurisprudence to see that a century and a half of OIA restrictions upon Indians' free actions was unlawful. John Collier was not a lawyer; Secretary Ickes was, and could understand Cohen's breakthrough. For that reason, Ickes brought Cohen and his *Handbook* staff back into Interior when the Department of Justice, equally realizing where Cohen was going with the *Handbook*, scuttled the project. With the *Handbook* published, Indians' struggles to live according to their treaties could assert a Constitutional foundation. The evolution of Jeffersonian policy ended, and a new legal environment framed a new evolutionary direction.

Collier's Goals

John Collier's crusade for Indians began with the 1920s fight for Pueblo land titles and religious freedom. Then when he became part of the Department of the Interior, he turned to restoring tribal lands and cultures through the Indian Reorganization Act. When only two of its four sections passed, he pushed further legislation to create an Indian Arts and Crafts Board for the goal of cultural restoration. The Court of Indian Affairs seems to have been more easily let go. Eastern Indian nations overrun by colonists before the United States was formed were also let go. Section 18 of the IRA exempted reservations that voted against accepting it from proceeding with its demand for constitutions; the section did not limit the act to federally recognized tribes. A number of Eastern First Nations held small reservations under state decrees, some since the eighteenth century. Collier instructed his staff to ignore those, such as the Shinnecock and Unkechaugs of Long Island, New York, whose members appeared "submerged by the Negro." Felix Cohen questioned the exclusion, and another Interior lawyer sent Collier a memorandum clarifying that Indians on reservations are descendant communities, their status based on genealogical data rather than physical appearance (Strong 2011:220–28).

For Collier, providing Indian self-government through instituting tribal constitutions and corporate charters was the prime order of business once Wheeler-Howard passed in June 1934. He had a model constitution drafted and allocated OIA funds to operate an Indian Organization Division within the office, hiring staff to work in the field with tribes and their superintendents. Even though Collier and his staff had repeatedly emphasized that tribes could vote against a constitution or a charter, understandably there was considerable distrust over whether failure to adopt the OIA's recommendations would penalize a tribe. Furthermore, there was a fundamental problem with the assumption that tribal self-government should proceed under a Euro-American form of governance. Moreover, 1934 was fewer than seventy years after the end of the Indian Wars. Many reservation people knew firsthand, or heard from their parents, how their society had governed itself. Band and village communities had often survived allotment. How could self-government be promoted by imposition of a foreign code?

Fundamentally, Collier failed to see the crucial paradox of restoring Indian cultures through a thoroughly Western modern form of organized activities. Surely customary First Nations governance forms were integral to their cultures. The gap between these and Collier's charters and corporations was well expressed by the chairman of the Rosebud (Reservation) Sioux Council when he apologized that he had difficulty translating the Wheeler-Howard bill presented to the Rapid City Congress, because Lakota did not have equivalent words for many of the terms in the bill. Indians who did speak English were daunted by the verbiage in the fifty-two-page original bill, not to mention its legal terminology. Hence, the field representatives' oral talks could be critical when reservations came to vote on accepting or rejecting charters and corporations.

To facilitate establishing local self-government, the OIA offered a draft model constitution. Its principal sections covered tribal land, tribal rolls, the form of the governing council with rules for election and for removal from office, and how amendments could be made. Collier reiterated often that a constitution is a legal document under US laws, expected to address certain procedures and actions and constrained by federal laws. Tribal constitutions had to fit within the basic form if they were to be legally recognized, and their language had to use proper terminology. Throughout the Indian congresses of 1934, Collier talked of constitutions and charters as if they were linked, although articles of incorporation, that is to say, a corporate charter, could be granted to any business enterprise. Indian enterprises would be under the purview of the OIA by custom, a point made by Felix Cohen (1942:122) in the *Handbook of Federal Indian Law*. A constitution is another matter, a set of principles governing an organization. Constitutions and charters may look similar to the layperson. For Indian tribes in 1934, there was a very significant difference, in that charters are granted by a regulatory agency, while constitutions are generated by the organization they are to govern and approved by the body of persons to whom they will apply.

Collier also insisted that the Secretary of the Interior possess ultimate power over American Indian tribes, so that any actions of tribal governments could be reviewed by the Secretary or his delegated administrators (primarily, the OIA and reservation superintendents) and would be subject to his approval. This would be a very broad interpretation of the commerce clause of the Constitution's Article I, Section 8, Clause 3: "[The Congress shall have Power] to regulate Commerce with foreign Nations, and among the several States, and with the Indian tribes."

Cohen (1942:46) would negate the overly broad interpretation in his *Handbook*. His insistence that the United States' dealings with its First Nations are based upon its treaties with them as independent sovereign nations clashed with the dominant, often reiterated and seldom questioned, view that Indians are incompetent to manage their own affairs. Guardianship or wardship was held to be benevolent, and protestations to the contrary by Indians to be naïve. Indians who actively opposed the government's power over them were labeled troublemakers or accused of favoring "mixed-blood" entrepreneurs against "traditional full-bloods." With the force of centuries of denigrating as "backward" those peoples conquered by Western imperialists (for example, Slavic-speaking peoples incorporated into the Austrian-Hungarian empire), Indians' alleged childlike inability to manage their lives was a self-fulfilling prophecy, operating through agents' denials of adult Indians' plans and Indian schools' program of rural vocational training rather than academic preparation

Collier's goals were not emancipation of Indians from federal government control. Instead, he envisioned what the British termed "indirect rule," letting traditional or government-selected headmen manage their communities as intermediaries between the colonial power and the conquered people. Indirect rule was much less expensive than the United States' practice of building agencies and paying white agents, farm instructors, teachers, and medical personnel to live in the field. It also preserved the indigenous communities and their local system of governance, as Collier wished. It did not "civilize" the natives. Many Indians who had become Christians, literate, and economically self-sufficient feared they would lose their advantages. Already in the 1920s there had been cases in which Pueblo Indians cast out Christian families who refused to participate in rituals integral to the structure and functioning of traditional life. Collier assured "progressive" Indians that their assets would be protected. This issue opened up the diversity within Indian communities, in contrast to Collier's conviction that they were, or should again be, cohesive islands of cooperation built upon unique cultures. Indirect rule had developed in Africa and Asia where Europeans had not immigrated en masse, intermarried, and infiltrated reservations via leases and buying allotments to the point that tribal territories were checkerboarded with non-Indian properties. Collier believed indigenous communities could be reconstituted when allotment stopped and land was bought back. His crusading drive could not manage the nuances and complexities of actual reservations or even pueblos. Nor did he accept the logical conclusion to promoting self-government, that tribes might construct communities quite different from the communalism Collier believed to be native to American First Nations.

Communalism was the beautiful principle Collier yearned to see. His visits to Taos, mediated by Mabel Luhan, seemed to afford glimpses of cooperative, constructive communalism contrasting with the aggressive striving he disliked in his own social class, and from which he took refuge by camping. Collier apparently did not consult closely with the Columbia University anthropologists working in southwestern pueblos, led by Elsie Clews Parsons. At the same time the Indian New Deal was being implemented, Margaret Mead, also of Columbia, was commissioned by the Social Science Research Council's Subcommittee on Cooperative and Competitive Habits (comprising three social psychologists: Mark May, Gardner Murphy, and Gordon Allport) to prepare a book describing, as the title says, *Cooperation and Competition Among Primitive Peoples* (Mead 1937). Mead used a 1934 Columbia University graduate seminar to compile a world sample. Irving Goldman, then a student, wrote the chapter "The Zuni Indians of New Mexico," acknowledging assistance from Professor Ruth Benedict and Ruth Bunzel, who had carried out ethnography in Zuni. Goldman (1937:346) described surface amicability underlain by "malicious scandalmongering" and attributed competition between Zuni sheep owners to white contact, sheep having been introduced by Spanish colonizers. As was standard for his time, colonial pressures were not directly discussed. Goldman's account is gritty, rendering Zuni daily life as stressful rather than peaceful. If that was what communalism looked like, it wasn't especially pleasant.

"Malicious scandalmongering" wasn't confined to Zuni Pueblo. Charges of communism were hurled at many New Dealers from Franklin Roosevelt and Harold Ickes to John Collier. As would happen a generation later with Senator Joseph McCarthy, the slanderers seldom bothered to distinguish between Marxism, communism as political ideology, the Communist Party, Stalinism, socialism, Social Democrat ideology, the Socialist Party, and anarchy. In the 1930s, slowly growing apprehension of the threat posed by Hitler and Mussolini added Nazism (an acronym for National Socialist, Nationalsozialismus in German) to the cacophony. By May 1938, the House of Representatives established a permanent House Committee on Un-American Activities, chaired by Congressman Martin Dies. Among citizens who testified before this committee was Alice Lee Jemison, a Seneca. Quite familiar with Iroquois governance (her uncle was president of the Seneca Nation and she assisted him and other incumbents in that position), Jemison campaigned tirelessly to abolish the OIA and restore Iroquois rights of sovereignty. Her nation's dire poverty during the Depression was in part effected by OIA rule, she believed. Jemison was supported by the American Indian Federation, an intertribal organization formed in 1934 of Indian people disgruntled by the IRA and by Collier. With Jemison, the Federation lobbied to abolish the OIA and thus "free the Indian." Collier's vision of cooperative, communal tribal governments easily led to cries that he was a communist. Harold Ickes and Collier countercharged that the American Indian Federation and Alice Jemison were Nazi puppets, pointing to a few Federation members who spoke in favor of Nazism, sporting swastika armbands. Although FBI records eventually showed that Jemison was not a Nazi, the Federation was besmirched. Its legitimate message that the IRA did not substantially change the fundamental position of US First Nations was lost in the clamor of "Communists!" "Nazis!"

John Collier seems never to have perceived the paternalism he practiced, telling Indians what would be good for them. He truly believed the OIA, rightly led, should and could benevolently protect Indians and their tribes. Harold Ickes cared about social justice, and although John Collier was the face of Ickes's policies affecting Indians, the Secretary astutely relied on his Solicitor, Nathan Margold, and Margold's hire, Felix Cohen. Margold had the track record of working with prominent African American attorney Charles H. Houston on NAACP strategy to overcome segregation, using a $100,000 grant (1930 dollars—more like $1 million today) from the American Fund for Public Service (Garland Fund). Margold had also been legal counsel to the Pueblos during their fight for land titles. Felix Cohen had a Harvard PhD in philosophy and a recent LLB from Columbia University. While Cohen had no experience with Indians or even with racial minority cases, Margold and his Harvard mentor Felix Frankfurter were confident he had both the conviction and legal skills to carry out Secretary Ickes's powerful commitment to Progressive social justice. Felix Cohen, after all, carried Frankfurter's name; his father and Frankfurter had been graduate school roommates.

CHAPTER THREE

"Frankfurter's Jewish Cabal"

John Collier's passion, coupled with the glamor of Mabel Luhan's anti-, modern artists' circle, made him the icon of the Indian New Deal—the selfless radical battling entrenched genocidal policy. Historians generally took him at his own measure, a visionary struggling against both governmental inertia and Indians' ignorance. That his goal of limited local tribal governance within federal guardianship was far from the emancipation First Nations wanted has not generally been stressed. Nor have historians of the Indian New Deal focused on its actual architects, the Jewish lawyers Felix Cohen and his boss, Nathan Margold. A little attention to Roosevelt's New Deal appointees reveals social justice for American Indians was only one facet of the President's and Harold Ickes's determination to bring to all American citizens the rights lawfully theirs. Indians, Negroes, and Jews must no longer be second-class Americans. Across the Atlantic, Hitler launched his campaign of racial purification, denying rights to Jews, gypsies, and Slavs. That parallel and opposite movement gives poignancy to Roosevelt's principled inclusiveness.

During the Roosevelt presidency, the Jewish jurist Felix Frankfurter served as one of the president's close advisors (figure 3.1), earning in 1938 a seat on the Supreme Court—considered, in effect, the Jewish seat, since he succeeded Benjamin Cardozo and was in turn succeeded, in 1962, by Arthur Goldberg (Cardozo had replaced that quintessential WASP Oliver Wendell Holmes Jr.). Explaining his role as personal advisor, Frankfurter recalled that he had known Franklin Roosevelt since both were working in the War Department in 1913, Frankfurter as an assistant attorney to

Figure 3.1. Felix Frankfurter. Photo from Library of Congress.

Secretary of War Henry Stimson, Roosevelt as assistant secretary of the Navy. During World War I, both served on the War Labor Policies Board. In March 1933, Roosevelt asked Frankfurter to be Solicitor General in his administration: "I want you down here [in Washington, DC], because I need you for all sorts of things, and in all sorts of ways. As you know, we are going in heavily for utility regulation, reorganization of the various Commissions, amendment to the Sherman [Antitrust] Law and a lot of other things. I need your help on all these matters, and I want you to come very much" (Frankfurter 1960:244). Frankfurter replied, "I can do much more to be of use to you by staying in Cambridge [at Harvard Law School] than by becoming Solicitor General. The fact of the matter is that I could not have anything to do on any of the matters on which you would want my help and [still] do my job as Solicitor General—it just can't be done" (Frankfurter 1960:245).

Frankfurter unabashedly recommended young Jewish lawyers for federal positions; to the point that newspapers wrote of the unprecedented number of Jews hired and of fears that "a Jewish cabal" was taking over America. Nathan Margold was named on these lists. The whole story of how, in Karen Brodkin's (1998) words, "Jews became white folks" in the first half of the twentieth century reverberates in the Roosevelt New Deal. This chapter looks at Felix Frankfurter and his student Nathan Margold, the men who put Frankfurter's namesake Felix Cohen in place to revolutionize American First Nations' position under US law. They played on a large stage, so visible that more than half a century later, a diatribe against Frankfurter and his "cabal" remains on the Lyndon LaRouche Watch website.[1]

Felix Frankfurter of Harvard Law

Felix Frankfurter was born in Vienna, Austria, in 1882. He was twelve when his family emigrated to New York, his father selling linens to support his wife and six children. Like Morris Cohen, two years older, Frankfurter spoke no English when he landed in New York. He recalled, gratefully, that his PS 25 teacher, Miss Hogan, forbade his classmates to speak German with him, forcing him to use English (Frankfurter 1960:4–5). In 1902, he graduated from City College of New York (CCNY). After working for New York City's Tenement House Department to earn enough to continue his education, he entered Harvard Law School, rooming with another Jewish student a year ahead in the school. During his third year, Frankfurter shared an apartment with Morris Cohen, CCNY '00, who was there to study philosophy. The two brilliant, idealistic young Jewish immigrants became lifelong friends, Frankfurter's passion for law inspiring Morris's fascination with the philosophy of jurisprudence and, in turn, that of Morris's son Felix.

Like Louis Brandeis, a Kentucky-born Jew who in 1916 became the first Jewish justice on the US Supreme Court, Felix Frankfurter was first in his class at Harvard Law and an editor of the *Harvard Law Review*. He was hired by a prestigious law firm, its only Jew, soon leaving it to assist Henry Stimson, the US attorney for the Southern District of New York, an earlier Harvard Law graduate. Frankfurter remembered the dean of Harvard Law promoting the value of public service over mere corporate legal business. Using law to help ordinary people and thus the country fit the principles of the Progressive Party (that is, Harold Ickes's party), principles that two decades later would foster friendship between Ickes and Frankfurter, and Ickes and Frankfurter's protégés. Stimson left the New York attorney position to become Secretary of War in 1911, taking Frankfurter with him to Washington.

Three years later, only thirty-one, Frankfurter was asked to return to Cambridge to teach in Harvard Law School. The dean and the faculty, alumnus Stimson, the great Supreme Court justice Oliver Wendell Holmes Jr.—friend of Frankfurter and later, of Morris Cohen and his son Felix—and Justice Brandeis all favored the appointment. Frankfurter had unusual experience in administrative law involving regulations and labor issues, plus a "liberal" view toward law, by which was meant at the time, an understanding that law is not, as he put it, "a closed system . . . but . . . a response to life" (Frankfurter 1960:168). Harvard Law already had a liberal professor with such an outlook, Roscoe Pound, and its dean wanted two such men interested in how the social sciences might illuminate law and jurisprudence. According to Frankfurter, Pound was timid and the dean hoped Frankfurter "would bring . . . the kind of ardor that was precisely what, in his opinion, the school needed" (167). With no faculty openings in 1913, the dean proposed asking the Jewish financier Jacob Schiff to endow a chair for Frankfurter, as a fellow Jew. Fortuitously, one of the law faculty resigned after discovery that he had lied about a retainer from New Haven Railroad. The position was given to Frankfurter, beginning with the 1914–1915 academic year. With a hiatus to serve the Secretary of War in Washington during World War I and as a legal advisor to Woodrow Wilson at Versailles in 1919, Frankfurter taught at Harvard until he joined the Supreme Court in 1939.

A deep friendship had developed between Louis Brandeis and Frankfurter while Brandeis lived in Boston, before he joined the Supreme Court. A prominent lawyer whose southern gentility made him socially acceptable to upper-class legal firms, Brandeis was scholarly and without ostentation. Frankfurter, a generation younger and of a lively temperament, delighted the Brandeis family, becoming like a son among their two daughters. Brandeis's support of Zionism, raised by his experience with the

New York (mostly Jewish) garment workers' strike in 1910 and with refugees from pogroms in Europe, brought Frankfurter in to help Jewish causes, although neither Brandeis nor Frankfurter (whose wife was Protestant) were observant of Jewish ritual. They exemplified the "secular Jew," proud of his heritage of learning and righteousness while committed to the nation in which he was a citizen.

Once he was raised to serve on the Supreme Court, it became unseemly for Justice Brandeis to meddle in politics; instead, he took the pose of a sage advising those active in worldly affairs. Voluble, extroverted Frankfurter fed all the news to his revered elder, in turn receiving advice on how to further their Progressive goals. Their partnership was so marked that three academic books have been written on it (Murphy 1982; Baker 1984; Burt 1988). Given that both men were Jews and active in American support for Zionism, rabid anti-Semites saw them as conspirators aiming to surreptitiously rule America (Crockett 1961:12). Even less foolish men spoke like this Boston politician about Brandeis when the Senate was considering his appointment to the Supreme Court: "a slimy fellow of this kind by his smoothness and intrigue, together with his Jewish instinct, can almost land in the Cabinet and probably on the bench of the Supreme Court" (quoted in Baker 1984:102).[2]

President of Harvard A. Lawrence Lowell had not opposed hiring Frankfurter in 1913. Harvard took the best and brightest, that was that. Then, after World War I, Harvard and other great universities and colleges saw a curious phenomenon: the brightest were, increasingly, Jews. Only 3 percent of the US population, Jews were 6 percent of Harvard students in 1908 and 21 percent in 1922. These students were not content with gentlemen's Cs. They sought and won scholarships, prizes, firsts in their classes, and *Law Review* staff positions. They even won places on athletic teams, to the height of captain of three sports (Synnott 1979:75). Harvard alumni started writing to President Lowell, telling him that the "plague" of Jews deterred other students from applying. Lowell remembered how such a plague of Jews had ruined summer hotels in New England. Lowell decided that the best way to combat anti-Semitism would be to limit the number of Jews at Harvard to 15 percent of the student body, thereby lessening the forced association that he believed would provoke anti-Semitism in the Gentile students. He introduced a new policy to limit the freshman class to one thousand entrants (counting the total would be necessary to keep Jews to 15 percent). Harvard's faculty was, in the main, against quotas for Jews. An appointed committee recommended increasing geographic diversity by imposing higher entrance standards upon boys in the northeastern quarter of the United States—excepting, of course, "lega-cies," the sons of alumni. By this ruse, southern and western WASPs took places that academic ranking would have given to northeastern Jews. Rab-bis's recommendations might not count as heavily as letters from Epis-copal ministers. Lowell also broadened admissions criteria to include "personality" and "character," assessed in interviews and letters of recom-mendation. Boys from eastern European Jewish immigrant families tended to show less attractive personalities, it seemed, than others.

Here was the crux. Lowell had been vice president of the Immigration Restriction League, an elite organization influential in persuading Con-gress to pass the 1924 Johnson-Reed Immigration Restriction Act. Care-fully crafted by Representative Johnson's aristocratic eugenicist friend Madison Grant, the act stipulated that immigration would be limited to 2 percent of each ethnic or national group or race living in the United States in 1890, the last census before southern and eastern Europeans, including eastern European Jews, came "flooding" in response to industrial demands for cheap labor. Lowell was not anti-Semitic, he insisted; some of his good friends were Jews, millionaire financiers and businessmen of German Jew-ish stock whose sons went to Harvard. Such Hebrew gentlemen donated generously to the university. Jacob Schiff had been ready to endow a pro-fessorial chair for Felix Frankfurter. Lowell's 15 percent would accommo-date the millionaires' well-bred sons.

Historians tend to follow the protestations of elite leaders that it was the unwashed boorish emigrants from shtetls they wished to exclude, in con-trast to German Jews whose families were Western educated. Both Louis Brandeis and Felix Frankfurter came of such stock. Brandeis was, more-over, restrained in manner, somewhat aloof. Nevertheless, Lowell disliked him as well as the extroverted New Yorker, Frankfurter. Lowell had led a segment of opposition to Brandeis's 1916 nomination to the Supreme Court. It is easy to presume anti-Semitism, but Lowell and his fellow Bos-ton Brahmins had quite good reason to recoil from Brandeis and Frank-furter.[3] Brandeis had become notorious, in their eyes, in 1910 when he mediated the New York garment workers' strike and a New England shoe manufacturer employees' strike, skillfully bringing owners to compromise with unions, and also in 1910 when he defended conservationists strug-gling against private exploitation of public lands. Much of his work was pro bono. For Brandeis, and for Frankfurter, public service was a moral obli-gation, rooted in Judaic moral philosophy. Lowell avowed an obligation toward public service, encouraging Harvard faculty and students to em-brace it as noblesse oblige, the duty of the educated upper class to govern.

Brandeis and Frankfurter felt themselves standing with the mass of the citizenry, not over them. Unlike the Brahmins, they believed themselves born to leadership not through family but through their intellectual gifts — they represented meritocracy, not aristocracy.

As a professor teaching administrative law at Harvard, Felix Frankfurter could advocate and demonstrate his "admiration for undiluted meritocracy" (Lipset and Riesman 1975:330). Despite its appeal on grounds of Enlightenment rationality, meritocracy could not but be contentious. Sociologists Seymour Martin Lipset and David Riesman list fourteen entries, most with subentries, under the topic "meritocracy" in their 1975 Carnegie Commission on Higher Education study, *Education and Politics at Harvard*. Riesman in this book contrasts the laid-back attitude cultivated by Harvard undergraduates in the 1920s and 1930s with the "ferocious competitiveness" at Harvard Law School. (Riesman entered Harvard as a freshman in 1927, graduated in 1931, and went on to Harvard Law, following that with a year as clerk for Justice Brandeis.) During this time, Harvard Law students' papers were identified by numbers rather than names, to prevent faculty from playing favorites (Lipset and Riesman 1975:330). Such clear pursuit of merit in the law school mirrored a shift in law firms' personnel and orientation. Aristocrats like eugenicist Madison Grant had taken degrees in law, had their names inscribed in Brahmin law firms, and occasionally stopped in on the way to their clubs.

Industrialization slowly changed American social classes. With more and more of the populace employees instead of farmers, labor challenged unregulated capitalism, the robber barons. The Progressive Party of the early twentieth century preached social welfare while leading churchmen taught a social gospel. Congress responded by fits and starts, curbing cartels, for example with the Sherman Antitrust Act of 1890. Businessmen now sought lawyers to strategize ways to circumvent populist regulatory laws, as well as to defend their businesses in court. Corporate law became a major business in itself. Lowell of Harvard, trained in the law, saw his brethren in these firms arguing for corporations; to him, these lawyers did public service. Brandeis and Frankfurter had each joined WASP law firms, and were the only Jews in the firms, where they saw this concept of public service and felt repulsed. Frankfurter's courses in administrative law were calculated to awaken in students that zeal for helping the underdogs, the unenfranchised, that invigorated him and his esteemed elder friend. Predictably, the advocates for social welfare reforms were accused of socialism.

The Bugaboo of Socialism

After the 1917 Bolshevik Revolution in Russia frightened capitalists, eastern European Jews were often stereotypically associated with socialism and communism. Earlier, these labels had more often been associated with utopian communitarian sects such as the Shakers or John Humphrey Noyes's Oneida Community. Nineteenth-century publics most feared the loose political movement termed anarchy, climaxed by self-announced anarchist Leon Czolgosz assassinating President McKinley in 1901. Bolsheviks became the new bugbear after World War I. Wartime calls for patriotic solidarity had lapsed, replaced in 1919 by calls from several unions for better conditions for their workers. "Wobblies" (members of Industrial Workers of the World, a broadly based international union focusing on class-based struggle) and anarchist radicals joined the struggles, sometimes throwing bombs. Congress passed Espionage and Sedition Acts in 1917 and 1918 respectively, authorizing imprisonment and deportation of persons heard to express opposition to US policies.

A case that ended up in the Supreme Court in 1929 involved denial of citizenship to an immigrant woman, fifty years of age, a declared pacifist. Upon examination, she had stated she would refuse to bear arms. Ridiculous as it would appear to demand that a middle-aged intellectual woman bear arms in war, the majority on the Supreme Court upheld the denial of citizenship. In dissent, Justice Oliver Wendell Holmes Jr. wrote, "If there is any principle of the Constitution that more imperatively calls for attachment than any other it is the principle of free thought . . . [even for those who] believe more than some of us do in the teachings of the Sermon on the Mount" (quoted in Bowen 1943:373–74).

Justice Holmes was a Boston Brahmin of impeccable ancestry, descended from David Holmes of Massachusetts Bay Colony, his grandfather the minister of First Parish Church of Cambridge, his father an eminent professor in Harvard Medical School. Holmes Jr. matriculated at Harvard, of course, chose Harvard Law School for professional preparation, and was admitted to the Massachusetts Bar after reading law at a leading Boston firm. If anyone should have been staid and prejudiced against "the unwashed," it should have been Oliver Wendell Holmes Jr. Instead, on the bench he became the "Great Dissenter," famous for his cogent, literate arguments for First Amendment rights, the constitutionality of legislation protecting labor, and his reading of the Fourteenth Amendment, especially its clause "nor shall any State deprive any person of life, liberty, or property, without due process of law." Holmes stated in dissenting from *Truax v. Corrigan*, 1921, that the majority on the Court erred in the "fallacy of delusive exactness," looking upon a business operation—necessitating dealing with employees—as if it were real property (in land), liable to simple damage by physical trespass. "There is nothing that I more deprecate than the use of the Fourteenth Amendment . . . to prevent the making of social experiments that an important part of the community desires," he wrote (quoted in Bowen 1943:365).

From 1916 until he at last retired in 1932, Justice Holmes had one staunch ally in most of his dissents: Justice Louis Brandeis. The Jew whose parents had emigrated to Kentucky from the revolutions of 1848 in Europe and the Boston Brahmin became, also, close personal friends. So did younger men in Washington serving their government during World War I, among them Felix Frankfurter. Frankfurter's Cambridge roommate Morris Cohen was another whose sharp analytical mind coupled with passion for humanity entranced Justice Holmes. They all were drawn to observing social experiments that communities desire. None were active in the Socialist Party. Instead, they joined the American Civil Liberties Union (ACLU), formed in 1920.

Conservatives viewed the ACLU as tantamount to radicalism. A March 28, 1934, article in the *New York Times* was headlined "12 in 'Brain Trust' Called Socialists; They Are Members of Civil Liberties Union." The Brain Trust members listed included Rex Tugwell, Jerome Frank, James Landis, Robert Marshall (OIA forester), Rose Schneiderman, Nathan Margold, and that lawyer famous for arguing for evolution in the Scopes trial, Clarence Darrow. Rep. Hamilton Fish (NY) was quoted by the *Times*: "It is estimated that there are about a score or more of young radicals, so-called economic experts and lawyers of the Felix Frankfurter school of thought, most of whom are disciples of Karl Marx, doing work for the government." Keeping balance, the same article then quoted Rep. Foulkes of Michigan: "America is not afraid of champions of the poor and lowly—call them 'red' or what you may. What it should be fearful of, and what it should strike down with swift and sturdy hand, are those evil instruments of Herr Hitler and the stupid fools who in their ignorance become blind allies."

Brandeis, Holmes, Frankfurter, Ickes and his friend Hiram Johnson of California, Franklin Roosevelt, and many thousands of others espoused the principles of the Progressive Party formed in 1912 under Theodore Roosevelt. They had no quarrel with capitalism per se, only with robberbaron exploitation of workers. Government, they held, should take a larger role in the United States by regulating employment hours and conditions

and labor's right to collective bargaining and unions, by setting up federally supported health and social security insurance, by expanding direct
election of senators and other officials, antitrust measures, and women's
suffrage. None of this went as far as the Socialist Party of America's plat-
forms calling for a cooperative commonwealth. Nonetheless, the epithet
"socialist" was hurled at all these liberals. The postwar Red Scare that
brought the Espionage and Sedition Acts turned the epithet dangerous.

Political invective and hate mongering have no truck with nice distinc-
tions. American Socialists (as a party) ranged from impoverished farmers
in Oklahoma and Texas to Jewish immigrants from Russia, refugees from
the failed 1905 revolution there. The twentieth-century United States saw
surges of Red Scare like plagues of seventeen-year locusts. Between epi-
sodes of deafening whirring wings and chomping jaws, memory persisted
with its box of ready labels to pin on political opponents. Fear of socialism,
that is, of a cooperative commonwealth instead of capitalism, stimulated
the New York legislative assembly to refuse to seat five elected Socialist
Party candidates in 1920, and Wisconsin Representative Victor Berger was
twice refused his seat in Congress, 1919 and 1920. Like Progressives in
1912, although American Socialists talked about revolution, they sensibly
rejected it, preferring to seek power through the ballot box.

Milwaukee, Victor Berger's home, elected several Socialist mayors, one
of whom earned the label "sewer socialist" for announcing he cared more
for providing clean water and good sewers than for Marxist theory. Ignoring real American Socialists' and liberals' pacifist leanings, Bolshevik hys-
teria tarred all socialist thinking with the charge of insurrection. If the
liberals or socialists happened to be Jewish, they could be accused of sabo-
taging America, according to the notorious, fabricated *Protocols of the Elders of Zion*. Henry Ford used his millions to print and distribute, beginning in 1920, much of this dangerously libelous material. Leading
American Jews such as Louis Marshall demanded that Ford retract the
lies, until in 1925 a Jewish agricultural labor organizer, Aaron Sapiro,
threatened a libel suit against him for defamatory untruths (Woeste 2012:
371 n. 65). *Sapiro v. Ford* came to trial in 1927 and was settled out of court,
exposing without really abating entrenched anti-Semitism.

Frankfurter's Hires

Felix Frankfurter had for years been supplying his best (in his opinion)
Harvard Law graduates as clerks and secretaries to justices Brandeis and

Holmes. Not all were Jewish; Frankfurter's criteria were brains, sound legal knowledge, a strong work ethic, and desire for public service. If many were Jewish, that reflected the commitment to hard mental work that President Lowell considered the distinction between the Jews and WASPs at Harvard. *Time* magazine in a 1934 article, "National Affairs: Jobs and Jews," commented that "the Jews of the [Roosevelt] Administration" were significant due to "their great industry, their extraordinary mental ability and their crusading fervor for what they conceive to be the high and remote ideals of the New Deal."

Time's response, in 1934, to suspicions that Roosevelt's Jewish advisors and hires represented a "Jewish cabal" is worth quoting at length. Noting that the President had no hand in electing ten Jews to the House of Representatives, and that the Jewish Supreme Court justices Brandeis and Cardozo had been appointed by previous presidents, the magazine counted:

Only 30 [Jews] in the 1,000 top jobs of the Federal Government, or 3%.

This proportion of Jews to jobs is slightly less than that of Jews to Gentiles in the whole U.S. population. . . . [Frankfurter] he [Roosevelt] uses less as an adviser than as an agent through whom to find and employ bright young legalites to do spade work for the Brain Trust. Undoubtedly the young Jews in second-string positions are not so much personal appointees of the President as they are the choices of the President's Gentile advisers. . . . [Although these Jews] are not many and do not hold high posts, the fact remains that because their brains and ability are used by their superiors and because they are frequently deputed to carry out the Administration's policies and write its bills, their importance exceeds their numbers and their official rank. . . . Secretary of Interior Ickes has Nathan R. Margold, Harvard Law School graduate, as his solicitor, and Robert D. Kohn as his director of PWA housing. Madam Secretary Perkins has two able Jewish helpers, Isador Lubin as labor statistician and Charles E. Wyzanski Jr. as solicitor. Lawyer Wyzanski has spent most of his 28 years winning prizes: as a high school boy, from the Daughters of the American Revolution; as a student at Phillips Exeter, the Walter Hines Page, Merrill and Teschemacher prizes (all in one year) and a four-year scholarship at Harvard; as a junior at Harvard the *New York Times*'s intercollegiate current events contest ($750). He was serving the Boston law firm of Ropes, Gray, Boyden & Perkins when Miss Perkins asked Professor Frankfurter to suggest a solicitor for her. Wyzanski was the answer. . . . [Another Jewish hire] is

Rose Schneiderman (Labor Advisory Board) who last January went to Puerto Rico to iron out its labor difficulties and, more recently, has threatened to sue Dr. Wirt for calling her "Red Rose of Anarchy." ("National Affairs: Jobs and Jews" 1934)

Not singled out by the magazine was yet another bright young Jew in the New Deal, Bob Marshall. Robert Marshall's father was Louis Marshall, a highly successful lawyer with a strong Jewish conscience (a founder of the national American Jewish Committee) who had worked with Louis Brandeis in 1910 to mediate the New York cloakmakers' strike, as well as mediating with Ford in the *Sapiro* case. Louis Marshall, like Morris Cohen, loved the Adirondacks, his family summering on Lower Saranac Lake and two of his sons, Bob and George, pioneering summiting Adirondack peaks. Bob earned a PhD in plant physiology to work as a forestry expert, coming to Washington in 1932 to the Forest Service and then transferring for three years to the Office of Indian Affairs as its chief forester before returning to the Forest Service. He and his economist brother George were founders of the Wilderness Society. Bob died unexpectedly in 1939, at age thirty-eight; the huge Bob Marshall Wilderness in Montana along the Rockies is his memorial.

Jews were not as absent from American political positions as would be inferred from most general American histories. Wikipedia lists these firsts for American Jews in politics:

First Jewish member of a colonial legislature (South Carolina): Francis Salvador (1775)

First Jewish governor of a US state: David Emanuel (Georgia, 1801)

First Jewish member of the US Congress/US House of Representatives: Lewis Charles Levin (Pennsylvania, 1845)

First Jewish member of the US Senate: David Levy Yulee (Florida, 1845)

First Jewish mayor of a major American city (Iowa City, Iowa): Moses Bloom (1873)

Two years later, Bailey Gatzert became mayor of Seattle (1875)

First Jewish cabinet member/Secretary of Commerce and Labor: Oscar Straus (1906)

Not including Judah P. Benjamin, who served in the Confederate cabinet as Secretary of State and War. President Millard Fillmore had offered to appoint Judah P. Benjamin to the Supreme Court in 1853, but Benjamin declined.

First elected Jewish governor of a US state: Washington Bartlett (California, 1887)

First Jewish justice of the Supreme Court of the United States: Louis Brandeis (1916)

First Jewish woman member of the US Congress/US House of Representatives: Florence Prag Kahn (California, 1925)[4]

Wikipedia missed Solomon Bibo, first Jewish governor of Acoma Pueblo, 1885; he had married into the pueblo and was chosen governor to deal with US officials troubling Acoma. Much too late to be a first, Fiorello LaGuardia was an outstanding mayor of New York City, 1934–1945, after twelve years as a congressman; his mother, Irene Coen LaGuardia, came from the noted Luzzato family of Italian Jews.

Not quite eligible for the list, Belle Moskowitz should be noted as the first American Jewish woman to serve as campaign manager and chief assistant to a governor of New York. Al Smith, like Mrs. Moskowitz, grew up in New York City among immigrants. When he ran for governor in 1918, after years in New York City politics, she became his most trusted advisor, supporting his Progressive goals. Smith, a Catholic, ran unsuccessfully for President in 1928, losing to Herbert Hoover, partly because of anti-Catholic propaganda. In 1932, he lost the Democratic presidential nomination to his successor as governor of New York, Franklin Roosevelt. He and Belle Moskowitz remained friends until she died from a winter fall, January 2, 1933, although he was shifting away from the Progressive principles she had firmly urged during the decade he served in Albany (Howe 1976:388–91). Mrs. Moskowitz was a precursor for the Roosevelt New Deal willingness to hire Jews when they were the best for a job.

Of all Frankfurter's hires for the early New Deal, Nathan Margold was pivotal for the Indian New Deal. Born in Iasi, Romania, Margold came to the United States with his family as a toddler at the beginning of the twentieth century. Attending CCNY, he took classes in philosophy from Morris Raphael Cohen, imbibing Cohen's inspiring combination of pragmatism with the ideal of socially sensitive, humane jurisprudence. Taking a law degree from Harvard in 1922, Margold was on the *Harvard Law Review*'s editorial board when it published an article commencing with a quotation from the school's dean, Roscoe Pound, calling for "an adjustment of principles and doctrines to the human conditions they are to govern rather than to assumed first principles; for putting the human factor in the central place, and relegating logic to its true position as an instrument."[5] Harvard

Law hired Margold to teach immediately after his graduation, a position he resigned to work as an assistant US attorney for the Southern District of New York, and then to become special counsel for the New York Transit Company in a protracted battle over raising some subway fares above the five cents charged since 1886. Already in 1926, Margold published an article in *The Nation*, "The Plight of the Pueblos," describing their "eleventh-hour resort to litigation" to retain their irrigation rights, litigation he assisted beginning in 1930, after a year with the Institute for Government Research, drafting a bill for Indian claims. Barely thirty, Margold prepared a report for the National Association for the Advancement of Colored People (NAACP) suggesting strategies for desegregating schools. His advocacy of sweeping challenges at every level of education was rejected by the experienced African-American lawyer Charles Houston in favor of targeting the most blatantly unequal sector, graduate programs. Margold was tagged as a brilliant young lawyer fighting for minorities, just the man Harold Ickes wanted for Solicitor for Interior. Frankfurter's recommendation was quickly accepted.

Margold's admiration for Professor Cohen led to a friendship with Cohen's family. He collaborated with Morris's son Felix on a brief for a struggle at CCNY over student rights. Possibly it was Felix's mother who urged Nathan to give her son a job in the New Deal (Tsuk Mitchell 2007: 63). Probably Margold needed no Jewish mother's urging to hire Felix Cohen, CCNY 1926, PhD, philosophy, Harvard 1929, LLB Columbia 1931. That the young Cohen, twenty-six, had neither knowledge nor experience with Indian people was no barrier to the work Margold directed on the Indian Reorganization Act. Because Felix Cohen had chosen Columbia Law after taking a doctorate in philosophy from Harvard, he was not one of Frankfurter's students (to Frankfurter's disappointment), yet his choice by Margold fit him into that company, not only through Margold's training with Frankfurter, but also through the lifelong friendship between Frankfurter and Morris Cohen beginning when the two men roomed together at Harvard.

Nathan Margold was an extremely busy man at Interior, implementing Harold Ickes's radical goal of making President Roosevelt's New Deal a revolution for the common people. Felix Cohen could be relied upon to work like a dog for the humanitarian principles his professor father had imbued in so many CCNY students. Felix's legal mind was as brilliant and well-trained as Nathan's. Felix had an additional advantage—the very bright anthropology graduate student he brought to Washington as his wife. When research on Indian tribes was needed, Lucy Kramer was eager to take part. Her papers in the Beinecke Library archives at Yale include many sheets with tribal names and topics in Felix's bold large masculine hand, and the spaces between filled in with Lucy's tiny neat handwriting, the result of her searches in the Library of Congress, Department of Interior files, and anthropological sources.

Felix and Lucy brought into the Office of Indian Affairs an admiration for social democratic principles and their embodiment in the rather odd WASP version of socialism preached by Norman Thomas. Both Felix and Lucy were literally card-carrying members of the Socialist Party of America through the 1930s.[6] Norman Thomas was the party's leader, over six feet tall, an inspiring orator along the lines of his Ohio Presbyterian father and grandfathers. Thoroughly middle-class American, Thomas abhorred violence. That brought him into conflict with Marxist expectations of revolution, as well as with the often violent outbursts of labor grievances. At the same time, Thomas belittled Milwaukee mayor Daniel Hoan's "sewer socialism" targeting public welfare rather than abstract socialist principles. Franklin Roosevelt's opportunism galled the Puritan-descended Thomas. When Roosevelt's and Ickes's New Deal espousal of labor, for example creating the National Labor Relations Board, drew many socialist labor leaders into the Democratic Party, Thomas struggled against their defection, as he saw it, and also against more Marxist members of the party, resulting in a breakdown of party spirit and significant loss of members by 1936 (Soyer 2012:221). Princeton-educated Thomas nevertheless gained respect for his deep pacifist faith in humanity, in the face of Axis militarism and then World War II, and his personal integrity. The Cohen family asked him to be a pallbearer for Felix Cohen at Felix's funeral (Bickel 2000).

Felix Cohen wrote to Norman Thomas on November 8, 1933, three weeks after Cohen's provisional appointment to Interior and a week before he was confirmed as an assistant solicitor. Combating "capitalist individualism" and supporting "a communal ceremony" would be his goal, Cohen told Thomas. Thomas replied promptly that Cohen's position would be an opportunity both to actualize socialist principles and to enhance the young man's government experience that later could be used to advance the party's goals.[7] There can be no question of Felix Cohen's dedication to socialism, nor of Felix Frankfurter's lack of support for socialism, not because of any love for capitalism, but because Frankfurter was pragmatic. In his memoir, Frankfurter mentions a meeting with Franklin Roosevelt during his 1932 campaign, when a wealthy contributor assured Roosevelt he would get her donation but not her vote, for she wanted to vote for Norman Thomas. Roosevelt replied that he considered Thomas "a fine man," in spite of his refusal to join Governor Roosevelt's New York state commission on the unemployment problem (Frankfurter 1960:241). Exactly that, principles before pragmatics, characterized Norman Thomas and drew young idealists like Felix Cohen, while "mugwumps" like Felix Frankfurter (his own term; Frankfurter 1960:240) got on with lawsuits and politicking toward achievable goals.

Roosevelt's New Deal was an extraordinary interlude in American history, a brief period of little more than two years, 1933–1936, when Progressive politics succeeded in revolutionizing life for the masses. Perhaps it was the crucible of crippling paralysis that forged Roosevelt's indomitable demand to ignore social criteria that had excluded highly talented men and women from influential positions. The Depression's pervasive unemployment made jobs in Washington lucrative; the mission of saving the country from its crisis drew creative thinkers and gave them latitude to initiate radical programs. Doctrinaire socialism, like doctrinaire laissez-faire economics, could not hold against Roosevelt's anything-goes spirit. Frankfurter and Ickes, along with numbers of other former adherents of the Progressive Party, let the party itself founder. To save the nation, its most extraordinarily competent and hardworking men and even some women must be recruited to serve their government.

Children of the great wave of European Jewish immigration of the 1890s had a cadre of brilliant young scholars (in the Jewish cultural tradition) ablaze with love of America, eager to work unstintingly. Frankfurter supplied the names of many he had taught, not to infiltrate with a Jewish cabal but to get the best and brightest Americans into government. Nathan Margold fit the need. So did his revered professor's son Felix Cohen. These men in Interior became a counterweight to John Collier's antimodern sensibility with its residue of paternalism. Not until Richard Nixon's Indian Self-Determination Act did policy shift toward the position codified by Cohen in his *Handbook*. Histories of the Indian New Deal have tended to take Collier at his word and trace the Indian New Deal to his advocacy for the Pueblo Indians he met through Mabel Dodge Luhan. The boys from CCNY, Margold and Cohen, and Boas's student Lucy Kramer Cohen need to be introduced into Indian history. The next chapter looks at those Jewish kids from New York.

CHAPTER FOUR

Felix and Lucy

Felix was tall, lean, fair. Lucy was petite, dark-haired, vivacious. Canoeing in the Adirondacks, tenting at night, was their idea of paradise (figure 4.1). Hardly your stereotypical New York Jews. At a Halloween party in 1925, eighteen-year-old Felix was boyishly acting up; he noticed bright-eyed "Little One" in a light lavender dress and asked to escort her home, but she properly returned with the young man who had brought her to the party. That night, Lucy confided in her Aunt Yetty (Yetty Kramer Mager) that if she ever married, it would be to that youth Felix Cohen. Felix would tell people that Lucy caught his eye because lavender is the school color of his college, City College of New York (CCNY).

Both Felix Solomon Cohen and Louise ("Lucy") Michelle Kramer were born in New York in 1907 to immigrant parents. Felix's father, Morris Raphael Cohen, came to the United States with his family from Minsk, Russia, in 1892 as a boy of twelve, speaking no English. Fourteen years later, he had earned a PhD in philosophy at Harvard University. As Jews were not usually considered for appointment as professors of philosophy at that time, Morris taught mathematics until a position in philosophy became open in 1912 at his alma mater. CCNY was attended by most of the city's immigrant Jewish boys and a few of its black youths. Morris Cohen remained professor of philosophy at CCNY until he retired in 1938. Morris married Mary Ryshpan, born in the United States to parents recently immigrated from Poland; she was a fellow student of the peripatetic Scottish philosopher Thomas Davidson at the Educational Alliance, a kind of settlement house created by a group of New York Jewish agencies

Figure 4.1. Felix and Lucy hiking in the forest. Photo courtesy of the Felix S. and Lucy Kramer Cohen Photograph Collection.

in 1889. Morris called her "May." Acceding to expectations of the time, Mary devoted herself to maintaining a household where her husband, freed of mundane tasks, could devote himself to his scholarly and bread-winning vocation. Morris had little time for his children—again, a commonplace for educated men of his time—whom Mary brought up in the Enlightenment spirit induced by Davidson.

Lucy's parents were Aaron and Annie Kramer. The Kramer family already espoused Enlightenment: Lucy was told that her father's grandfather had studied with Moses Mendelsohn, the eighteenth-century German Jew accepted as a modern philosopher in Frederick the Great's Berlin. Love of books, museums, and dance was instilled in Lucy and her siblings by their Aunt Fanny, who had attended Hunter College (New York's free college for women, as CCNY accepted only male students). Tuberculosis had forced Fanny to drop out of Hunter. Married and with her own child, she used her education to foster and guide the Kramer children, choosing Erasmus Hall high school for Lucy and then seeing that she enrolled in Barnard College. Sidney, the only boy among the five Kramer siblings, developed a passion for books in that book-loving family, earning a doctorate in library science and in 1946, with his wife Miriam, opening Sidney Kramer Books in Washington, DC, specializing in researchers' needs. (His son Bill Kramer opened Kramer Books and Afterwords on Connecticut Avenue, a mecca for lovers of books and coffee.) Neither the Cohens nor the Kramers followed orthodox Judaism, instead keeping the principal holidays as family celebrations and sending the children to synagogue classes for religious education. The Kramers and Cohens knew they should be proud of their Jewish heritage of learning and justice.

Barnard College was, and is, the women's college of Columbia University, one of the Seven Sisters eastern women's colleges paralleling the men's Ivy League universities. Charging tuition, Barnard had fewer immigrants' daughters than the city-supported Hunter College. Because Columbia's Franz Boas was committed to bringing talented women into anthropology—his mother in Germany was a suffragist—he taught in Barnard classrooms and encouraged Barnard students to continue in his graduate program at Columbia. Margaret Mead (Barnard 1923) was the best known; another was the African-American Zora Neale Hurston (Barnard 1928). Lucy Kramer, enrolled 1924–1928 and living on campus, knew both. While majoring in anthropology to find out everything possible about humans, she felt strongly attracted to the pure beauty of mathematics. Happily, Professor Boas needed a mathematically minded research assistant; he had her help analyze Kwakiutl linguistics and use his own statistical modes of analysis to handle anthropometric data. His innovations were not published as such, and were instead buried in anthropological reports, resulting in his English contemporary Karl Pearson receiving public credit for some formulas Boas had also developed.

Lucy Kramer quickly earned an MA in mathematics in 1929, going on through 1933 with doctoral-level courses in both mathematics and anthropology while working as one of Boas's research assistants. Anticipating fieldwork toward a dissertation by accompanying Edward Sapir to an Apache reservation in the summer of 1932, Lucy was frustrated by a new reluctance to let young women work on reservations, the result of the 1931 murder of a Columbia graduate student by an Apache man who misunderstood, and was angered by, her insistence on asking about Apache sexual customs. To save money, Lucy audited several graduate courses, thereby not receiving transcript credits that would have been valuable when she applied for federal employment years later.[1]

Felix Cohen chose to enroll in Columbia in 1928–1931 for his law degree, in part to be with Lucy after his two years in Cambridge for his PhD in philosophy, awarded in 1929. At Harvard, Felix had taken anthropology courses; he had known Boas both through Lucy and as a family acquaintance. If technically Felix was not a Boas student, his immersion in Lucy's life ensured familiarity with Boasian anthropology, its uncompromising hostility to popular nineteenth-century racist cultural evolutionist schemas and its voracious demand for empirical observations and data. Franz Boas, by example, also influenced Lucy and Felix to respect and actively support women pursuing scholarly research. His example showed, too, that a brilliant, leading scientist could find time to be with his children, to take the fatherly interest in students that prompted the women to call him Papa Boas, and to make music a daily joy. To be a Boasian anthropologist one did not require a diploma—it was a way of living in the world of humans.

During their years at Columbia and into the 1930s, Lucy and Felix were active in a lively group of mostly Jewish young people eager to change the world for the better (figure 4.2). They belonged to the League for Industrial Democracy, founded in 1905 by Norman Thomas, Harry W. Laidler, Clarence Darrow, and others as the Intercollegiate Socialist Society. Membership overlapped, in the case of the Cohens as well as many others, with the American Civil Liberties Union, causing the ACLU to be hounded by conservatives as "Red" or even as a Communist front organization. Laidler knew the young couple personally, writing in 1938 on a card reminding them of their pledge of twenty dollars to the League for Industrial Democracy and that prompt payment "would be doubly appreciated. Hope you have a fine vacation," and adding next to their names on the address side of the card, "to those lucky in their parents!"[2] Morris and Mary Cohen, and Aaron and Annie Kramer, promoted for their children a secular outlook ostensibly built upon science and humanitarian respect for fellow humans. Underlying their rational principles was Judaism's traditional mitzvah, a person's moral obligation, literally commandment, to perform good deeds. The young Jews' Industrial Research Group (IRG)

Figure 4.2. Felix, Lucy, and friends, 1931–1933. Back row, George Bronz, Ted Haas (later OIA colleague), Felix's sister Leonora Cohen; middle row, unidentified man, Lucy Kramer, Felix Cohen in front of her, two unidentified women. Photo courtesy of Felix S. and Lucy Kramer Cohen Photograph Collection.

was for them a mitzvah, a means to live righteously as their forebears had striven to do.

Lucy was the secretary for the IRG, a subgroup of the League for Industrial Democracy. Its postal address was Schermerhorn Hall, Columbia University, home of the Department of Anthropology. A year after the group had published a set of articles, 1931, and sent them to professors of economics, suggesting students could use the materials and especially the bibliographies for research papers, Lucy mailed out a mimeographed form requesting the professors' feedback on the articles' distribution and whether they had proved useful. Not many professors bothered to reply. Lucy then, in 1932, submitted a letter to the *New York Times*:

INDUSTRIAL RESEARCH GROUP New York N.Y. To the Editor: Those of your readers who are interested in research on the labor problem, whether as producers of research studies or as consumers, may be interested to know of the existence of the Industrial Research Group. This organization attempts to act as a clearing-house for students of labor problems and for those who may wish to build upon their work.

Guides to research with bibliographical notes are available for free distribution to students interested in the following subjects: (1) The Intellectual and the Labor Movement; (2) Consumers' Power; (3) Managers in the Profit System; (4) The Labor Injunction; (5) Agricultural Prosperity and Labor Unionism. LUCY M. KRAMER, Secretary, Industrial Research Group, Columbia University, New York City.[3]

The following year, 1933, the IRG deposited $100 in May and withdrew $99 in November and December, the lonely last dollar languishing in the bank until 1936 when the IRG treasurer took it out, extinguishing the bank account.[4] The money apparently was used for mimeographing the papers and for postage. After Felix was hired by the Department of the Interior and Lucy moved with him to Washington, assisting him with research on Indians, she procrastinated with an article she had undertaken as an IRG outgrowth, on assignment to Meredith B. Givens, head of the Industrial Section of the Social Science Research Council: "A Survey of Social Problems in the Production and Consumption of Food: An Analysis of Fields for Further Research." Givens had to pressure her to finish that commitment, a forty-eight-page essay she turned in during November 1934, receiving an honorarium of $250.[5] To be fair, she had suffered bouts of ill health a year previously, spending some time recuperating at the Mountain Meadows Inn in Asheville, North Carolina.[6]

Felix's role in the IRG and their circle of young intellectual socialists was to collegially frame and lead discussions. He wrote in 1931, on behalf of the IRG, to Edward Pease, a founder of the Fabian Society in England, sending him copies of reports on social problems written by IRG members. Pease replied, "The Fabian Society as you know was never primarily a research organization. We started with a theory, or at any rate an object, & researched to prove or attain it." He noted that the Fabians had recently organized the New Fabian Research Bureau informally affiliated with the London School of Economics.[7] Ironically, "starting with a theory . . . and researching to prove or attain it" was the modus operandi of IRG and its friends. Felix's doctorate in philosophy and his law degree both trained him to think in this manner. His father, Morris, was famous for relentlessly challenging students' arguments, perhaps not consciously in the Talmudic argumentation tradition he had heard with his grandfather in Russia; Morris coauthored with his student Ernest Nagel a well-received text, *An Introduction to Logic and Scientific Method* (1934). Most of Morris's CCNY students, the majority born into the Ashkenazi tradition, manfully bore the sharp-edged interlocution, grateful for its honing of their critical powers.

Felix with his peers was soft spoken, his breadth of knowledge and analytic faculty generously serving their gatherings.

Yearly in the 1930s, in August or early September, the Cohens' circle held a ten-day conference, a young intellectual adults' version of camp. Thomas Davidson had purchased Glenmore, a farm in the Adirondacks, to use as a writing retreat and for a summer school. Morris Cohen attended in 1899 and 1900, living in a tent and doing work around the school in return for board. Between the beauty of the mountains and the provocative discourses on philosophy, Morris was entranced, "joyful and inspired," he said (M. Cohen 1949:108). Summering in the Adirondacks, hiking and swimming, became Cohen family practice—the Jewish hotels in the Catskills were not for them. The IRG's annual conference must have owed something to Davidson's school at Glenmore. Lucy, secretary to the IRG, organized the conferences, always making sure there would be camping space for those who preferred to sleep outdoors. In 1933 and 1937 it was at the Manumit School in Pawling, New York, a Progressive Christian socialist boarding school offering modest dormitory, dining, and lecture rooms and a pleasant campus appreciated by the IRG "kids." Discussions were mapped out for each day, serious reading lists sent out, song-fests drawing on the Rebel Arts songbook, and finally each year a play written and performed by the members.[8] The quality of the discussions can be inferred from the organizers: in addition to Felix and Lucy and Joe Lash, later to be Eleanor Roosevelt's close friend, they included political philosopher Lewis Feuer and Felix's future colleague in Interior, Theodore Haas.[9]

The mundane need to make a living brought Felix, after obtaining his LLB, to clerk, in 1931–1932, for Judge Bernard Shientag of the New York Supreme Court. Upon Shientag's recommendation, he was then employed by the New York law firm Hays, Podell, and Shulman (a "Jewish firm"; Jews were seldom hired by firms whose partners were not Jewish). Judge Shientag was Orthodox, observing Sabbath on Saturdays and expecting his clerks to adjust weekends accordingly. Shientag was fatherly with Felix, who deeply respected and liked him. Hays, Podell, and Shulman showed concern for social justice that was comfortable for Felix. Meanwhile, Lucy translated articles in German for the *Encyclopedia of the Social Sciences* and taught mathematics at George Washington High School in New York in 1933, and the next year worked as a librarian in Columbia's Classics Library, in addition to assisting Professor Boas. Two summers, 1925 and 1931, she worked as a statistician for the National Bureau of Economic Research, and in the summers of 1927 and 1928 she assisted professors in Columbia's Teachers College with statistics and biometrics. Lucy needed income to pay off her student loan from Columbia University, finally completed in August 1935.[10] Typical of the time, Felix had a career; his wife had jobs. Because she was a woman, her graduate work in mathematics was considered to qualify her to teach high school mathematics, nothing more.

When his slightly older friend Nathan Margold invited Felix to take a position as assistant solicitor under him in the Department of the Interior in October 1933, he had an opportunity to leave the routine of a junior man in a New York firm for unprecedented attacks upon injustice, supported by the charismatic new president and his Progressive stalwart Secretary of the Interior. Lucy applied for government positions as research specialist senior anthropologist and as assistant ethnologist in the spring of 1935, passed the qualifying exams, but worked as a volunteer researcher for Felix from 1934 to 1937. Thanks to a suggestion from Barnard College's dean's assistant, Lucy was employed in 1937 as a statistician in the Department of Agriculture's Bureau of Home Economics, on a project analyzing dietary factors in children's growth; the director of the project was Dr. Eleanor Phelps Hunt (Barnard 1923, PhD in anthropology). From April through July 1938, Lucy had similar paid work in the same Bureau of Home Economics for Dr. Louise Stanley, preparing charts and statistics on growth of black children.[11] Then Lucy took "maternity leave," she stated, to bear Gene Maura in 1939, and Karen Annie in 1943, both large babies for whom she underwent caesarean delivery. Ruth Morris, an African-American, joined the family, relieving Lucy of household tasks and sharing mothering the girls (Mrs. Morris had her own children, too). With Ruth in the house, Lucy was able to work as a statistician for the National War Labor Board, becoming head, by 1947, of its Bureau of Labor Statistics.[12] Her years with the IRG gave her a knowledge of labor economics that, with her expertise in statistics, at last gave her a position particularly suited to her interests and experience. For the rest of her long life, Lucy worked at editorial and analytical tasks calling upon her anthropological background and familiarity with a broad range of sciences and projects.

Felix had found his field when he began working for Margold in Washington. Neither familiar with, nor particularly interested in, American Indians before he came to Washington, Felix quickly realized that Collier's goal of providing limited self-government to his Indian wards could be, as he wrote to Norman Thomas, an opening wedge for constructing social democratic communities in the United States (Tsuk Mitchell 2007:74).

Collier believed that many federally recognized tribes retained a sense of community, valuing communal institutions more than individual wealth and high status. If the siphoning off of communal lands via allotment, leasing, and sales could be halted and larger land bases restored, he foretold revived egalitarian villages nurturing traditional arts and religions, strong enough to withstand the consumer capitalism vitiating American society. The United States being a nation of laws, legislative acts needed to be drawn up to translate the vision into action. For that, Margold had hired Cohen and another young Jewish lawyer, Melvin Siegel, who had clerked for Supreme Court justice Cardozo, 1932–1933, after graduating from Harvard Law School. To introduce the young men to their new assignment, Margold ordered them to spend the month of November 1933 visiting reservations, first Fort Berthold in central North Dakota, the last refuge of Mandan, Hidatsa, and Arikara, then to Gallup, New Mexico, where they could see Navajos, Zuni, and, to the east, the Pueblos along the Rio Grande north of Albuquerque, and finally in that month to Oklahoma, erstwhile Indian Territory.

No sooner were the young lawyers back in Washington than Collier told them he and Margold wanted a draft of Indian reform legislation by the end of December. Ward Shepard, who had been director of Harvard University's Harvard Forest, had moved to the US Forest Service and assisted a senior government conservationist, Ayers Brinser, in writing *The American Way: Our Use of the Land* (1939), then had moved to the OIA to advise on land policies. Shepard's orientation can be surmised from the title of the book he published in 1945, *Food or Famine: The Challenge of Erosion*. Collier and Shepard, sharing a passion for the primeval, became close friends. Shepard decried deforestation, plowing without regard to land contours, and overgrazing. That brought him, and Collier with him, in conflict with Navajos and those pueblos, including Acoma, where sheep and goats were raised; from 1932 to 1936, a quarter million Navajo sheep and goats and uncounted thousands of horses were killed to reduce grazing pressure on Navajo land. Sheep and goats were the mainstay of Navajo subsistence. Hundreds of families were stripped of their only means of independent living, and anger at the high-handed, wasteful slaughter fueled Navajo refusal to vote for the Indian Reorganization Act (IRA) in 1934. Anger would have been even greater had officials told the Navajos that the real reason for curbing erosion on the reservation was a prediction that eroded soil would wash into the Colorado River and silt up the reservoir behind the much-touted Boulder Dam (now called Hoover Dam) completed in 1936. Sheep, goats, and horses were anathema to

Shepard and Collier as invasive species infecting Indians with lascivious, unnatural greed. Neophyte lawyers Cohen and Siegel did not have enough time in the Southwest to grasp any of this. They accepted the critical importance of reversing loss of Indian lands. That the United States had unjustly exercised a taking—the legal term—without adequate compensation of Indians was clear. Congress should pass a bill to rectify the United States' failure to fulfill the principle underlying the Fifth Amendment to the Constitution.

Without question, dispossession of Indians from their lands had to end. Jefferson's ideal of the yeoman on his land, for which Indians had been dispossessed, had been proffered as justification for the Dawes General Allotment Act. In the crisis of Depression and Dust Bowl forcing thousands of settler families off their farms, the plight of Indians could fit into America's populist ethos: Indians, too, were gouged by robber baron land speculators and railroad magnates. Cohen and Siegel understood that the legislation they were to draft must place priority on an end to allotment and means to restore tribal lands. They understood that not only Collier but Ward Shepard also envisioned Indian communities residing on communal lands—a Social Democrat vision—to build feasible sustainable Indian economies, given some initial infusion of capital. The lawyers recommended that the federal government charter such communities to incorporate, on the model of municipalities. Cohen pushed for recognition that Indians' right to self-governance must allow their communities to enact ordinances, exercise jurisdiction over their members, and challenge Bureau of Indian Affairs (BIA) administration and employees. Proposing a federal Court of Indian Affairs that would develop case law focused on Indians reflected Felix's deep concern with jurisprudence, a concern that was a bond between him and his father.

Morris Cohen wrote in his autobiography, "Reflection on law was a major part of the Talmudic studies of my childhood. The Hebraic God is primarily a law-giver, and . . . Moses has always been regarded as primarily a law teacher" (M. Cohen 1949:175). Morris felt the mitzvah, as an American citizen and trained philosopher, to familiarize himself with, and analyze, contemporary politics. At the height of the Progressive movement in 1912, he critiqued political axioms from the perspective of philosophy. Felix Frankfurter and other legal scholar friends advised him as he wrote it. Although the essay was not published, writing it launched Morris into decades of studying jurisprudence. He and son Felix coedited *Selected Readings in the Philosophy of Law* in 1930 for a CCNY course, and in 1933 Morris published *Law and the Social Order*. As a philosopher, Morris

Cohen was a pragmatist like his Harvard professor William James and, earlier at Harvard, Charles Peirce, whose articles he edited for publication, and his own friend John Dewey. Regarding law, Morris was a legal realist like Roscoe Pound. Felix Cohen followed his father and Pound in the conviction that laws are societal constructs, not embodiments of immutable natural axioms. Hence the importance he gave to creating an Indian court responsive to the social dimensions of jurisprudence in Indian country.

Cohen and Siegel initially sent Collier, in late January 1934, drafts of two bills for Indian reorganization. Collier told them to combine everything into one omnibus bill to submit to Congress—a slam-dunk shot. Less than three weeks later, they gave him that. From the point of view of congressmen reeling from Roosevelt's radical New Deal of revolutionary welfare such as Social Security and the plethora of New Deal alphabet-soup acronyms—NRA, WPA, SEC, CCC, FERA, TVA—a bill to reorganize Indian administration was of regional interest, affecting less-populated western states. This was why Burton Wheeler and Edgar Howard, representing two such states, chaired the congressional committees on Indian affairs and were asked to cosponsor the IRA. Senator Wheeler remembered, "when I began looking over the original draft, there were many provisions I didn't like. It set up a special judicial system for the Indians, with a federal judge to try only Indian cases. I thought it was a crazy idea and had it thrown out in committee" (quoted in Rusco 2000:234).

Wheeler and Howard had their staffs drastically prune the young lawyers' detailed expositions. Editing the mind-numbing lawyer jargon revealed more clearly the revolutionary purpose of the bill. Worse yet was its socialist leaning. Congressman Thomas O'Malley of Wisconsin thought it might be Soviet "collectivism"—this is the same representative who gave his name, that spring of 1934, to the Johnson-O'Malley Act enabling the federal government to contract with states to provide education, medical needs, and other welfare to Indians. O'Malley's legislation illustrates the other tack that reformers in Congress were taking, decentralizing federal control by devolving Indian affairs onto states rather than Indians.

Indian Congresses and Anthropologists

Indian reorganization was going to happen; it had been already set in motion under Hoover's presidency. An end to allotment was generally favored, allotment's iniquities evident to all. Collier and his comrade Ward

Shepard wanted the BIA to end the policy of assimilation and instead work toward creating local self-government on the model of municipalities for its Indian wards, but communal rather than hierarchically structured upon individually owned properties. Felix Cohen did not, at this point, disagree; he accepted Collier's belief that some Indian tribes, particularly in the Southwest, retained considerable indigenous governmental structure but that paternal oversight by the Bureau remained critical to Indian survival. A month's tour shepherded by BIA field agents left him and Siegel barely acquainted with Indian country, nor had the lawyers time to search policies and case law for legal foundation for the multiple proposals in the bill they were set to draft. A third assistant solicitor hired by Collier, Charles Fahy, did have experience similar to Margold's, working with Collier's American Indian Defense Association.

Already when Cohen and Siegel were hired in October, Collier was requesting, via circulars sent to reservations, that Indians tell him what issues they considered urgent. Agency superintendents tended to answer these circulars rather than have their wards do so directly. Collier then convened a conference at the Cosmos Club in Washington early in January 1934, asking leaders of friends-of-the-Indian organizations for their opinions on major sections of the draft IRA. Bureau staff attending included Collier, his deputy William Zimmerman, other employees, and the solicitor's men Margold, Cohen, Siegel, and Fahy. Alma Wilmarth Ickes, Harold's wife, was a member. "Indians" invited were only three, Captain and Mrs. Raymond Bonnin and Princess Chinquilla. The Bonnins were Nakoda, he an Army captain working with the OIA and she the writer Zitkala-Ša, while Princess Chinquilla was a New York woman performing as a "Cheyenne princess," whose claim to Indian birth aroused Mrs. Bonnin's skepticism (Carpenter 2005). Minutes of the conference endorsed that "the Secretary of the Interior should have the power and duty to recognize and establish Indian communities and endow them with any or all of the powers of existing communities *of like size and purpose* . . . the above process be made by *progressive stages* . . . [according to] the present varying capacities of the tribes" (quoted in Rusco 2000:210, emphasis added). The tenor of the conference fit well the private-club chamber within which it sat.

Felix Cohen was not impressed with the Cosmos Club conference. His "very limited experience on several reservations last November," he told Collier, let him glimpse "a large degree of misaprehension [*sic*]" about the Commissioner's goals and means (quoted in Rusco 2000:211). No one else in Washington seemed concerned about this, he noted. Nevertheless he urged Collier to send a letter he drafted to "Superintendents, Tribal Councils, *and Individual Indians*" requesting discussion and comments on a summary of the proposed legislation, attached to the circular (Rusco 2000:212, emphasis added). This Collier did promptly. Collier's next move was to seriously, substantially reach out to masses of Indians, proposing in February a series of "Indian congresses" in the West and Midwest to speak face-to-face with hundreds of reservation leaders. His purpose was to elicit Indian support of the IRA, channeled to congressmen who would be voting on the bill. Collier and his staff traveling across half the country were like a shadow of the 1853 journey of Isaac Stevens, Washington Territory governor, sitting in council with large gatherings of Indian leaders—a shadow, or a mirror image, because where Stevens was palavering with independent Indian nations, not yet in treaty, to take over their lands, Collier was declaring his intention to restore land to those Indians. Lucy Kramer Cohen made a list of the congresses:

II Conference Section / A Minutes (1) Plains Congress—Rapid City, So. Dak. March 2–5, 1934 / (2) Navajo Tribal Council—Ft. Defiance, Ariz. March 12–13, 1934 / (3) All Pueblo Council—Santo Domingo, N. Mex. March 15, 1934 / (4) Southern Arizona Indian Conference—Phoenix, Ariz. Mar. 15–16, 1934 / (5) Riverside Conference—Riverside, Calif. Mar 17–18, 1934 / (6) Anadarko Conference—Anadarko, Okla. March 20, 1934 / (7) Muskogee Conference—Muskogee, Okla. March 22, 1934 / (8) Miami Conference—Miami, Okla. March 24, 1934 / (9) Chemawa Conference—Chemama [*sic*], Oregon April 8, 9, 1934 / (10) Hayward Conference—Hayward, Wisc. April 23–24, 1934.[13]

Lucy recalled, "One of the things I and some other people did, we drew up a questionnaire that was sent to all the tribes in the country asking them what they thought their needs were in education . . . in occupations and training, in credit . . . everything" (Bickel 2000, reel 7, 26:17:27).

Office of Indian Affairs delegations to the congresses usually consisted of Commissioner Collier; Ward Shepard as land policies specialist; James C. Stewart, chief of the OIA Land Division; Walker Woehlke, the commissioner's field representative; Robert Marshall, the chief of the OIA Forestry Division; and Cohen and/or Siegel. From this set it is clear that the focus of the congresses, as of Collier's policy and its predecessor under Hoover, was to be on land. At the Anadarko, Oklahoma, congress, Collier said, "I shall not talk but about a minute about the court, the Court of Indian Affairs, because I don't think that will interest you very much" (Deloria 2002:270). Equally clear, in Lucy's memory, was the Cohens' far more holistic outlook reflecting their anthropological background. At the Pueblo and Navajo congresses, more OIA staff plus friends-of-the-Indians organization leaders attended. Cohen came along to the Rapid City (South Dakota), Chemawa (Oregon), Pueblo, and Navajo congresses; he did not attend those for southern Arizona, Southern California, Miami (Oklahoma) (Siegel did), or Hayward, Wisconsin (it got John Reeves, longtime chief counsel of the OIA). At Anadarko, Oklahoma, Collier did not bring staff, relying on respected Winnebago educator Henry Roe Cloud to manage the meeting and answer some of the questions, and at Muskogee (Oklahoma), Collier alone presented the government view. Each congress was a large affair, usually with several hundred Indian people present of whom more than one hundred would be elected delegates from the federally recognized tribes of the region. Official delegates sat in the front and could ask questions aloud; the rest of the audience was behind them and obliged to write their questions, hoping that the meeting chairman would have time to read them into the discussion. From stenographers' transcripts the presence of women can be glimpsed—"crying babies" should be taken from the hall; "Lady in the Audience" calls out that non-English speakers did not understand Collier's inquiry in English as to whether any in the audience needed interpreters; and, tellingly, the unsigned comment from "a member of the Pine Ridge Sioux delegation": "Honorable Commissioner of Indian Affairs, Mr. Collier—Not one Indian woman had a voice in this Indian council and may I submit it in writing—this new plan is our only salvation. Let's all join in and accept the new Bill and make the best of our advantages" (Deloria 2002:97).

Following the March 1934 congresses, returned questionnaires and communications from the tribes, delegates, and audiences rolled into Washington. Lucy kept a running tabulation of "how the different tribes were voting on which aspects of the thing. And that went to the different committees, while the committees were in session, when they were going over the legislation" (Bickel 2000, reel 7, 27:09:18). For two months, Felix and Lucy together worked unabated to collect written evidence supporting the bill in committee (Bickel 2011:25). Lucy's work on the perishable foods report she had been hired to do for Meredith Givens was put aside.[14] She wrote to Givens, "The survey would have been completed long before this had I not been unexpectedly drafted into work for the Indian Bureau on the Indian legislation, work which occupied all of my time until the early summer."[15]

Lucy welcomed a fun break in the routine when Richard Sanderville, a Carlisle graduate from the Blackfeet Reservation who usually interpreted for politicians visiting there, was in Washington in 1934 to help complete a visual dictionary of Plains sign language. Outside the Smithsonian, he put on a demonstration of the language, telling a story that Lucy noted on small notepaper with the letterhead "Smithsonian Institution Bureau of American Ethnology Memorandum _____193": "Man asks chief's daughter (1) 'Will you marry me?' (2) Woman answers (3) 'No.' 4. Man is sad 5 Man goes to war 6. Kills 2 Sioux Indians 7 Steals 10 horses and 2 guns 8 Man returns after 10 days Man asks 9 woman 'Will you marry me?' 10 She says, 'yes.' 11. Man says, 'No. You don't love me. 12 You love my horses.'"[16] Sanderville presented Lucy with a handsome parchment-like sheet (figure 4.3): "Washington, D.C. July 13, 1934. To Mrs. Lucy K. Cohen [drawing of calumet pipe with stem through card saying] The Blue Smoke of Friendship, From Your Blackfeet friend. Chief Bull [drawings, Indian man head with one feather, bison bull] or Richard Sanderville."[17]

The quantity and quality of Lucy's contributions were summarized by John Collier:

> From March, 1934, through June, 1934, Mrs. Cohen compiled, ana-lyzed, and edited the expressions of opinion submitted to the Office of Indian Affairs by Indian tribes throughout the country on the subject of the then pending Wheeler-Howard Bill. The results of such work as of April 30 and May 7 are printed in "Hearings before the Committee on Indian Affairs, H. R., 73rd Cong., 2nd Sess., on H. R. 7902," at pp. 399 (mimeographed copy in this folder), 422–425. This work, although accomplished under pressure of time, was performed with accuracy and intelligence and was of material assistance to this Office in presenting the facts to the committees of Congress in a clear manner. During this same period Mrs. Cohen prepared a compilation of comments and criticisms by American anthropologists on the problems dealt with in the pending Wheeler-Howard Bill. These comments and criticisms were received in answer to a questionnaire which Mrs. Cohen helped to pre-pare, and the task of arranging the material thus received was entirely in her hands. The results appear in the printed hearings above referred to, at pp. 361–370. Sincerely yours, John Collier, Commissioner.[18]

Attending all the hearings on the bill in the Senate and the House, Lucy reported to Felix the discussions and, good ethnographer that she was, what she observed. "I enjoyed watching the Indians sitting around the ta-ble discussing the various provisions in sign language, much to the chagrin of the chairman. It was a very good way for the Indians to secretly get a consensus" (Kramer Cohen 1986:71).

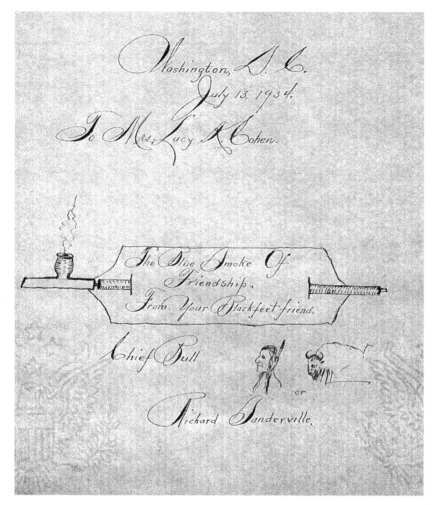

Figure 4.3. Gift from Richard Sanderville "Chief Bull" (Blackfeet), Plains Sign Language demonstrator, to Lucy Kramer Cohen, July 13, 1934. Photo from Yale Collection of Western Americana, Beinecke Rare Book and Manuscript Library.

Lucy was not the only anthropologist involved with creating the Indian New Deal. Questionnaires were mailed in November 1933 to a number of anthropologists asking for information on Indians they had worked with, and for comments for the proposed IRA. Response was good, with Felix telling Ward Shepard early in January 1934 that he had found them "extremely useful." He mentioned by name Franz Boas, Alfred Kroeber, John

Swanton, Harold Colton, Oliver La Farge, Cora DuBois, Scudder Me-
keel, and Alfred Bowers (Rusco 2000:189–90). Privately, Felix wrote to
Boas about his disappointment that Boas's Nez Perce graduate, Archie
Phinney, could not participate:

> Dear Professor Boas / In view of the fact that Archie Phinney is at pres-
> ent in Russia [1933–1934] & not immediately available, the position we
> had in mind will have to be filled otherwise. (for the time being). How-
> ever, at the beginning of next year when the appropriation becomes
> available, other positions will develop, particularly work involving the
> drawing up of community charters and constitutions (based on a knowl-
> edge of the history—& culture of particular Indian tribes). It is in the
> latter field we feel Archie Phinney, with his anthrop. training & recent
> work on racial Minorities in Russia, may prove of great real value.
>
> We should like to have your candid opinion of his qualifications &
> ability for this particular kind of work.
>
> (We understand Archie Phinney has a research fellowship at Yale for
> the coming year.)
>
> We should be glad to have your suggestions from time to time [sev-
> eral crossed-out words, then in Lucy's handwriting] qualified individuals
> who might be of assistance [back to Felix's handwriting] in the work of
> rehabilitating Indian tribal organization & social life. Sincerely yours.[19]

This letter draft, in Felix's bold hand in red pencil, with emendations in
Lucy's small neat hand, shows how closely the couple worked together,
how Felix could rely on Lucy for detailed amplification of ideas and, as
would prove especially invaluable in preparing and proofreading the
Handbook of Federal Indian Law, for her keen sense of clarity, syntax, and
style.

Acknowledgments of the anthropologists' responses, ostensibly by Indian Commissioner Collier, were at least sometimes drafted by Lucy, in
this case on three pages of a small notepad:

> Zingg [Robert M. Zingg] Please accept the thanks (of the I.C.) for your
> letter of April 14 (in which the present policies of I. Bur)
>
> The support of (by) anthropologists of the present policies of the I.B.
> is peculiarly/particularly {appropriate / helpful} at this time with (ap-
> propriate) legislation embodying those prin. pending in Congress.
>
> Should the Wheeler-Howard Bill go through

despite

even in a modified form become law, head B will not stop there in its attempt to correct past evils abuses in Indian administration with the scientific knowledge but will make an even more determined effort to extend the right—privileges accorded to other Amer. to the Indians.

We look forward to further aid from anthropologists. Sincerely yours, Commissioner

On another page of the same notepad, she wrote:

Hodge which the pressure of pending legislation made impossible for me to answer {earlier / until now} even a modified

Should W-ld Bill become law {despite the organized} terrific opposites by exploiting whites cattlemen missionaries politicians.[20]

Presumably this short and rather impolitic draft was for Frederick W. Hodge, formerly of the Bureau of American Ethnology and then with the Heye Foundation in New York.

Inexplicably, John Collier denied in his autobiography that anthropologists had any significant impact on the Indian New Deal, and this denial seems not to be challenged by historians (e.g., Rusco 2000:189). Dave Warren, enrolled in Santa Clara Pueblo and an anthropologist (PhD, University of New Mexico, 1955), testified in the 1983 conference commemorating the IRA's fiftieth anniversary that Collier did institutionalize using anthropologists and their work in the BIA, in its educational division under Willard Beatty, and in the Applied Anthropological Unit he created to work with the Smithsonian's Bureau of American Ethnology to obtain data from Indian communities pursuant to drawing up constitutions under the IRA. The crux of the idea that anthropologists had no significant impact seems to be lack of direct documentation of anthropologists' input. IRA constitutions were written quickly, more or less to the blueprint model provided by the OIA, instead of over a period of years of delving into particular histories and circumstances and discussing possible tribal governments. In other words, Collier agreed with Cohen that knowledge needed to be brought in from the diverse reservations and that anthropologists should be hired for the purpose, but Collier could not allow necessary time for this slow process of gaining nuanced knowledge.

Dave Warren emphasized that in regard to Indian education, 350 teachers were trained, mostly in summer courses, to be more sensitive to Indian ways; these were lessons in Progressive pedagogy (Beatty's background) that, Warren suggested, required a generation to be absorbed and to revolutionize Indian education. World War II stopped this process a scant three years after it began (Warren 1986:63). Insignificant as the impact of anthropologists upon the Indian New Deal may seem, John van Willigen (2002:26–29), a leader in applied anthropology practice, states in his textbook on the field that "Collier's advocacy of the utility of anthropology is widely viewed as crucial to the rapid expansion of federal employment of anthropologists" in studies of rural life, nutrition (Lucy worked in this) and other health needs, and, during the war, relocation camps, military intelligence, and propaganda.

Another perspective on the role of anthropologists in the Indian New Deal would look at the Indian Claims Commission. Margold had proposed it before he joined Interior; Cohen wrote legislation for it in 1935, 1940, and 1943. Then in 1944, Congress decided it was important to end the nuisance of Indian claims and the Indian Claims Commission Act was passed in 1946, a bill drafted by the National Congress of American Indians. It launched a business occupying hundreds of lawyers, historians, and anthropologists for a generation. Ethnohistory, a new discipline, was born from the voluminous testimonies before the Claims Commission. Anthropologists were in the foreground, forcing historians to recognize that all groups have histories, however scanty their written documentation. Ethnohistory embodied the core of Boasian anthropology, historical particularism. Ironically, Congress's willingness to create a commission to hear Indian claims—that is to say, Indian histories—arose from its eagerness to get rid of Indians as Indians, to terminate reservations and special statuses. The 1946 Indian Claims Commission Act was one face of the postwar policy of termination that seems a perverse reading of the Indian New Deal. Extended beyond the original cutoff year for claims, the commission finally closed in 1978, three years after the turning-point 1975 American Indian Self-Determination Act. Insofar as an Indian claims commission was advocated and attempted during the Indian New Deal, and anthropologists dominated its testimonies, anthropology can be said to have been significant in the Indian New Deal.

The Bill Is Passed

Once the Wheeler-Howard Indian Reorganization Act was passed on June 18, 1934, the Cohen team again sought the Indians' views. An undated eight inch by ten inch map of the United States, surely from this time, has red-pencil annotations in Lucy's tiny hand: "Colville, Blackfeet, Ft. Belknap, Ft. Berthold, Grand Portage, Ft. Hall, Pyramid Lake, Ft. Yuma, Haskell." With this map are two pages of paper with entries in Felix's larger handwriting, each page filled in with Lucy's tiny notes. For example, "Rosebud, ? [Felix] [Lucy writes in:] S.D. F. H. D. considers it O.K. One Sioux group should be organized. Supt. Robarts [?] sympathetic. Political situation bad. Former supt (dismissed) now Dem. State chairman has embarrassed Roberts [?] & administration again and again. Influences Indians. Would be well to have them organized."

A list in Felix's hand, with some names entered twice, on one page and then on the other:

Blackfeet
Carson Indian School
Consol Chip[pewa?]
Eastern Cherokee
Grand Portage
Flandreau
Ft. Belknap
Ft. Hall
Ft. Totten
Ft. Yuma
Cayugas
Piute, Utah
Pima
Tulalip Tabolah;
Red Lake—Bitney?
Walker River
Rocky Boys—Linderman La Vatta
Rosebud; Idea
Grand Ronde
San Carlos—working on const[titution]
San Ildefonso (?)
Standing Rock
Walapai (Valentine, Ariz.)
Turtle Mt.
Western Shoshone
Laguna Pueblo
Zuni

Then, boxed off: "12 [IRA corporations to be] established by Jan. 1 Collier; Stewart; Zimmerman; Cohen; Woechler; Smith; Shepard; Welpley."

Felix continues with a list of topics, each underlined, on the lower right side of the first page:

Index of Materials
Maps
Copy of Const. [Lucy writes in here "charter"]
Resolutions
Statistics Summary
Social History
Recommendations to Supt. — Indians

On the back of page 2, a list in Lucy's hand of anthropologists to consult (figure 4.4):

Stewart & *Ralph Beals* — on S.W.
Park Service
Wm. Fenton — NY Indians c/o Yale Univ. Dept. of Anth.
JND. [sic] Hewitt — Beureau [sic] Ethnology. — Historical material
Miss Helen Blish — Pine Ridge
Michigan (Teacher) West Branch — allow to go for a while
Re Pine Ridge {Ella Deloria — on situation at Pine Ridge
Mr. Jennings — Supt. Ed. Pine Ridge}
Mrs. Sargent (Oliver La Farge Group) Re San Ildefonso[21]

Parallel with their collaboration researching and summarizing Indian situations, the Cohens helped plan their socialist group's annual conference, at the Manumit School. In mid-July, Ruth Schechter wrote,

> Dear Felix and Lucy, I'm sending the outline of the conference that Adolph, Violet, etc. drew up. . . .
>   4.4. The structure of society
>   . . . What is a constitution? In what respects is a constitution a social contract? A system of social habits? A treaty of peace between warring classes? A code of rules of warfare? What gives force to a constitution?
>   5. The constitution of a socialist society
>   What political outlines may a socialist society assume? How completely can economic life be assimilated within the structure of government? How serious is the danger of over-centralization, regimentation,

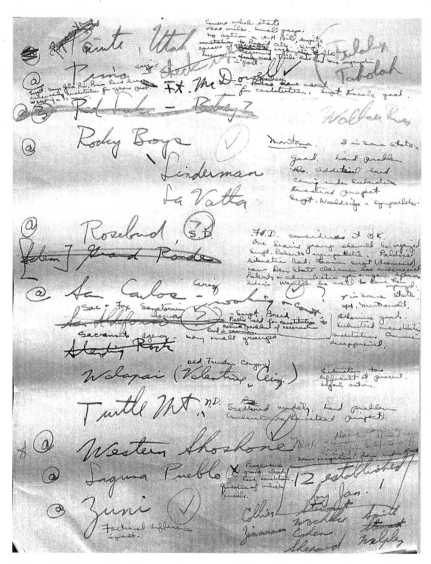

Figure 4.4. Page of Lucy's research notes on Indians for Felix, working on the Indian Reorganization Act. Photo from Yale Collection of Western Americana, Beinecke Rare Book and Manuscript Library.

bureaucracy, loss of individual initiative and sense of individual freedom and importance? How can this danger be overcome? By the allocation of political power to voluntary groups, e.g., semi-autonomous regions, communities, industrial organizations? By the political and economic guarantees to non-conformists? How can the values of freedom and experiment be reconciled with the values of social planning and social efficiency? Is a liberal civilization essentially unstable? What is the place of art, religion, science, philosophy under socialism? . . .

Bibliography:

Towards the Understanding of Karl Marx—Sidney Hook

The State and Revolution—N. Lenin

Prospects of Industrial Civilization—Russell

Constitution for a Socialist British Commonwealth—Sidney & Beatrice Webb[22]

Ideal constitutions for ideal communities could be debated; real constitutions for real Indian communities had to be worked out on the ground with variously eager or reluctant, determined or confused, united or fractured Indian "tribes" that in many cases were BIA administrative units rather than descendant First Nations.

To implement the reorganization of Indians, in July 1934, Felix was placed in charge of the Immediate Program for Organization of Indian Tribes. He asked Collier to supply data on tribes' conditions, so that constitutions and charters could be tailored to each tribe, and when subsequently he saw constitutions that appeared to merely copy a sample or one from another tribe, he urged the tribal councils to invite general discussion with their constituents. Legal staff within the office traveled to reservations to explain what a constitution needed to cover (such as specifying territory and membership criteria) and assist in formulating language in accord with legal usage. Charlotte Tuttle (Westwood), hired by Cohen for his staff soon after she graduated from Columbia Law School,[23] recalled that when she was sent to South Dakota Lakota reservations, Ben Reifel, an educated Lakota employed by the OIA who had attended the Rapid City congress in March 1934, was assigned to accompany her. Fluent in Lakota, Reifel explained and when necessary translated Tuttle's presentations and the questions asked of her, and facilitated discussions with tribal councils and in open meetings. (After serving in World War II, Reifel earned a PhD in public administration from Harvard and served five terms in the House of Representatives.) Tuttle spent a week or more on reservations ranging from the Hopi to the Winnebago.

Felix himself traveled to the Southwest in late December, noted by Lucy: "Itinerary—Dec. 15, 1934 Chic. 16 Sun. 244 E. Pearson St. Chic.[;] Pima Ariz. Tues. morn. 18–19 (20?) Pima Agency, Sacaton Ariz c/o Kneale, Supt.[;] Yuma 20–23 Herbert B. Jolley[;] San Carlos Eve 23, 24, 25 Jas B. Kitch[;] Chic[ago]. morn 28—Pittsburgh eve. 28." Pittsburgh was where the American Anthropological Association would be holding its annual meeting. On Christmas Day, Felix telegrammed Lucy from Arizona, "Work finished here could return and meet you in Pittsburgh Thursday evening however Woehlke wants me to come to Los Angeles for a conference on Friday about Californian situation which in a mess perhaps this is best in view of your advise about Woehlke and legislation please wire what you think dayletter to me care Southern Pacific Railway station Bowie Arizona."

Lucy composed a day letter, carefully limiting the number of words, crossing out "Please don't travel by air," and undecided how to sign herself, "your lonesome [sensible [sane]] Lucy." Later that afternoon, happy, Felix replied, "Got your telegrams at Bowie also one from Woehlke advising return for legislative program more important than California know not how or why this came here but overjoyed see you Pittsburg meeting Thursday evening New York trip Monday or Tuesday probable warmest greetings from poor lonesome cowboy make hotel reservations = Felix."[24] It did matter to both Lucy and Felix to keep up their participation in the community of anthropologists.

Once the process began of writing constitutions and holding referenda on them, Collier's well-founded distrust of agency superintendents' reports enabled Lucy as well as Felix to travel to reservations to learn firsthand what was happening in Indian country (figure 4.5). Already in November 1934, the salutation in a letter from a friend from New York City was, "Lucy Lily, Lucy Much, So, wench of the Indians, how have you been?"[25] The month after enjoying Richard Sanderville's lively demonstration of Plains sign language, Lucy met him again on his own reservation in Montana, after visiting Standing Rock and Pine Ridge Lakota reservations in South Dakota in August 1935. A small notebook lists her purchases there, from Mrs. Jule Ecoffe (a belt), Mrs. Laura Whirlwind Soldier (belt), Mrs. Cow Killer (moccasins), and names of other "Indian Friends," among them Mrs. American Horse and Mrs. Julia Red Bear (Good Voice Spirit Hawk) (figure 4.6). Her friends taught her to say, "Eha ke nape oci yu/spe / Aha ka napa oshi u spa ("a" long in ka, second 'a' in napa, first 'a' short) [sic] / I shake your hand in parting."[26]

Figure 4.5. Lucy and Felix with Indian friends, 1937. Photo from Felix S. and Lucy Kramer Cohen Photograph Collection.

Lucy's Columbia anthropology friend Ella Deloria, a Lakota from Standing Rock working with Boas on a Lakota dictionary, met her and Felix in Pine Ridge for a meeting was called for women to discuss the IRA. Deloria reported the women were concerned that they were excluded from working on the proposed Oglala constitution, that they had specific issues including requesting clarification—which Felix provided—on how a turkey-raising cooperative would operate, and that "it was very interesting to contrast the formal Dakota when each got up to speak, and then the comments in colloquial Dakota when each matter was discussed among the women themselves."[27] In addition to meeting and talking with Indian women, Lucy was researching winter-count calendars with the expectation that Willard Beatty would use them as experimental history texts in Sioux schools; in 1936, Scudder Mekeel, head of the OIA's Anthropology Unit, told her that eminent ethnographer Clark Wissler was interested and

Figure 4.6. Lucy dressed in Oglala Lakota regalia; Oglala Lakota woman with her is probably Rose Ecoffey, who performed in Wild West shows as Princess Blue Water. August 1935. Photo from Felix S. and Lucy Kramer Cohen Photograph Collection.

might cooperate with her if the school use brought to light additional winter counts.[28] Lucy did publish two winter counts in the OIA magazine *Indians at Work*, in 1939 and 1942 (personal communication, Linea Sundstrom, November 22, 2010).

Again, in May 1936, Lucy accompanied Felix to reservations, this time to the Pima (Akimel O'odham) at Sacaton, Arizona. What they observed disturbed Felix: he wrote "Anthropology and the Problems of Indian Administration" at this time. His conviction that democratic socialism offered the best principles for sustainable and decent communities did not abate, nor did opponents' attacks upon the Indian New Deal. Friend and colleague Theodore Haas wrote to Lucy, August 25, 1936, "I was thinking about Felix to-day when I read in the New Masses that an anti-Semite had charged Nathan R. Margold with communizing the American Indians. I supposed that the Redmen are so indoctrinated with fine American principles of freedom as to be inoculated against alien red ideas. . . . With best regards to you and Big Chief Red Pants. Ted."[29]

Officially describing this period of initial implementation of the IRA, Haas in 1947 wrote,

> As was to be anticipated, some opponents of the new administration including selfish vested interests, conducted a nation-wide campaign of false propaganda to defeat the measure. Real estate interests which had been acquiring Indian lands by devious methods, and stockmen and lumber interests which had profited by the inability of the Indians to protect their own resources, waged a campaign designed to perpetuate their privileges, often through hired Indians. Fantastic rumors were spread, such as: the bill was designed to deprive the Indians of the interests in their lands, to take away their allotments and communize them, to put the church out of business, and forbid missionaries to work among the Indians. (Haas 1947:6–7)

Caught up in the campaign to turn the tide of Indian affairs, Lucy had the idea of writing a book:

> Dear Mr. Zimmerman [Assistant Commissioner of Indian Affairs]: I am enclosing a copy of the first draft of "Red Man's Gifts to Modern America," which was to have been one section of a chapter on "Native America," according to the enclosed outline.
>
> Originally, this was to have been part of an introduction to a semi-popular book which would correct certain current misconceptions, and

at the same time be accurate enough for official use. In view of that purpose, I tried to put into the body the popular material, and into the footnotes the sources and more detailed material.

This material, in its present form, was submitted to Mr. Collier for the Secretary in November, 1935.

Since Mr. Collier advised me this spring that the Secretary was no longer interested in the proposed publication, and that I might use the material as I pleased, I have submitted copies of this draft to Dr. Mekeel and Dr. Beatty.

Dr. Mekeel advised me that this would be of use to him in his courses this summer for Indian Service people. I understand that Dr. Beatty thinks the material, in its present form, too popular for school use, but plans to use some revision of the paper.

I should like very much to have your criticisms and suggestions, to guide me in any rewriting I may attempt. Sincerely

Zimmerman did not like the draft. An undated penciled sheet, marked in the corner "Type please," gives her his evaluation:

Notes on Mrs. Cohen's material: 1. Sounds too much as tho ballyhooing Something which she wants to believe. If her statements are factual they can be more strongly presented by understatement. 2. If true, the material would be greatly strengthened & made more interesting by telling who, where and how regarding these various "gifts." Pride on the part of the Indian groups could be stimulated by an accurate statement which credited the group with an actual contribution—such as "Hopi beans," "Zuni," check damming, etc. 3. More material, verified as above, would make interesting basis for series of readers valuable alike to whites & Indians. In present form, too much generalization. 4. Do anthropologists subscribe to her many claims? WWZ[30]

Lucy tried several versions of the "Indian book" over the years, none completed. Some of the material she used in preparing radio scripts for a regular Indian Affairs broadcast and for articles in the Bureau's magazine, *Indians at Work*. "Red Man's Gifts to Modern America" was a topic she worked over several times, for the radio and for use in Indian Service schools.[31]

Meanwhile, ominous news was reaching America from Europe. Morris Cohen organized the Conference on Jewish Relations, incorporated in May 1936. Lucy's father-in-law mailed "Miss Lucy Kramer" the printed letter announcing the conference's first formal meeting, at Temple Emanu-El in New York City. "Your chairman," presumably Morris, planned an "address on the Future of the Jews in America" followed by discussion. Two months earlier, at a meeting at the New School for Social Research, the not-yet-incorporated conference had discussed "the pogroms in Poland and proposed law to prohibit kosher slaughter." Seeking to rescue European Jews would escalate to become Morris Cohen's principal activity as Nazism turned kosher slaughter into slaughter of those who kept kosher. Franz Boas joined Morris in these endeavors generally unwelcome in America outside Jewish circles.

Eventually, in 1939, Harold Ickes put Felix to work on a proposal to settle Jewish refugees in Alaska; Ickes, as Secretary of the Interior, shrewdly pushed the idea as a means to develop that "vast undeveloped" territory.[32] Congress, except for its few Jewish members, chose to reject the proposal as tending to draw the United States into an unwanted war. Perhaps it was when his father was organizing the Conference on Jewish Relations that Felix copied out, on a sheet of paper with the printed letterhead "Felix S. Cohen 401–23 Street N.W. Washington, D.C.," a Yiddish poem:

Ich leib in shrek
in grosse secunes
Zures hab ich un
a shir
Antloffen mus ich
bei der levuna,
veil men ferfolk mich
men lost nicht mich
mein kopf aufhäben
Alles bes thit man mir
austeilen, men shreit
Yedish gezendil ihr
lebt nor von shvendel
ihr berobt das Kristentum
Yireshuliam –
mein theier eiliges land
(I live in fear /And great danger, /My suffering knows no bounds. /I must flee /By the light of the moon /Because I am oppressed, /I am not allowed /To raise my head. / They inflict every evil upon us / They yell "Jews, /You live by swindling, /You prey on the Christians." /Jerusalem--My dear holy land.)

By June 1938, Morris's printed letter on the conference began, "The fact that you have joined the Conference on Jewish Relations indicates that you share our conviction that the forces which threaten to degrade or exterminate the Jewish people (and ultimately to destroy liberal civilization by destroying all elemental human rights) cannot be effectively met by willful or ostrich-like ignorance."[34]

It was in the shadow of Nazi forces that Felix Cohen was given the assignment to prepare a handbook of federal Indian law for the Department of Justice. Lucy and Charlotte Tuttle joined the project staff.

CHAPTER FIVE

The Handbook of
Federal Indian Law

The *Handbook of Federal Indian Law* did what the Indian Reorganization Act failed to do: it made untenable the United States' Indian policy prevailing since Jefferson. Felix Cohen, assisted by his team, constructed the legal case for First Nations' continuing inherent sovereignty. Harold Ickes supported Cohen's position. The *Handbook* has been called "one of the greatest treatises in all of the law" (Wilkinson 2005:60).

If Felix had, in 1933, no particular interest in Indians or laws affecting them, his firsthand experience at the March 1934 Indian congresses, his trips to reservations, and his work with Indians writing tribal constitutions impressed him with the fundamental wrongness of federal Indian policy, including that established by the IRA. Indians, he saw, were not childlike. To hold them wards of a benign paternal government was contrary to their rights as adult citizens.

Lucy Kramer knew how difficult it was for Indians, such as her Columbia anthropology friends Ella Deloria and Archie Phinney, to obtain higher education and professional employment. Section 11 of the IRA states that Treasury funds up to $250,000 annually may be appropriated "for loans to Indians for the payment of tuition and other expenses in recognized vocational and trade schools"—the act does not direct funds toward liberal arts colleges or postgraduate or professional programs, and the funds are only loans to be repaid. This clause in the act, continuing the long-standing policy of restricting Indians to primary schooling and manual training, quite obviously reflects a racist denigration of Indians' intellectual capacities. Charged with advising tribes on writing constitutions,

Felix met many astute, intelligent men and women frustrated over and over by autocratic Indian agents and the OIA's refusal to let reservation residents run their businesses as they thought best. Increasingly, his initial hope to guide Indian communities into democratic socialist villages gave way to a realization that severe injustices called for immediate relief.

Fundamentally, Cohen's *Handbook of Federal Indian Law* reflects Franz Boas's articulation of historical particularism, that is, recognition that every society has its own, long history of adaptations to environments and societal contacts. Boas reiterated again and again, most notably in his 1911 *The Mind of Primitive Man*, that the races Americans identify are social classes, not biologically distinct populations. (His book title misleads twenty-first-century readers. He attacks the idea that the modern world contains less-evolved primitive men.) Historical particularism implies cultural relativism, that societies' histories of experiences have brought about their variant cultures, each reasonably successful in meeting their people's needs for survival. Understanding this power manifest in living societies lays the groundwork for respecting American Indian First Nations' inherent sovereignty. Competent over millennia in enabling their populations' survival, Indian societies should be respected and freed from the burden of conquerors' tyrannies.

When, in 1939, an interdepartmental agreement was signed to appoint Felix Cohen chief of the Indian Law Survey in the Department of Justice, the sponsoring department, Justice, intended an indexed compilation of statutes and cases that lawyers could consult. Nothing like it existed; Justice's lawyers had to waste time searching through law libraries for possibly relevant materials. Felix had been dealing with laws relating to Indians for five years. He had prodigious memory and analytic powers. What Justice's bureaucrats hadn't reckoned on was his unwavering commitment to understanding jurisprudence and how it reflected and directed social conditions, a commitment he shared with his father. A simple handy manual to keep Justice's work consistent and save lawyers time in preparation would seem, to Felix, prostitution of the law. So there was no Blackstone on Indian law? Then the Indian Law Survey needed to create one, a historical survey of foundational principles, statutes, cases, and their sources and effects in the nation.

The team assembled for the Indian Law Survey included the Cohens' friend Ted Haas, Charlotte Tuttle (Westwood) Lloyd, and Lucy. Lucy was entrusted with the critical chapter on Indian treaties, which Felix would insist remain the basis of relationships between Indians—as we say now, First Nations—and the United States. Preparing for actually writing a handbook, the team searched law libraries and Justice Department files to compile all US statutes relating to Indians, cases and judicial opinions, and treaties and public acts. Typists copied these thousands of documents onto stencils and mimeographed them, indexed and collated into forty-six volumes published in 1940. While this compendium was reaching completion, Justice officials became upset that the handbook was oriented toward protecting Indians' rights rather than expediting government lawyers' defense against Indians' complaints. Abruptly, the Department of Justice terminated the project.

Margold refused to condone Justice's determination to protect the government rather than its wards. The Department of the Interior took over the project, reassigning Cohen to its staff. The *Handbook* itself was completed in manuscript not long after, by summer 1940. To print the exhaustive treatise as the handsome book Felix envisioned would be far more expensive than the Indian Law Survey's budget had anticipated, even though the job would be done by the Government Printing Office. Thus, the August 1941 first edition is in two-column pages of small print.

Open the *Handbook* and the reason for Justice's dismay leaps out: "Chapter 1—The Field of Indian Law: Indians and the Indian Country. . . . Most of the land in the United States . . . was purchased from Indians, and therefore almost any title must depend for its validity upon issues of Indian law even though the last Indian owners and all their descendants be long forgotten" (Cohen 1942:1). This is indeed radical. It recognizes that the right of first discovery lies with Indian nations, not the United States or its colonial predecessors. It states that a handbook of federal Indian law must concern the rights of those First Nations as they affect the entire United States. Until Felix and his enablers Ickes and Margold insisted on this standpoint, the departments of Justice and Interior had litigated cases involving Indians from the standpoint of the United States imposing its power upon its wards. The government's fiduciary responsibility was interpreted to require parental control over the wards, similar to parents' power over children. Like children, Indians basically had only the right to enough food, shelter, and clothing to prevent starvation and death from cold. Like children, Indians' money was withheld, eventually leading to the *Cobell* lawsuit, 1996–2011, blowing open the gross misappropriation of millions of dollars of Indians' money. By the end of his opening section, Cohen allows that Interior's Indian Law and Order Regulations of November 27, 1935, define "Indian" pragmatically as "any person of Indian descent who is a member of any recognized Indian tribe now under Federal jurisdiction," that is, "members of certain social-political groups towards which the Federal Government assumes special responsibilities" (Cohen 1942:5).

Cohen's dramatic opening line is startling: "Indians are human beings." We think of Shylock:

> I am a Jew. Hath not a Jew eyes? Hath not a Jew hands, organs, dimensions, senses, affections, passions; fed with the same food, hurt with the same weapons, subject to the same diseases, heal'd by the same means, warm'd and cool'd by the same winter and summer, as a Christian is? If you prick us, do we not bleed? If you tickle us, do we not laugh? If you poison us, do we not die? And if you wrong us, do we not revenge? (Shakespeare, *The Merchant of Venice*, act 3, scene 1, lines 58–68)[1]

Merely declaring Indians to be human beings, not Jefferson's "merciless savages," didn't guarantee them human rights.[2] In 455 pages the *Handbook* densely demonstrates the huge amalgamation of legal documents that the Cohen team winnowed to the kernels of foundational principles. Under them all, as it were the turtle on which rests the cosmos, is the principle of inherent sovereignty.

The Issue of Sovereignty

Indian rights and federal powers hinge upon the jurisdictional issue of sovereignty. From 1803, Jefferson's policy of dispossessing Indians robbed them of standing in US courts. After the 1924 granting of US citizenship to Indians—ten years before the IRA—they had the rights of citizens, if they could prevail against biased courts. Cohen realized from observing the drastic cuts to his original IRA bill, and the effects of the bill after June 1934, that there had been no real change in federal Indian policy other than reversing dispossession. His and Lucy's growing acquaintance with Indian people, coming to Washington or out on reservations, convinced him that paternalism was not only cruel and crippling but contrary to the Founding Fathers' intent. Even Jefferson, devious and prone to propaganda rhetoric as he was, respected Indians as adults. It became clear to Felix that Indian nations were similar to states, that they had signed treaties with the federal government that paralleled the thirteen states confederating in 1781. The Tenth Amendment to the Constitution enshrined the principle of sovereignty within the federation: "The powers not delegated to the United States by the Constitution, nor prohibited by it to the States, are reserved to the States respectively, or to the people."

"*Those powers which are lawfully vested in an Indian tribe are not, in general, delegated powers granted by express acts of Congress, but rather*

inherent powers of a limited sovereignty which has never been extinguished.
Each Indian tribe begins its relationship with the Federal Government as
a sovereign power, recognized as such in treaty and legislation. . . . What
is not expressly limited remains within the domain of tribal sovereignty"
(Cohen 1942:122, emphasis in original). From this paragraph comes its
restatement by Congress, signed into law by the president in 1975, in the
American Indian Self-Determination Act that at last repudiated Jeffersonian policy. Asserting precedent in Justice Marshall's 1832 decision in
Worcester v. Georgia, Cohen quoted from it: "The Indian nations had always been considered as distinct independent, political communities"
(1942:123). Where states or federal administrators "presumed to govern
the Indian tribes," such acts were trespass (Cohen 1942:125).

Countering Felix's extraordinary affirmation of inherent sovereignty was
the century-long concept invented by Justice Marshall, that Indian nations
making treaty with the United States become "domestic dependent nations." On page 170, Cohen carefully explained that Marshall did not say
that individual Indians become wards of the government: "He did not say
that Indian tribes were wards of the Government but only that the relation
to the United States of the Indian tribes within its territorial limits *resembles*
that of a ward to his guardian" (Cohen 1942:170, emphasis in original).
That is, encapsulated Indian nations perforce look to the federal government for protection against enemies, in the manner of smaller nation-states
allied with more powerful neighbors, and for succor against famine and
catastrophes. Cohen reiterated the principle of inherent sovereignty:

> The whole course of judicial decision on the nature of Indian tribal
> powers is marked by adherence to three fundamental principles: (1) An
> Indian tribe possesses, in the first instance, all the powers of any sover-
> eign state. (2) Conquest renders the tribe subject to the legislative power
> of the United States and, in substance, terminates the external powers of
> sovereignty of the tribe, e.g., its power to enter into treaties with foreign
> nations, but does not by itself affect the internal sovereignty of the tribe,
> i.e., its powers of local self-government. (3) These powers are subject to
> qualification by treaties and by express legislation of Congress, but, save
> as thus expressly qualified, full powers of internal sovereignty are vested
> in the Indian tribes and in their duly constituted organs of government.
> (Cohen 1942:123)

Very important to this interpretation, although discussed in detail else-
where in the treatise, were the 1790s Trade and Intercourse Acts that

reserve to the federal government all dealings with Indian nations, and Marshall's opinions in *Johnson v. M'Intosh*, 1823, and *Worcester v. Georgia*, 1832, recognizing aboriginal possession of usufruct (occupancy) without legal title under international law (Cohen 1942:291–93). Burying these critical precedents in the middle of the dense treatise, many wearying pages beyond the forthright statements of inherent sovereignty, was rhetorically shrewd.

Cohen's position understands "domestic" to be opposed to "foreign," and "dependent" to be construed strictly according to Marshall's recognition of the smaller nations' desire for protection. "A principal responsibility of Congress [is] ' . . . to secure them [Indian tribes] in the title and possession of their lands, in the exercise of self-government, and to defend them from domestic strife and foreign enemies'" (Cohen 1942:91, quoting from the Twenty-Third Congress, 1834). In a word, its treaties with First Nations placed the United States as suzerain over the other signatories. "Suzerainty" connotes a feudal relationship, wherein an autonomous estate places itself under the protection of a more powerful lord. Although Felix did not pursue this line of interpretation, it underlies his insistence that conquest did not obliterate tribes' internal sovereignty, any more than feudal vassals lose their autonomy. Yes, relations between tribes and federal government, as between lord and vassals, are fraught with tension, exemplified by the Magna Carta. Cohen, Margold, and Ickes—all three men who, unlike John Collier, had struggled against the complacent dominance of upper-class gentlemen—were determined to fulfill America's promise of true democracy by freeing the Indians from their quasi-slavery under the OIA. "Our treatment of Indians, even more than our treatment of other minorities, reflects the rise and fall in our democratic faith," Felix reiterated in his last essay (Cohen 1953:389).

Using a historical approach more broad than usual in legal handbooks, Cohen established the primacy of treaties in Indian law and his larger goal of restoring America to the moral high ground he and his circle fervently believed in. Congress had repeatedly failed to ratify treaties made in the field, usually without informing the signing Indians, and unilaterally abrogated treaties it had ratified, most blatantly in 1889, breaking up the Great Sioux Reservation of Dakota Territory into five parcels for Indians and opening up half the land for sale to settlers. Pursuant to the just-passed Dawes Act, the five reservations were to be allotted in severalty to their Indians, irrespective of their wishes. Cohen made clear in the *Handbook* that such actions were not only illegal, they were contrary to the most fundamental principle of US governance:

The substance of treaty-making was destined . . . to continue for many decades [after formal cession in 1871]. For in substance a treaty was an agreement between the Federal Government and an Indian tribe. And so long as the Federal Government and the tribes continue to have common dealings, occasions for agreements are likely to recur. . . . Legislation based on Indian consent does not come to an end with the close of the period of Indian land cessions and the stoppage of Indian land losses in 1934. . . . Thus, while the form of treaty-making no longer obtains, the fact that Indian tribes are governed primarily on a basis established by common agreement remains, and is likely to remain so long as the Indian tribes maintain their existence and the Federal government maintains the traditional democratic faith that all Government derives its just powers from the consent of the governed. (Cohen 1942:67)

On a less lofty plane, Cohen invoked the right of escheat, a feudal law about land reverting to the Crown or mesne lord when a vassal died without heirs, or committed a felony. "This right of escheat was not, strictly speaking, a form of inheritance but was a sovereign right superior to the property right of any landlord. . . . Land held by a tribe in fee simple would be subject to escheat and it is unnecessary to assume any peculiarity of 'Indian title' to explain this result" (Cohen 1942:311). The 1982 edition of the *Handbook* drops the argument against elaborating "Indian title," mentioning merely that the land of an allottee dying intestate without heirs would revert to the tribe by escheat (Strickland et al. 1982:480). Burying Felix Cohen's fervent vision of transcendent principle under a mass of decisions, the 1982 and 2005 revisions of the *Handbook* are more textbooks on Indian law than the primary document Felix and his team created.

Accompanying these revised editions are compedia of cases of Indian law, with notes, for use in law school courses. The third edition of *Cases and Materials on Federal Indian Law* added a critical legal scholar who is a Lumbee Indian, Robert A. Williams Jr., to the earlier editions' team of David Getches and Charles Wilkinson, whose authority derived from long-standing and extensive practice of Indian law as well as teaching. Williams brought back that sense of outrage invigorating Cohen. In their introduction, the three authors highlight the value of studying Indian law to obtain "the understanding it fosters for the dominant society and its legal system. Consider the reaction of the system to Indian legal rights. . . . Congress considers abrogation of Indian rights on the basis that they are 'old' or 'inequitable'" (Getches, Wilkinson, and Williams 1993:7). Above all, Congress can unilaterally abrogate Indians' treaty or statute rights. Putting that into legal terminology, "all aspects of Indian sovereignty are subject to defeasance by Congress" (Williams in Getches et al. 1993:331). Defeasance means annulment.

Cohen's enormous effort to unequivocally state the primacy of treaties in Indian law, and their basis in consent of the governed, polarized positions on the plenary power of Congress. Ickes, Margold, the Cohens, and Felix's team on the *Handbook* all saw the Indian person, a citizen of his First Nation and since 1924 of the United States as well, as the raison d'être of the *Handbook of Federal Indian Law*. His rights and well-being, like those of all citizens in every civilized country, must be protected by law. The Department of Justice and most members of Congress had the opposite standpoint, that Congress is the organ of America's representative democracy and its plenary power cannot be compromised. Its power over Indians rests on the commerce clause in the Constitution, that Congress holds power over intercourse with Indian tribes. Cohen (1942:156) insisted that this does not conflict with Indians' rights of citizenship. Rebutting this position on the Indian as citizen, Interior's opponents emphasized Marshall's ruling on Indians' dependency on the federal government. That is, Congress exercises its plenary power over Indians because it accepted their requests for protection—in this sense, it obtained consent of the governed.

Did Indians signing treaties request protection because they knew themselves to be incompetent to carry out adult responsibilities in a civilized country? Or did they ask only that the strong military ally assist in their struggles against aggression by colonial invaders and competing First Nations? Interior's team took this view, bolstering it with the long history of treaties signed by Indians whose adult competency was never questioned in the treaty negotiations. Federal policy from the Marshall decisions on— including the Wheeler-Howard Act—presumed that Indians as a class (a "race") needed to be protected not as allies but as wards. Indian formal rhetoric calling upon the federal "Father" to be generous to his "Children" (as Indian speeches were conventionally translated into English) did not mean the Indians considered themselves childlike. Their formal speech to whites may in many instances have been influenced by familiarity with Catholic missionaries who taught that they represented the Pope (English version of Greek *pappas*, "father") and were themselves to be addressed as Father. Treaties were negotiations in which each side sought to gain concessions. However politely he professed himself humble and needy, no Indian delegate felt himself to be like a child. The United States' assertion of fiduciary responsibility extending far beyond terms of treaties into guardianship came from the racism that negated the doctrine of discovery for Indians, claiming that they were only savages in a wilderness.

Robert Williams, the Lumbee legal scholar, vehemently argued, in a 1986 law review article, that Congress's plenary power respecting Indians "is ultimately genocidal in both its practice and intent" (Williams reprinted in Getches, Wilkinson, and Williams 1993:328). Strong words, provoking a carefully sober counterarticle by a law professor who, refraining from pointing out that Indians are still here, affirms his own confidence in Congress's good faith toward its Indian citizens (Robert Laurence, reprinted in Getches, Wilkinson, and Williams 1993:328–29). Paternalism survives. Laurence did acknowledge that Congress's plenary power is counterbalanced by tribes' inherent sovereignty, a statement indicating Cohen's position has carried weight (ibid.).

Presumptive Bias and Coercive Tutelage

Overall, blatant racism, if not genocide, has been the basis of Congress's policies toward American First Nations. Beginning with Jefferson's citing "merciless savages on our frontiers" in the Declaration of Independence's twenty-seventh Fact, it continued with Justice Marshall in *Johnson v. M'Intosh*: "the character and religion of its [America's] inhabitants afforded an apology for considering them as a people over whom the superior genius of Europe might claim an ascendancy" (quoted in Robertson 2005:99). Cohen discussed racism in the *Handbook*'s section on civil liberties: "The principle of government protection of the Indians runs through the course of federal legislation and administration. *The line of distinction between protection and oppression is often difficult to draw*. What may seem to administrative officials and even to Congress to be a wise measure to protect the Indian against *supposed infirmities of his own character*, may seem to the Indian concerned a piece of presumptuous and intolerable interference with precious individual rights" (1942:173, emphasis added). Here in one sentence, "The line of distinction between protection and oppression is often difficult to draw," is the problem in Marshall's "domestic, dependent nations."

Canadian anthropologist Noel Dyck has written extensively about Canada's Indian "Problem" (a word he always puts in quotes). Canadian and US Indian policy being alike derived from Anglo culture, Dyck's analysis works for the United States, too. Dyck selects "coercive tutelage" as the central problem with the nation-states' administration of their First Nations populations; it is precisely what Cohen described in the passage quoted above. Dyck says,

> With a remarkable degree of sincerity, generation after generation of "tutors" have mounted programs to deliver Indians from the stigma and vulnerability, poverty and misery associated with Indianness in the Euro-Canadian mind. . . . Tutelage constitutes a relentless assault upon the survival and integrity of Indian communities in the name of "helping" Indian persons to rid themselves of their stigmatized status and inappropriate customs and beliefs. . . . The survival of Indian communities subjected to this unrelenting siege has entailed staggering human costs. (Dyck 1991:24, 26–27)

Darcy McNickle, a Cree scholar from the Flathead (now Salish-Kootenay) Reservation, wrote of "the presumptive bias" that has underlain European and descendant nations' policies since Columbus (McNickle 1973:166). It is the foundation of coercive tutelage and a long series of adverse rulings against Indian plaintiffs, including the 1903 landmark *Lone Wolf v. Hitchcock* that set a precedent for Congress claiming plenary power to abrogate treaties. Lone Wolf, a Kiowa, was lead plaintiff challenging the federal taking of Kiowa reservation land to open it to settlers. One facet of the *Lone Wolf* decision, remarked historian Blue Clark (himself Muskogee Creek), was that under it, "no tribe or Indian individual could prove competency. . . . The necessity for restrictive oversight was presumed from the mere fact of 'Indianness'" (1994:101). Ruling in 1955 against a Tlingit community's suit for compensation for timber taken from their land, the Supreme Court majority declared, "The American people have compassion for the descendants of those Indians who were deprived of their homes and hunting grounds by the drive of civilization. . . . The Tee-Hit-Tons [the Tlingit community] were in a hunting and fishing stage of civilization, with shelters fitted to their environment, and claims to rights to use identified territory for these activities as well as the gathering of wild products of the earth . . . with claims to that effect carved on totem poles" (Reed 1955). Somehow the majority of the Supreme Court failed to understand an anthropological report they cited, on Tlingit society and claims, written by Felix and Lucy's close friend Ted Haas with Walter Goldschmidt, an eminent anthropologist (Goldschmidt and Haas 1946). Tlingit are, and before Russian invasion were, essentially commercial fishermen in societies resembling feudal baronial territories, their shelters timber halls housing the aristocratic head of a clan and his noble relatives, commoners, and slaves. Land and harbor rights were formally recognized and titles recited by trained official historians. Goods traded along regular sea, river, and overland routes included metal knives and ornaments and cultivated tubers. Only presumptive bias could allow the Court to say Tlingit were nomadic, implying they were savages.

Over in British Columbia, a decision entered in 1991 in *Delgamuukw v. Regina* exposed the appalling bias held even by highly educated jurists at the end of the twentieth century. Several Tsimshian and Wet'suwet'un communities on the Upper Skeena River sued, like the Tlingit in the 1940s, for royalties on timber cut from the land around their villages. The lead plaintiff was the Delgamuukw, hereditary head of one of the Gitskan Tsimshian clans. Allan McEachern, chief justice of the British Columbia Supreme Court, heard the case. His judgment against the plaintiffs is worth quoting at some length:

> It is common, when one thinks of Indian land claims, to think of Indians living off the land in pristine wilderness. . . . Similarly, it would not be accurate to assume that even pre-contact existence in the territory was in the least bit idyllic. . . . There is no doubt, to quote Hobbs [*sic*], that aboriginal life in the territory was, at best, "nasty, brutish and short." . . . (McEachern 1991, quoted in Culhane 1998:236 and other pages as cited)
>
> It is asked whether a nation may lawfully take possession of some part of a vast country in which there are none but erratic nations, whose scanty population is incapable of occupying the whole? . . . Their unsettled habitation . . . cannot be accounted a true and legal possession, and the people of Europe . . . finding land of which the Savage stood in no particular need, and of which they made no actual and constant use, were lawfully entitled to take possession. . . . (239)
>
> Some tribes are so low in the scale of social organization that their usages and conceptions of rights and duties are not to be reconciled with the institutions or the legal ideas of civilized society. . . . (246)
>
> I do not accept the ancestors "on the ground" behaved as they did because of "institutions." Rather I find they more likely acted as they did because of survival instincts. . . . (248)
>
> The Indians of the territory were, by historical standards, a primitive people without any form of writing, horses, or wheeled wagons. . . . (247)
>
> Aboriginal life, in my view, was far from stable. . . . It is my conclusion that Gitksan and Wet'suwet'en laws and customs are not sufficiently

certain to permit a finding they or their ancestors governed the territory. (249)

The Indians' appeal was upheld by the British Columbia Court of Appeals in 1993, ruling that McEachern erred in finding extinguishment of aboriginal title, and by the Supreme Court of Canada in 1997 on procedural error in his refusing to allow testimonies by official Gitskan and Wet'suwet'en historians on grounds that, being orally transmitted, they were "hearsay." Adverse rulings in two courts were not enough to discourage the University of British Columbia from naming McEachern its chancellor in 2002, disregarding strong protests by faculty and students.

The *Tee-Hit-Ton* and *Delgamuukw* cases demonstrate the wall of ingrained bias Felix Cohen intended to demolish. Not only did he fail to do so, the backlash from Congress against the IRA policy reversals and from the Department of Justice against the *Handbook* perversely reads that Congress does have plenary power to terminate treaties. If Cohen in the *Handbook* reiterates that Indians are now citizens, thus entitled to civil liberties, the 1943 Senate Survey of Conditions Among the Indians of the United States urged that these citizens be now totally freed of their peculiar status: "While the original aim [of federal policy] was to make the Indian a citizen, the present aim [the Indian New Deal] appears to be to keep the Indian an Indian and to make him satisfied with all the limitations of a primitive life. We are striving mightily to help him recapture his ancient, worn-out cultures which are now a vague memory to him and are absolutely unable to function in his present world" (Senate Report 310, quoted in Getches, Wilkinson, and Williams 1993:229).

Presumptive bias once again. Commissioner Collier was requested to "give us concrete suggestions as to what the Congress can do to absolve the Government from its responsibility under treaties and statutes" (Rep. Karl Mundt, House Committee on Indian Affairs, 1943, quoted in Wilkinson 2005:63). After World War II ended, the Hoover Commission studying federal government efficiency continued the attack: "The basis for historic Indian culture has been swept away. Traditional tribal organization was smashed a generation ago [i.e., by the IRA]. . . . Assimilation must be the dominant goal of public policy" (quoted in Wilkinson 2005:64).

Felix Cohen died (only forty-six years old) in 1953, the year House Concurrent Resolution 108 passed: "At the earliest possible time, all of the Indian tribes . . . should be freed from Federal supervision and control" (quoted in Getches, Wilkinson, and Williams 1993:231)—in other words, an end to the United States' burdensome fiduciary responsibility. Congress had unilaterally made all Indians in the United States its citizens in 1924; now they would be nothing but citizens of the United States. The authors of the 1982 revision of the *Handbook of Federal Indian Law*, a revision made to reinstate Cohen's standpoint, note that "the Supreme Court has repeatedly held that Congress can abrogate a treaty provision unilaterally without consent of the tribe, even to the point of terminating entirely the trust obligation" (Strickland et al. 1982:222). Here, the constitutional clause giving Congress exclusive power over intercourse with Indian nations takes precedence over Marshall's "domestic dependent nations" opinion of 1831. Presumptive bias let the white men in Congress and the White House in 1953 believe that their fiduciary responsibility included its termination in order to free the wards from lawfully negotiated relationships.

Justice (that is, the Department of) had its way at last in this backlash era. It revised Cohen's *Handbook* to focus on Congress's plenary power rather than Indians' historic and civil rights. If Felix felt the final Wheeler-Howard Act "emasculated" his original legislation, this government-sponsored revision of his *Handbook* left him not only emasculated but drawn and quartered. Published in 1958 to replace the 1942 *Handbook*, the revision did not even properly update the sections it retained (Strickland et al. 1982:ix). Lest anyone misunderstand the purpose of the gutted and distorted 1958 edition, its introduction made clear that it was intended for "foreclosing, if possible, further uncritical use of the earlier edition by judges, lawyers, and laymen" (quoted in Strickland et al. 1982:ix).

Public Law 280, passed by Congress in August 1953, authorized states to take over both civil and criminal jurisdiction of Indians. In effect, reservations lost their sovereignty, and Indians their status under their treaties. "Indians not taxed" is a venerable phrase, in Article I of the Constitution relating to apportionment of congressional representatives according to state populations—Indians not being citizens then and under the jurisdiction of the federal, not state, governments, they were not to be counted in apportioning representatives, and "Indians not taxed" was shorthand for the separate status Indians held under treaties. Public Law 280 was interpreted to say that Indians' incomes are subject to income tax except where treaties specifically exempt a tribe from income tax, but the Sixteenth Amendment to the Constitution imposing a federal income tax was not passed until 1913, forty-two years after Congress ended treaty making, a point made by Spokan leader Joseph Garry (1954:37).

How far the reversal of policy went can be gauged by a case in Alaska concerning the Indian village of Hydaburg, which had been granted three thousand feet of coastal water as part of a reservation ordered under the Alaska Welfare Act. Libby and other large commercial canneries challenged this restriction on their business. The Alaskan district judge ruled in 1953 that this extension of the Indians' economic base was invalid. Theodore Haas, Cohen's friend and colleague on the *Handbook*, commented, "Undoubtedly the Government's decision not to appeal this ruling was influenced by the fear of the Justice Department that the appellate court in reversing the trial court might hand down a legal opinion which might help the Alaskan natives in their land claims against the United States" (Haas 1954:23). A judge in another Alaskan case at this time even held that the Hydaburg reservation had not been properly established, and to set up reservations for Alaskan native communities actually constituted racial discrimination (Strickland et al. 1982:765).

Termination proved to be disastrous in human terms, and surprisingly costly to the federal government. The Indian Relocation Act of 1956 dumped Indian families in cities where employment and housing discrimination doomed them to ghetto poverty. Funds were appropriated to pay for Indians' transportation off reservations, to subsidize the first month in a city, and to open and staff employment and assistance offices in principal cities of relocation. Monroe Price, in his 1973 casebook on American Indian law, remarks that in the nineteenth century, reservations were to be "schools of civilization" taught by missionaries; the termination program "suggests that the new school for civilization was to be the city. Jobs and not farming became the key to civilization" (1973:584). Senator Chavez of New Mexico, speaking at a hearing on HR 3790, 1952, summed up the termination principle: "The American background is one of suffering. The winning of the West is one of suffering, and they [Indians] have to suffer, and they are willing to suffer and are willing to try. But treat them as citizens, as human beings, as part of the country. The Indian does not need special attention except in the American way of life" (quoted in Price 1973:589).

Cohen's insistence on the primacy of treaties was nevertheless acknowledged. Senator Arthur Watkins of Utah, leader of the termination policy in Congress, declared that the Termination Act "in no way violates any treaty obligation with this tribe [Menominee]" (quoted in Getches, Wilkinson, and Williams 1993:243, opinion of Supreme Court Justice Douglas in the 1968 case arguing for Menominees' hunting and fishing rights even after termination). Terminations had to be enacted piecemeal for each tribe after detailed negotiations on land, services, and funds. The notion that termination would be a simple end to federal responsibility came up short against the legal history embedded in Cohen's *Handbook*. President John Kennedy's administration in the early 1960s ceased promulgating proposals to terminate tribes, and his successor, Lyndon Johnson, formally announced a new policy in 1968 to include Indians in his Great Society economic programs.

Ironically, termination was pursued simultaneously with the third prong of Cohen's construction of an enlightened federal Indian policy, the resolution of tribes' claims against the federal government. The Indian Claims Commission was not meant to end federal responsibility, since that was founded upon the treaties. Lacking the force the *Handbook* earned, the Claims Commission instead created a business that employed anthropologists, historians, and of course lawyers for two decades, and a new discipline, ethnohistory.

CHAPTER SIX

The Indian Claims Commission

Felix Cohen saw the Indian New Deal in three parts: the Indian Reorganization Act restoring Indian land and creating limited self-government through tribal constitutions; the *Handbook of Federal Indian Law* arguing for Indian Country and its sovereignties; and the Claims Commission to adjudicate tribes' claims against the federal government. As a scholar committed to social democratic principles of "revolution through the ballot box" and the rule of just laws, he believed these three efforts should free the tribes from onerous restrictions, allowing them to retain their cultures while rising out of poverty.

Two of his three efforts missed the mark. The IRA, even in its initial lengthy draft by Cohen, continued the federal government's unwarranted paternalism, and Felix's youthful faith in constitutions imposed a foreign instrument of governance upon the tribes.[1] By the time he came to write the *Handbook*, with five years' experience dealing with Indian people, including visits to reservations, Felix realized he had acquiesced in John Collier's limited goal of reforming the Office of Indian Affairs. Radically liberating Indians from federal control—control by the bureau he now headed—was not Collier's aim. In the *Handbook*, Felix and his team worked to establish inherent sovereignty and the primacy of treaties over Congress's plenary power, including its power to delegate Indian affairs to one of its agencies. Now Felix wanted to level the playing field by restoring to tribes what had been unjustly and illegally (if one accepts the *Handbook*) seized from them by the federal government. Tribes had been making claims against the government for more than a century, for example

Taos Pueblo's repeated efforts to regain its holy Blue Lake from US Forest Service control, hampered by an 1863 congressional statute denying US Court of Claims jurisdiction in Indian claims stemming from treaties. (The Court of Claims itself had been established only in 1855.) Only specific legislation from Congress could exempt a tribe's claim from this prohibition. Interior's team—Ickes, Margold, Collier, and Cohen—favored a congressional Indian Claims Commission empowered to hear and resolve tribes' claims. Note that this would be a commission, not a court of claims. Most Americans saw this move as just and fair. Indians perceived an irredeemable flaw in the commission's authority: it could only order monetary compensation, not restoration of land.

Framers of the commission assumed Indian tribes would simply use the money gained through successful claims to buy whatever land they wanted. Two considerations made this untenable. First, a great deal of disputed property was not for sale, such as Taos's Blue Lake. Second, many Indian people were antagonized by the idea that a dollar value could be put on land significant to them as holy or a homeland. Offering dollars for the Lakotas' Black Hills appeared to be the grossest misunderstanding of the value of the hills, ignoring the locales immortalized in legendary events, ignoring its soul-refreshing beauty, ignoring its valuable hunting unavailable on the Plains. For all the Cohens' and Margold's socialism, they still believed land is property. Morris Raphael Cohen, Felix's father and Margold's professor, in 1927 published a classic article stating that "property and sovereignty, as every student knows, belong to entirely different branches of the law. Sovereignty is a concept of political or public law and property belongs to civil or private law" (Cohen 1927:8). Cohen *père's* essay goes on to clarify the harm done to the body politic by rejection of a minimum wage law in favor of an employer's absolute power (sovereignty) over employees' wages and their ability to join trade unions. Perhaps this seems a far cry from the Lakotas' Black Hills claim, but the point Morris Cohen makes is that under Western law, "property as sovereign power compelling service and obedience may be obscured for us in a commercial economy" (1927:12). American Indians understood this. Lakota do not want dollars to buy land somewhere, or to buy parcels in the Black Hills, they want the valuable and holy Black Hills to be acknowledged as their property under their sovereign power secured in their 1868 treaty.

Nathan Margold had been hired in 1929 by the Institute for Government Research to draft a bill that could resolve the many outstanding claims by Indians and tribes against the federal government, an obstacle to helping Indians identified by the 1928 Meriam Report. Margold proposed a limited-tenure six-person claims commission, not a court, to hear and decide Indian claims of whatever nature. After Cohen joined Margold at Interior, bills were drawn up for such a commission in 1935 and again in 1940, but President Roosevelt did not believe such a commission could succeed in settling Indian claims. Then World War II forced a hiatus in programs unrelated to the war. Once the tide of war had turned, in December 1944, the House Committee on Indian Affairs, spurred by the backlash against the IRA and also by the competency and heroism displayed by Indians in the armed services, recommended an Indian claims commission as part of the growing sentiment for termination of Indian status.

Strong support for a claims commission came from the new National Congress of American Indians, organized by the Cohens' friend Archie Phinney (Kaplatsilpilp, a Nimipu or Nez Percé), D'Arcy McNickle (Salish-Métis), and Charles Heacock (Lakota), all employed by the OIA. Encouraged by Collier and his assistant commissioner William Zimmerman to form an independent national Indian congress from among the bureau's several dozen Indian employees, meetings were held in 1944, including some with a representative of the sympathetic white American Association on Indian Affairs (later Association on American Indian Affairs), of which Felix and Lucy were members. Phinney told McNickle that it was of paramount importance for their congress to be Indian and independent of any white group, so they could choose whom they wished for assistance, for instance "the good knowledge of Felix Cohen and others" (quoted in Cowger 1999:36).

A part-Choctaw congressman from Oklahoma, William Stigler, brought the National Congress of American Indians' draft Indian Claims Commission bill to Congress in 1945. It called for a three-person commission of which at least one member would be an enrolled Indian. After several months of hearings before the House Indian Affairs Committee, a revised bill omitting the requirement for at least one Indian commissioner went to the House, then to the Senate, passing in August 1946. Ickes had assigned Felix to work with a Washington lawyer experienced in Indian cases, Ernest L. Wilkerson, to amend the House bill so that the commission would answer to Congress, not an executive-branch agency, that its decisions would be final (although subject to federal Court of Claims and Supreme Court review), and that it would have authority to hear an unusually broad range of claims. Felix added clauses to make the commission proactive in itself, notifying tribes and other Indian groups of its mission and inviting claims, and to fund an investigative section to assist tribes in researching necessary documents—prompted by his experience with the *Handbook*.

Pleased with his work, the House committee appointed Felix to redraft the bill. Somehow, he neglected to put back the stipulation that at least one member of the commission should be Indian. The Department of Justice, true to its conservative bent, objected to practically everything Felix put into the bill, persuading the Senate Committee on Indian Affairs to gut it. House committee members argued for their version, and most of Felix's bill was incorporated into the final congressional bill of August 1946. Felix had the further satisfaction of preparing President Harry Truman's statement upon signing the bill (Tsuk Mitchell 2007:226).

The Indian Claims Commission Act built upon the *Handbook* in accepting the primacy of treaties in Indian affairs. By this time, Felix saw wisdom in emphasizing treaties as contracts between the Indian signatories and the federal government. Like his father, he realized Americans can be better reached through the language of business than through abstruse moral discourse. The United States had conquered America's First Nations, yes, but instead of seizing their properties, the Founding Fathers had reserved to the federal government commerce with Indians—"intercourse"—and negotiated contracts (treaties) to purchase their lands. Contracts are sacrosanct in capitalist America. The Indian Claims Commission would review Indian claims of breaches of contract, of failure to make legitimate compensation, rectifying these lapses of businessmen's morality. Felix even wrote a popular article for the mass-market national magazine *Collier's* (not related to the OIA commissioner), called "How We Bought the United States," explaining this position underlying, in his view, the Indian Claims Commission Act.

However honest in fulfilling its contracts the United States should be, in 1946 it wanted to terminate all those it held with Indians. The Indian Claims Commission Act would hear, "on behalf of any Indian tribe, band, or other identifiable group of American Indians residing within the territorial limits of the United States or Alaska" claims falling into these five categories:

(1) claims in law or equity arising under the Constitution, laws, treaties of the United States, and Executive orders of the President;

(2) all other claims in law or equity, including those sounding in tort, with respect to which the claimant would have been entitled to sue in a court of the United States if the United States was subject to suit;

(3) claims which would result if the treaties, contracts, and agreements between the claimant and the United States were revised on the
ground of fraud, duress, unconscionable consideration, mutual or unilateral mistake, whether of law or fact, or any other ground cognizable
by a court of equity;

(4) claims arising from the taking by the United States, whether as
the result of a treaty of cession or otherwise, of lands owned or occupied
by the claimant without the payment for such lands of compensation
agreed to by the claimant;

(5) claims based upon fair and honorable dealings that are not recognized by any existing rule of law or equity. (quoted in Strickland et al.
1982:161)

Against this fantastical breadth of allowance of claims, the act imposed a
limit of five years for filing claims, and the claims had to refer to situations
predating the August 1946 Act. After that date, new claims would go to the
US Court of Claims, under its normal rules. For Indians, the red flag in
the act was this: "A final determination against a claimant made and reported in accordance with this Act shall forever bar any further claim or
demand against the United States arising out of the matter involved in
the controversy" (quoted in Strickland et al. 1982:161). Furthermore, although the Act did not state in so many words that resolution could only
involve monetary compensation, it did say "payment of any claim," which
implied, and was understood to mean, monetary payment. A claim for a
homeland unjustly taken was not settled by handing descendants dollars
while the homeland could not be bought (the Black Hills are the prominent actual case, but think of Mahicans who might yearn for at least In-
wood Park on their homeland island, Manhattan). Felix wrote the Indian
Claims Commission Act to reflect and rectify injustices and perfidy suffered by American Indians at the hands of agents of the United States;
Congress passed the act to clear the decks of Indians' claims during the
same ten years it expected to terminate Indian status.

Indian New Deal goals clashed with Western states' interests, as evi-
denced in Senator Burton Wheeler's efforts to rescind the IRA. After World
War II, devastation abroad fed capitalist enterprise in America, fostering a
military-industrial complex that wanted more land in the West for huge
military test ranges as well as for power-generating installations, river controls, and urban and suburban development. Arthur V. Watkins, senator
from Utah, led the 1950s Congressional push to end special status for Indians, a move that would save many millions of federal dollars and would

complete assimilation of Indian lands into the capitalist economy. Watkins was motivated, according to historian H. Warren Metcalf (2002:45–46), by his Mormon faith, believing that American Indians are a fallen race who ought to be made "white and delightsome" through conversion to Mormon Christianity and its political-economic way of life. Ernest Wilkerson, the lawyer who worked with Cohen drafting the Indian Claims Commission Act, was also a devout Mormon, soon to be named president of Brigham Young University (Metcalf 2002:60–61). Although he had become wealthy through fees gained by successful litigation of Ute claims, Wilkerson anticipated an end to such lawsuits and the special status that he and Watkins believed impeded Indians' salvation in this world and the next. That these men may not have been moved primarily by crass land-grabbing desire made their ideological commitment to termination unwavering, especially in Watkins's case.

Altogether, 611 claims (dockets) were filed under the Indian Claims Commission Act before its last extension, to September 1978, was closed. Its three-person commission was expanded to five members. A revolving fund was eventually established in 1963 to assist Indian tribes in researching claims (recall that the government, defendant in these cases, had its own investigative unit under the Act). A number of claims were still in process of hearing in 1978 and were transferred to the US Court of Claims. By this time, the 1975 Indian Self-Determination Act had, at last, repudiated unilateral termination of Indian status by the federal government—in effect, the completion of an Indian New Deal interrupted by backlash.

Indian Claims and Aboriginal Title

In spite of Felix's wonderfully broad set of criteria for claims, and his *Handbook* making treaties and agreements the basis for relationships between the federal government and Indian tribes, the hearings revealed a gaping area needing exploration: aboriginal title. Felix had said in the *Handbook* that court cases on title to Indian lands differ in "whether they refer to the Indian right of occupancy as a 'mere' right of occupancy or as a 'sacred' right of occupancy" (Cohen 1942:293). Following British principle, still held in Canada, that conquest rendered Indian lands the exclusive property of the Crown, which it might convey to tribes or private persons in fee simple or other forms of deed, the United States upon its establishment in 1783 took exclusive power to purchase Indian lands from Indian nations, usually by treaty. Since Indians in the United States did

Figure 6.1. A Blackfeet soldier contests the forced ceding of Blackfeet land to make Glacier National Park (park entrance at bridge, background); sculpture by Jay Laber, commissioned by Blackfeet Nation; East Glacier, Montana. Photo by Alice B. Kehoe.

not have written titles to their estates (whereas Mesoamerican native lords did have written titles before conquest, many of them preserved in Spanish colonial archives), Indians could not be said to hold title to their lands in fee simple. Thus their possessory right was a right of occupancy. American courts recognized this. A right of occupancy ceased if the Indians left the land. Margold and Cohen wanted American courts to understand that abandonment under duress should not end a tribe's right to its land.

From this standpoint, compensating a tribe with money is irrelevant. The tribe did not seek to sell its land, and in filing a claim it asks for its right of occupancy back. Attorneys for Indian plaintiffs before the Indian Claims Commission generally advised their clients that it was more realistic to press for large monetary settlements—something most Americans think reasonable to settle litigation—in lieu of disputed land. Money could be used for buying back land. For American courts, making the issue one of adequate or inadequate payment for a taking is straightforward;

the value of the disputed land at time of taking is determined, the amount paid is compared to it, and compensation ordered for the difference. Interest on the amount owed by the government was seldom figured in. Attorneys would get their contingency fee, usually 10 percent of the settlement, various costs were deducted, and the remainder paid to the tribe to be used for tribal business and projects, perhaps buying land, and, often, one-time per capita payments to members of the tribe.

It was clearly stated in the Act that settlement constituted final extinguishment of the plaintiff's claim. Some tribes decided not to file a claim because they would not accept such terms. More tribes listened to attorneys advising that this unprecedented opportunity for broadly construed claims ought to be taken, that it might never be possible again, and that money was better than nothing. The Indian Claims Commission looked to be a generous, noble effort by the United States to settle wrongs suffered by the peoples it had dispossessed. To Indians, it could be read as one more step in the conquerors' "civilizing" coercive tutelage, that everything translates into money and money is the lifeblood of society.

Years after Felix Cohen died, a young attorney named Tom Tureen took a case for the Passamaquoddy tribe in Maine. Not recognized as a tribe by the federal government—common among the East Coast nations invaded by colonists long before there was a United States—the Passamaquoddy had signed a treaty with the state of Massachusetts in 1794 (Maine being still a part of Massachusetts then), leaving them with a small portion of their territory. Their descendants sought to recover some of this land. Tureen realized that their 1794 treaty with a state could not be valid because it was four years later than the federal 1790 Nonintercourse Act prohibiting purchases of Indian land except by treaty or agreement with the United States. Legally, the Passamaquoddy and neighboring Penobscot still held aboriginal title to the lands they occupied, then and continuing since they still lived on the remnants of their lands in 1970 when Tureen took the case. The two Maine tribes had not gone to the Indian Claims Commission, which could but seldom did hear federally nonrecognized tribes.

Tureen requested the United States to file suit against Maine for failing to observe the Nonintercourse Act. As might have been predicted, the Department of Justice did not wish to do so, but Tureen petitioned a federal district judge who ordered the suit. With uproar from thousands of Maine residents whose title to their properties was now in doubt, both the tribe and Maine retained top-rank lawyers, including former solicitor general and Watergate prosecutor Archibald Cox for the Passamaquoddy. President Jimmy Carter appointed a mediator with a staff to assist him. In 1980, Carter signed the Maine Indian Claims Settlement Act, which ratified the

1794 treaties (i.e., rectified the failure in 1794 to obtain US approval) and awarded the Passamaquoddy and Penobscot federal recognition with its entitlement to federal services to Indians, and monetary compensation for the taking that the tribes used to purchase three hundred thousand acres from non-Indians agreeing to sell. Aside from ameliorating the Maine tribes' economic disadvantages, the mediated settlement gave hope to other Eastern tribes to gain federal entitlement and possibly regain land that technically was still in aboriginal title.

Out in Nevada's high desert, a different case was pursued by the Western Shoshone. From the beginning of the Indian Claims Commission, a number of Western Shoshone refused the possibility of a monetary settlement for their claim to land recognized in their 1863 Treaty of Ruby Valley. The Indian Claims Commission ruled in 1962 that encroachment by white settlers had so displaced Shoshone that in 1863 they no longer held occupancy title: there was no taking in the legal sense. The Commission would value the land given up in 1863 under treaty (at its 1863 value, no less) and award monetary compensation. Some Shoshone, especially those in IRA tribal business councils, were willing to accept what they believed was the only possible outcome of their claims. Many others organized to continue resistance against extinguishment of Indian title. Then the federal Bureau of Land Management charged two Shoshone sisters, Mary and Catherine Dann, with illegally grazing their cattle on the Bureau's public land. The Danns filed countersuit in 1974 against the United States, insisting that their family had occupied the land in question before 1863 and continuously since. The case went through courts and appeals until August 1986 when the Reno district federal judge ruled that the Shoshone tribe's title to their 1863 lands had been extinguished by the 1979 Indian Claims Commission award of money, but the Dann sisters could continue to graze their cattle on their ancestral land because by continuously occupying it, the family had individual aboriginal rights to use it— usufruct, not title. This partial victory has not satisfied the large number of Shoshone, including the Dann family, who demand rejection of the Claims Commission finding that gradual encroachment dispossessed the Shoshone before 1863.

Ethnohistory

Although the Indian Claims Commission was not a court, it proceeded in the adversarial mode standard in American courts (Lurie 1956). Government attorneys defending the United States against Indian plaintiffs did their utmost to win for the government. The Department of Justice did not see "Indians not taxed" as their wards to be advocated for. Margold and Cohen had struggled against this bias in the Hulapai case against a railroad encroaching on their reservation (described at length in McMillen 2007). The Justice Department's persistent ignoring of the Indian New Deal shift in policy greatly escalated the cost and the time incurred by the cases brought to the Commission, demanding duplicate research efforts—by plaintiffs and by Justice's attorneys—and lengthy cross-examinations of witnesses before the Commission. Pitting professional anthropologists and historians against one another on the witness stand bred enmity that destroyed former collegiality. Ethnohistorian Arthur Ray recounts a proclivity of defendants to cite standard published sources on a tribe, never intended to be used in legal disputes, against plaintiffs' expert witnesses' in-depth archival source research on the specific localities in question (Ray 2010:46–48, 2011:147–152). Indians' own historical traditions were discouraged in favor of written documents, legally more acceptable than orally transmitted knowledge.

Ethnohistory as a scholarly discipline was born under the Indian Claims Commission (Krech 2012; McMillen 2007:173–77; Ray 2006, 2011:6, 43). Situated within the mental box of American legal practices, the Commission favored disputes focusing on real property, that is, land and its transformability into money. John Locke's argument that property in land "improved" by labor is the foundation of civil society informed the Commission as it had Locke's seventeenth-century aristocratic entrepreneur employers and their political descendants in the thirteen colonies (Locke 2003; Williams 1992:246–49). Aboriginal title based on occupancy being legally inferior to written title exchangeable for money (Locke's spin justifying his employers taking Carolina Colony), plaintiffs were advised to rely on historical documents such as treaties and explorers' accounts mentioning their forebears' occupancy of territories. That such-and-such a hill was the abode of a powerful nonhuman being was relegated to myth, and "the bones of my ancestors lie there" was sentiment, neither of these claims having actual—monetary—value. Anthropologists employed as expert witnesses, often because no professional historians had researched the tribe making a claim, had to learn to emphasize archives more than ethnography. They also learned that nuances dear to scholars were only nuisances to the legal mind. At the same time, historians slowly learned that archived documents might not be sufficient to build a case for, or against, tribal claims; anthropologists' experience with Indian people not only gave a different standpoint, it also might demonstrate bias in the documents.

Brought together in the claims cases, anthropologists and historians realized there was a large common ground between their disciplines, institutionalized in the American Society for Ethnohistory founded in 1954.

Disputations in Commission hearings were supposed to focus on facts. Few listeners were learned enough, and critical enough, in anthropological theory to pinpoint how theoretical positions influenced the collection of factual data, as well as their interpretation. A much-discussed, bitter disagreement occurred between Julian Steward, speaking as expert for the government on Paiute and Shoshone claims, Omer Stewart, an ethnographer working closely with Paiute, and Alfred Kroeber, dean of anthropologists after Boas's 1942 death. Julian Steward had been employed by the Bureau of Indian Affairs in 1935–1936 to carry out fieldwork in Nevada and adjacent Southern California on these Numa-speaking groups. Committed to a theory of cultural evolution from simple small bands to complex civilizations, Steward welcomed the salaried opportunity to create a picture of the most primitive stage of human social evolution. It would, he theorized, be patrilocal and patrilineal, fathers and sons the cores of family groups—men being active, armed hunters, in contrast to passive women tied to hearth and babies. After two years of speaking with hundreds of Paiute and Shoshone men, and a few women, Steward failed to elicit evidence of patrilocality or patrilineal principle. Steward lamely commented, "further investigations may require supplementary theories to fit facts not previously known" (1938:259). When he turned in his report to the BIA in 1936, Collier was disgusted. It wasn't factual reporting, and Steward's obvious belief that assimilation was necessary prejudiced him against a way of life that did not conform to academic theory. Collier had the superintendent of a Shoshone agency read the report; she noted many inaccuracies, agreeing with Collier's evaluation of few facts and too much bias (Kerns 2003:206–8).

In 1954, Steward appeared for the defense (Department of Justice) in a Northern Paiute claim on a taking of their aboriginal territory without compensation. Slotting Northern Paiute into his "family level" of sociocultural integration, Steward insisted that these Indians, like the neighboring Shoshone, represented the simplest way of life, independent families roaming about a sparse countryside always searching for food. From Steward's information, the Department of Justice stated as fact "that the Northern Paiute were not organized socially, religiously, politically, or even through kinship . . . [and] did not have 'property or territory'" (quoted in Ronaasen, Clemmer, and Rudden 1999:177–78). They formed "predatory bands," without defined territory, preying on settlers after they began arriving about 1845, and the Paiutes obtained horses. Steward disparaged the Paiutes' expert, Omer Stewart, saying he had been naïve in directly asking Paiute the names and territories of bands, that these were postcontact designations the Paiutes learned from settlers. Kroeber tried to mediate by stating that American Indian sociopolitical organizations were not generally congruent with US legal concepts and terminology, especially in the matter of sharply defined boundaries.

Julian Steward's dogged dogmatism against these Indian people was highly influential among anthropologists and archaeologists persuaded that theory should guide science (Ray 2011:38). Archaeologist Jesse Jennings taught for decades that, as Steward had stated, Great Basin people lived a nomadic hand-to-mouth existence virtually unchanged for millennia, and interpreted his excavations to demonstrate that. Steward and Jennings were finally challenged in the 1960s by young archaeologists cognizant of the Mormon invasion in the 1840s that had driven Indian settlements out of the watered valleys (Jennings 1973). Steward had assumed that the impoverished life of his marginalized Indian informants had been that of their ancestors, too, paying no attention to the relationship between this poverty and the prosperity of the Mormon agricultural communities instructed by Brigham Young to homestead where they saw remnants of Indian homes, for there would be water and vegetation. Steward's blindness to history stemmed from his determination to scientifically discover ecological laws determining levels of human sociopolitical organization (civilization or its lack). Fortunately for the Northern Paiute, the Indian Claims Commission preferred Omer Stewart's straightforward recitation of band names and associated territories, and awarded the plaintiffs compensation for the taking.

Not only did the claims hearings expose the bias incurred when academic theory is given more weight than empirical observations, the hearings exposed the inadequacy of ordinary historiography. Archived documents are only a portion of any nation's history. Plaintiffs' attorneys and expert witnesses in the hearings hammered at the issues of poor language interpretation in treaty negotiations, one-sided self-serving documents in archives, ignorance and corruption behind recorded statements, unrecorded events and situations, and, above all, refusal to respect Indian nations' oral histories. That Europeans had extraordinary systems for memorizing complex knowledge, "arts of memory," from classical Greece through the Renaissance, is not commonly known (Yates 1966); these remarkable methods for memorization indicate how orally transmitted knowledge can be systematized and preserved. Anthropologists cite studies of African oral histories by Vansina (1985), who corroborated them with European documents. Cursorily dismissing Indians' statements on history cannot be justified; neither can a court hold sacrosanct contemporary elders' statements on their forebears' actions (Ray 2008:23–24). Ethnohistory as a discipline tends to take the anthropological approach of looking at the social context of documents and weighing statements that superficially may seem to be poetic or mystical. Careful translations, often by the First Nations speakers themselves, may reveal factual historical knowledge—an example is the use of Hopi oral histories to find archaeological sites and construct historical maps of Hopi clan movements (Bernardini 2005).

Overview

The Indian Claims Commission Act was extraordinarily broad, as Felix Cohen wrote it, insofar as it would allow claims "not recognized by any existing rule of law or equity." Its foundational premise, however, was terribly flawed: from Nathan Margold's initial 1929 proposal to the 1946 Act, it assumed that American Indians would accept that land can be valued in dollars, and a claim for land can be settled with an award of dollars. The Act was supremely assimilationist, forcing Indian people to live in a Western legal system even as they challenged its validity for them.

At the end of his short life, Felix Cohen published a bitter reflection on the Indian New Deal and its vicissitudes (Cohen 1953). He reviewed the OIA commitment to bettering Indian lives beginning with Commissioner Rhoads in 1929 and continuing to 1950, then specified reversals occurring under Commissioner Dillon Myer beginning in 1950:

> The Bureau spent federal money to influence Indians voting on tribal matters, directly interfered with elections on the Blackfeet Reservation, and refused to recognize San Ildefonso Pueblo's elected Governor.
>
> Myer attempted to prevent Indian tribes from independently hiring legal counsel.
>
> Indians have been asking for repeal of statutes forbidding them to purchase alcoholic beverages, sell their cattle or crops without Reservation agent approval, buy ammunition, or even cooking utensils. Myer's BIA opposed Congressional bills to end these discriminations.
>
> Myer tried to sell off hospitals and clinics on reservations, although many of these had been built with tribal funds.

The BIA refused to respect a Pueblo request that no white person be within the pueblo territory during certain ceremonies.

The BIA wanted its employees to carry arms and make arrests without warrant for alleged violations of the Bureau's more than 2,200 regulations applying only to Indians.

Reservation superintendents were interfering with Indians' personal lives, for example, ordering that stick games in a Blackfeet village should not continue past six o'clock in the evening. Another example is an order to Rio Grande Pueblos that they are "putting too much labor" into their cornfields.

The BIA has not pursued the official policy to give preference to Indians in employment, and to train Indians for Bureau employment.

The BIA was attempting to lease Indian lands and mineral deposits without consent of the tribes, and forbidding Indians to use their own allotments to graze their animals.

The BIA ordered the Blackfeet Tribal Council to withdraw its funds in the local bank and deposit them with the Agency Superintendent. It refused to turn over buildings built with tribal funds to the tribe. It claimed title to Indian cattle that the Blackfeet had paid for.

The BIA wanted to charge "poor credit risks" higher interests on loans regardless of the tribe's assessment of credit risks.

With the Indian Claims Commission, the BIA has not cooperated with providing information plaintiff tribes require for their cases.

The BIA began extending individual trust land patents only year to year instead of the preceding usual twenty-five-year periods, rendering individual allotment holders unable to plan for the future.

Myer opposed turning over power to tribes, whether requested to approve tribal corporations or transfers of services, and did not obey the practice of having Interior review proposed BIA rulings.

What Cohen described was the paradox that under the congressional policy of terminating Indian status, Commissioner Myer was reinforcing the OIA's tyrannical control of its "wards."

Myer, the target of Cohen's 1953 attack, was an authoritarian who came to the OIA from administering the infamous Japanese relocation camps during World War II. "A blundering and dictatorial tin-Hitler," Harold Ickes called him, quoted by Cohen (1953:158 fn.). Considering the sickening similarity between Nazis herding Jews into death camps and the United States herding Japanese Americans into bleak desert camps, if not in most cases fatally, Felix Cohen's hatred of the "tin-Hitler" is understandable. Myer, like "good Germans," could defend himself by saying he was only carrying out his legitimate government's orders. He did not initiate Congress's termination policy. That policy was backlash against the Indian New Deal.

The Indian Claims Commission dramatically illustrates the enormous weight of Anglo culture, how its centuries-old adversarial process blew out what had been envisioned as mediation. Nor did Margold and Cohen foresee that settling injustices against Indian tribes would be equated with final termination of their special status, or realize the insult, the blasphemy, of trying to give First Nations money in lieu of land. The Commission became a Procrustean bed on which several hundred deep grievances were lopped and crammed into a highly structured alien procedure rigged against realizing Indian hopes. Whether it might have been softened if Margold and Cohen had lived beyond its launching, we shall never know.

Crisis in Indian Affairs

If Margold and Cohen thought settling claims against the federal government would realize the IRA's goal of establishing Indian communities on a solid land base, the postwar Congress saw the Claims Commission as the final solution to Indians' intransigence in meekly settling down. Extinguish their grievances with monetary compensation, facilitate younger families' movement into America's booming postwar cities, and the anachronistic peculiar status of domestic dependent nations should at last become past history. The political climate of the decade that saw *Brown v. Board of Education* break enforced segregation of African-Americans favored measures to abolish other races' marginalization (Metcalf 2002:5). Multiculturalism was a radical leftist notion (Katz 2012:192). Victorious America's return to normalcy celebrated unity unbesmirched by unjust practices, picturing Levittowns full of happy children playing together.

Backlash against the Indian New Deal engendered its own backlash as Indians, many veterans of World War II, rebelled against arbitrary termination. The National Congress of American Indians geared up to lobby Congress. In the 1960s, conservatism dimmed, giving John Kennedy and Lyndon Johnson presidential power to, in Kennedy's short term, drop termination action and then, with Johnson's succession, include Indians in the liberal Great Society welfare and entitlement programs. Movement toward implementation of the fundamental principle argued in Cohen's *Handbook*, inherent sovereignty, became a strong current during that radical decade. Chicago anthropologist Sol Tax organized and hosted a pan-Indian congress in 1961 that laid groundwork for effectively demanding political and legal reforms, while more militant Indians took note of Black Power activism. Red Power marches, attacks, and takeovers made headlines between 1968 and 1973, climaxing in the seventy-one-day siege of the hamlet of Wounded Knee, South Dakota. That wave of lobbying and protests culminated in the true reversal of federal Indian policy, the 1975 Indian Self-Determination and Education Assistance Act.

Richard Nixon turned out to be the US president who effectively revolutionized Indian policy, although Nixon's resignation resulting from the Watergate scandal left Gerald Ford to sign the act. Nixon had made a landmark speech in 1970 (HR Doc. No. 363, Ninety-First Congress, second session), calling for "a new era in which the Indian future is determined by Indian acts and Indian decisions. . . . The policy of forced termination is wrong. . . . We must make it clear that Indians can become independent of Federal control without being cut off from Federal concern and Federal support. . . . Termination is morally and legally unacceptable" (Nixon, quoted in Getches, Wilkinson, and Williams 1993: 253–54).

Behind these reasoned words was an emotional memory. When a student in Whittier College in California, a small Quaker institution, Richard Nixon was on its football team, coached by Wallace Newman, a Luiseño Indian (Mission Creek band). Coach Newman was like a second father to the ambitious young man. Seeing the coach's success in winning local league championships for the college in both football and baseball, but never receiving offers for positions in larger institutions, Nixon felt keenly the injustice of racism. His beloved coach lived until 1985, active with his own band and other Southern California Indians, pleased that Indian affairs of which he had spoken so often with students were turned at last toward self-determination (Malcolm F. Farmer, professor at Whittier College, personal communication, 2006, 2007). Cohen's and Margold's truncated lives had deprived them of seeing fulfillment of their efforts to truly turn the tide of Americanization forced upon Indians.

CHAPTER SEVEN

The Consequences of Being Jewish

Most discriminating employers are right in thinking that Negro or Jewish employees may be less effective from the standpoint of public relations than native white Protestants.[1]

Felix Cohen was replying to a request from the editor of the magazine *Common Ground* to recommend a person "without a Jewish name" to write an article counteracting the isolationist ideas that immigration costs jobs and lowers living standards for Americans. He said he had thought the magazine "a staunch opponent of name changing and other concessions to popular prejudices," since it was published by the liberal Common Council for American Unity. Felix mentioned that he himself had published an article such as the editor requested.[2] Wryly, he noted "*Harper's Magazine* later ran several paragraphs of it under the name of an author whom I don't know."[3]

This minor exchange between Felix Solomon Cohen and M. Margaret Anderson, a second-generation Swedish American (Beyer 1991:30), testifies to the power of anti-Semitism in 1930s America, notwithstanding Roosevelt's remarkable practice of hiring the best people regardless of party or race. When the president's attention turned to war, standard practice rebounded. Taken-for-granted anti-Semitism in the 1930s triggered *Time* magazine to count up the number of Jews in Roosevelt's top circle (see chapter 3). Felix Cohen was one of the Jewish "bright young legalites . . . [who] are not many and do not hold high posts, the fact remains that because their brains and ability are used by their superiors and because they are frequently deputed to carry out the Administration's policies and write its bills, their importance exceeds their numbers and their official rank" (*Time*, May 1, 1934). In this chapter, I explore the consequences of being seen as Jewish for Felix, Lucy, Nathan Margold, and their coterie.

On July 7, 1941, Nathan Margold wrote to Felix about hiring new people. On page 7 of the letter, Margold says,

> whether in connection with a Land Office job or some other vacancy, I should like to call your attention to a Mr. Drechsler / Drexler, on the staff of the Division of Investigation in our Dept. who has been a long-standing applicant for a lawyer's job in some *Washington, D.C.* branch of our office, who is, I believe, a good man and whom I should have recommended for appointment long ago except that he is Jewish and has his residence in New York. If you are in a spot where Jews from New York are again to be open for consideration, I feel obligated and also would on the merits want to urge you to give him the first preference for any appointment to a $3800 vacancy.[4]

A month later, Margold wrote to Felix,

> The only comment I have to make relates to the choice being put up to Flanery as between Hofflund, Seagle and Drexler. My own opinion is very strong and clear that if we do not *have* to eliminate both Seagle and Drexler for reasons of religion and geography i.e. if we consider merits only—Seagle is by far the ablest of the three and also has special qualifications for Indian work by reason of his past research and writings. He ought not to be asked to join our staff, however, at a salary of less than $4600 per annum.[5]

There were quotas for Jews in the Ivy League colleges and even in state medical schools (Halperin 2001); there were few Jewish professors; there were Jewish law firms because few other law firms would hire Jews. Jews were tagged, even if, like Bob and George Marshall, they bore Anglicized names. Jewish Americans like Felix and Lucy and the Marshall brothers might seem well assimilated, canoeing and climbing in the Adirondacks every summer, yet the friends they socialized with were Jewish. As Margold shows, being Jewish significantly affected American Jews in the 1930s, regardless of whether they observed religious practices. Discrimination was open, taken for granted (Hurtado 2012:148–51, 219–21).

Educated young Jewish Americans like the Cohens and their circle loved America. They were discriminated against in schools, housing, employment, and social events, but in contrast to their immigrant parents in their homelands, they did not fear being murdered in pogroms. They were a generation younger than Leo Frank, the innocent Jewish businessman lynched in 1915 in Georgia. America was indeed a land of golden opportunities for these grandchildren of the shtetls who attended CCNY and Hunter College for free, who could find employment and decent housing and holiday resorts and summer camps in the parallel economy of Jewish businesses. They were excited by America's rhetoric of democracy and freedom. For many of the brightest among them, that rhetoric echoed the Social Democrat ideals of their parents. They understood, as Albert Einstein emphasized in his autobiography, "The bond that has united Jews for thousands of years and unites them today is above all the democratic ideal of social justice, coupled with the ideal of mutual aid and tolerance among all men" (quoted in Fuchs 1958:601).

Ideals may inspire; daily life in the 1930s taught the limits of the US ideal of equality. World War II broke barriers not only for African-Americans and, to a lesser degree, American Indians, it challenged unofficial segregation of Jews. The year 1947 was the watershed marked by a wildly successful novel and its film dramatization, *Gentleman's Agreement*: a WASP journalist pretends to be Jewish to uncover restrictions against Jews purchasing or renting homes. The plot includes a Jewish secretary revealing she changed her name to get a job refused her under her Jewish name. Casting the Jewish John Garfield (né Jacob Garfinkle) in a supporting role dressed as an Army officer who is Jewish subtly expressed the patriotism most Jews maintained. Winning three Academy Awards, the film outraged the House Un-American Activities Committee, provoking it to call up Garfield, producer Darryl Zanuck (Protestant from Wahoo, Nebraska, sometimes presumed to be Jewish), director Elia Kazan (Greek-American), and supporting actress Anne Revere (a descendant of Paul Revere). Revolutionary ideas about discrimination in the United States? They must be communists.

Before the postwar House Un-American Activities Committee, there was a 1930s version, known as the Dies Committee. Martin Dies, a representative from Texas, led this congressional committee established in 1938 to ferret out Communist Party members and communists, that is, leftist liberals inclined toward socialism (Miller and Hall 1984). Roosevelt's New Deal Progressive enactments, particularly the WPA and federal projects for writers and for theater, drew the congressmen's suspicions. With a number of Jews in these projects and the New Deal generally, and the well-known social democratic liberalism of Ashkenazim (Miller and Hall 1984), the House Un-American Activities Committee inevitably called many Jews to testify. This fed anti-Semitism, pushed on by automobile baron Henry Ford's unremitting virulent claims that Jewish financiers were taking over the world. In addition to publishing vitriolic anti-Semitic and anticooperative journalism in his own newspaper, the Dearborn *Independent* (see chapter 3), Ford bankrolled demagogue Gerald L. K. Smith and Catholic Father Charles Coughlin's magazine *Social Justice*, serializing in it the satanic *Protocols of the Elders of Zion*. Coughlin preached popular radio sermons (on the CBS network) until forbidden to continue, in 1942, by his bishop (Kaplan 2000:68–71, 286–91). The same year, 1938, that the Dies Committee was formed, CCNY faculty fought for their College Teachers Union, affiliated with the New York Teachers Union. Unions were suspected of leftist sympathies, and of course a union of intelligentsia would be particularly suspect. Initially, the New York Board of Education refused to cooperate with Dies. Then in 1940, the New York state legislature in Albany formed its own investigation, the Rapp-Coudert Committee. CCNY was its main target. A year of closed hearings, with the subpoenaed teachers denied legal counsel, resulted in over fifty faculty being dismissed as "subversive." Besides the many Jews, Max Yergan, the first African-American to teach in a New York City public college, lost his appointment (Smith 2011).

No American Jew could pretend outpourings of anti-Semitism did not exist, nor contend against the entrenched exclusions dramatized by *Gentleman's Agreement*. Felix and Lucy Cohen knew they could never live in the suburban village of Bronxville, New York, that openly forbade Jewish residents. I mention Bronxville because my liberal, nonobservant Jewish family lived in the neighboring, open town of Mount Vernon, and my mother, Lena Rosenstock, had been told when she applied for a teaching position in Bronxville that the town would not employ Jews in its schools. Sociologist Nathan Glazer, describing the remarkable increase in "the attainment of middle-class rank" by American Jews between the 1930s and 1955, remarked, "The American Jew tries to avoid getting into a situation where discrimination may seriously affect him. . . . The Jew prefers a situation where his own merit receives objective confirmation, and he is not dependent on the good will or personal reaction of a person who may happen not to like Jews" (Glazer 1958:140; cf. Kobrin 2012:3). Glazer saw this avoidance steering immigrants' children such as Felix and Lucy into the professions and business ownership, except that (in the 1950s) "the number of Jewish doctors has continued to be artificially held down by discrimination" (1958:140).

Being Jewish and American

Glazer explained the extraordinarily rapid increase in the proportion of Jews who are middle class as a result of their immigrant parents' background. Max Weber ascribed capitalists' capacity to invest and forego immediate gratification to Calvin's stern Protestantism, but Glazer pointed to 1,500 years of Jews practicing middle-class virtues before Calvin was born, a "Jewish Protestantism" (Glazer 1958:143; see Gregory 2012:240–43 for a provocative rejection of the significance of Protestantism per se). Even more than foresight, moderation in personal habits, sobriety, and desire to work for oneself rather than a boss, Jewish culture prized the scholar. All Jewish boys spent their days in school. Parents wished their daughters to marry scholars, to the extent of supporting them. Scholars were expected to marry and father families. Where Roman Catholics favored celibate monkish scholars and American Protestants were leery of scholars (the weak bespectacled geek), Jews are the People of the Book. Where did those hard-studying Jewish boys come from who were jeopardizing the gentleman's C of Ivy League scions? From fathers and grandfathers who studied and were "highly learned," as Morris Cohen (1949:145) remembered, in Torah and Midrash. Being Jewish meant being literate, admiring intellectuals whether or not one was one (Sklare 1971:58, Lipset and Ladd 1974:259). It was a characteristic of Jews; Jews are smart (see Gilman 1996). Residential segregation led Jewish children to take for granted the expectation that they would work hard and do well in school—all the families around them, their playmates, shared this value. American Jews threw themselves into studying, their paths leading to the professions or business ownership. Even those whose immigrant parents in the interwar era had become farmers in back-to-the-land Jewish communities usually left for professions and business (Dubrovsky 1992). Metaphorically, brain power has been Ashkenazim's capital (Merton 1994:10).

Thorstein Veblen, the political economist best known for his *Theory of the Leisure Class* (1899), published in 1919 an influential essay, "The Intellectual Preeminence of Jews in Modern Europe." Veblen proposed that Jews' intellectual preeminence came from their outsider status. Those who left the ghetto or shtetl to pursue secular higher education saw their fathers' tradition to be archaic, yet the young Jew saw, likewise, that "the gentile world" was burdened by its own "prepossessions." "By consequence he is in a peculiar degree exposed to the unmediated facts of the current situation" and introduces "free-swung skeptical initiative . . . into the pursuit of the modern sciences" (Veblen [1919] 1993:291). David Hollinger (2002) comments that this could be a description of Veblen himself, born into a rural Norwegian-immigrant community that he escaped for higher education. Young Thorstein, like Jews, faced Yankee prejudice in Minnesota. "Alienation" is the usual tag for intellectuals' rejection of their natal culture coupled with a sharply critical view of the society they have moved toward. That word connotes a more total outsider status than either Veblen or twentieth-century American Jews felt. They would not conform to their parents' Old World culture, from countries that had driven out their impoverished families, and most of them would not blindly ape the WASP culture that did not want them, but they cared deeply for the promise of opportunity and democracy that their American schooling held out to them.

American-born children of the flood of East European Ashkenazi immigrants between 1880 and World War I bore the brunt of American anti-Semitism (Wenger 1996:200). For them, colleges and universities imposed Jewish quotas in the 1920s. Given their tradition of scholarly study, American-born Ashkenazim filled those quotas and almost overwhelmed CCNY and the one major university that did admit them without prejudice, New York University at its Washington Square campus. Jewish students from New York suburbs, such as my father from Bayonne, New Jersey, not eligible for CCNY because not New York City residents, enrolled at NYU's Washington Square. NYU maintained a second, wooded and dignified campus in the Bronx that kept a quota and thereby was a genteel ivory-tower retreat (Hollinger 1996:61). Besides colleges and restricted residential apartment buildings and communities, American Jews were openly refused by hotels, resorts, summer camps, and even hospitals. Cottages at Pewaukee Lake outside Milwaukee were burned and destroyed in 1929 because the owner and renters were Jewish (Feldstein 1978:284). Employment ads stated "Christians only" or "Christians preferred." The New York Telephone Company would not hire Jewish women as switchboard operators, and Western Union would not hire Jewish students for temporary holiday work (Feldstein 1978:294). To circumvent this barrier, many American Jews Anglicized their names, as Jacob Garfinkle was changed to John Garfield, and my grandfather changed Bauch to Beck. Historian Stanley Feldstein discovered that the 1926 edition of *Who's Who in American Jewry* noted that "some persons preferred to be omitted rather than associate their names with those of their racial colleagues. . . . A few even rejected . . . a volume where their Jewish identity would become a matter of public knowledge" (quoted in Feldstein 1978:296).

Illustrative of the prevalence and inescapability of American anti-Semitism is the case of Moses Friedman, surprising because he was made superintendent of Carlisle Indian School four years after the retirement of its founder, Richard Henry Pratt. Friedman was born in Cincinnati, Ohio, in 1874, and graduated from the University of Cincinnati in 1899. Embarking on a career as an educator, he first taught two years in Cincinnati, then between 1900 and 1904 at the Phoenix (Arizona) Indian School, from 1904 to 1906 instituted American-style vocational training in the newly conquered Philippines, from 1906 to 1908 was assistant superintendent at the Haskell Institute (for Indians), and, capping a rapid rise, became superintendent at Carlisle Indian School in 1908 (figure 7.1). Downplaying the military form beloved of Captain Pratt, Friedman demanded better academic work of the students, strengthened the vocational ("industrial") training, encouraged Indian crafts and designs in the art

Figure 7.1. Moses Friedman (center, front) with Blackfeet parents visiting Carlisle, 1913. (1) Lazy Boy. (2), Robert Hamilton, a mixed-blood (white-Blackfeet) who was a vocal advocate for full-bloods. Hamilton had been a Carlisle student. (3) Susan Two Guns, wife of Two Guns White Calf (No. 4). (4) Two Guns White Calf. (5) Superintendent Moses Friedman of Carlisle Indian School. (6) Medicine Owl. (7) Three Bears, who was about fifty-eight years old at the time (based on Blackfeet census information—born 1854). (8) Sheep Woman, Medicine Owl's wife. (9) Long Time Sleep. Photo from Archives and Special Collections, Dickinson College, Carlisle, PA.

program, and tolerated the win-or-die tough athletics led by "Pop" Warner that brought fame to Carlisle. (Jim Thorpe was one of several Olympic contenders Warner produced at Carlisle.)

Friedman ended the campus leadership of a YMCA resident secretary who was not a school employee, incurring the wrath of the man's student followers whom he had inculcated with the popular "muscular Christianity" of the time (Haley 1978:107–18). Students wrote "Dirty Jew" on the blackboard when Friedman appeared, threw shoes at him when he checked the boys' dormitory in the evening, and disrespected him because, as he testified to an OIA investigator, "I am not an active man, nor a prizefighter, and any blackguard can come into my office and say anything he pleases." The Christian men on campus, from the profane, gambling Pop Warner to the music teacher, punched male students, slapped girls, beat them with wooden paddles and a baseball bat, and knocked a Kutenai youth down stairs (Bentley 2012:170). Students nevertheless told the investigator that a Christian should replace the Jew, to restore the morals and morale of the school (Bentley 2012:158). "It is useless to maintain a school like this without having a strong, moral Christian man at the head as superintendent," asserted student Bertha Canfield, at the 1914 hearing on Carlisle problems (Matthew Bentley, personal e-mail, July 5, 2012).

Moses Friedman's assumed Jewish origin could not be countered by his baptism at Carlisle Episcopalian Church late in 1912. His wife, Mary, was the daughter of Major General Green Clay Smith, who became a Baptist minister in Washington, DC, after serving as territorial governor of Montana following the Civil War. General Smith died in 1895, so his son-in-law's conversion in 1912 was not at his immediate instigation. In Carlisle, the Friedmans attended the local Presbyterian church that Captain Pratt and other staff belonged to. The Friedmans lived on campus, under the eyes of the students. It may be that Mary Smith Friedman's deportment was more damaging to her husband's authority than his Jewishness. At the investigation, a female student (name redacted) complained, "his wife is not the woman that ought to be on the grounds for we girls to follow the example, because the way she goes around here on the campus sometimes is simply disgraceful. We girls have seen her time and again when the boys [in the school band] were playing on their instruments over here, when they happened to be coming from the club she would go out here and skirt-dance and kick until you could see up to her knees" (quoted in Bentley 2012:188). Not only did the woman dance, she held Suffrage League of Carlisle meetings at the superintendent's house (Bentley 2012:186).

At the end of the 1914 congressional hearings on Carlisle, Friedman was found not guilty of the charge of embezzlement, although his chief clerk was. There could be no continuation of his supervision of Carlisle; he was dismissed. He went from Carlisle to a position as superintendent of Anchor Ranch School for Defective Boys near Valdez, New Mexico, remaining until 1921 when he took over as superintendent of a vocational school in Pocono Pines, Pennsylvania. He lived until 1966 (Matthew Bentley, personal e-mail, July 5, 2012). Moses Friedman's career as an educator for marginalized youth and his marriage to an unconventional middle-class Protestant American woman reflect opportunities available to American-born Jews, while the insults he suffered from Carlisle students prove the prevalence of anti-Semitism early in the twentieth century.

Anti-Semitism's increased visibility in 1930s America was fed by tremendous unemployment and bankruptcies. Bank failures gave credence to Henry Ford's charges against Jewish financiers and "the Elders of Zion." Heightening American Jews' fear that escalation of anti-Semitism might bring pogroms in the United States was Christian American indifference to Hitler's successes in Europe. Morris Cohen reacted in 1933 by forming the Conference on Jewish Relations to bring together "liberal men and women who will not let their differences in regard to religious orthodoxy, zionism, socialism, or communism hinder them from cooperating to prevent the permanent degradation of Jews as human beings" (quoted in Rosenfield 1962:219–20). With the conference demanding ever more of his time, Morris resigned from CCNY in 1938 to devote all his energy to the life-or-death campaign to save Jews.

Like his daughter-in-law's Industrial Research Group, Morris Cohen's conference claimed its purpose was primarily research to collect and analyze data on "the true state of Jewish social, economic, and political activities in the present as well as in the past . . . in our educational system; . . . in the professions; . . . geographic and economic distribution of the Jews as regards agriculture, industry, and commerce; . . . in small communities as well as in large cities, . . . and . . . causes of anti-Semitism" (quoted in Rosenfield 1962:223–24). Conference projects produced data on Jews in the legal and medical professions, and on their occupations in New York City and Detroit. Money raised through Morris's fund appeals paid for a substantial report on the situation of Jews in Europe by Oscar Janowsky, who published in two books in 1937 and 1938. Membership in the Conference was more than six hundred in 1936, led by luminaries including Albert Einstein, Felix Frankfurter, Salo Baron, Edward Sapir, Isidor Loeb (dean at George Washington University), Max Radin (professor of law, University of California–Berkeley), and Monroe Deutsch (vice president of the University of California). Franz Boas and John Dewey gave lectures at Conference meetings. In spite of such distinguished sponsors, neither Franklin Roosevelt nor the Congress was persuaded the United States should do anything more than admit famous Jewish scholars as refugees. In 1939, a bill in Congress to admit Jewish children in excess of the immigration quota failed. Suffer not the little children to come unto me, said Roosevelt and Congress, if they are Jews.

The Great Epic

Morris Cohen saw as a "great epic . . . the generation which cut its roots in the old home and crossed the ocean into a strange land without any resources other than their own unconquerable fortitude" (quoted in Rosenfield 1962:xiv). His own father and two older brothers, educated only in the *cheder* in their Russian village, worked in sweatshops. The mother was, as common in the Old Country, an entrepreneur always trying to manipulate tiny profits from selling fruit or soda water or sewing or buying a house with rooms to rent. Some of her babies died; Morris was sickly. Age twelve when the family settled in New York, Morris went to public school where his remarkable intelligence carried him rapidly through the grades. This progress convinced his father to let him continue in school. Three years later, he took the examination for entrance into CCNY's preparatory class (in lieu of secondary school), coming in first and winning a gold medal — real gold; the family pawned it sometimes when money was really tight. An insatiable reader, the immigrant youth was especially inspired by Benjamin Franklin's *Autobiography*, vowing to follow his practice of keeping a diary to record thoughts.

The scraps of paper on which Morris preserved his adolescent thoughts are an understated epic. Working in a poolroom at his father's stand selling soda water, the boy's effort to assist his impoverished family, Morris tried, between customers in the dingy poolroom, to read Gibbon, Voltaire, Samuel Smiles's self-help books, and again and again, Franklin's *Autobiography*. He "resolved," one January Saturday, "to practice Jewish writing" (Rosenfield 1962:9), loath to abandon his forebears' wisdom simply because his path lay with secular authors. At home in his parents' tenement flat where he was called Meishele, where his father would question neither faith in the Lord God of his people nor their rituals, Morris felt himself a rebel. At CCNY and the Educational Alliance where Thomas Davidson, once a poor boy in Scotland, taught Yiddish youth a compatible philosophy of fulfillment through love of humanity, Morris leaped out of his parents' constricted world. Davidson had a farm in the Adirondacks where he gathered such friends as William James, John Dewey, Rabbi Stephen Wise, and psychologist Hugo Münsterberg to mingle with students. Both Morris, who helped out with chores for his board, and a young woman from the Educational Alliance classes, Mary Ryshpan, were welcomed into the circle. These two young Jews had literally climbed the mountain in their quest for freedom and knowledge. Their union in marriage begat three members of the generation of secular American Jews that completed the great epic: Felix the lawyer-philosopher, Leonora the professor of literature, and Victor William the physicist (figure 7.2).

Settlement houses like the Educational Alliance provided bridges to Americanization. Their classes in English, civics, domestic practices, and the arts, and their assistance in gaining employment enabled immigrants and especially their children to escape the ghetto. Exercise, gardens, and clinics countered the unhealthy conditions of the tenements. Wealthy Christians as well as Jewish philanthropists supported settlement houses

Figure 7.2. Morris and Mary Cohen. Photo from Felix S. and Lucy Kramer Cohen Photograph Collection.

geared toward Ashkenazim, and idealistic upper-class Christians like Jane Addams and John Collier were among their staff members. Bringing together the privileged and the poor was part of their vision. Because the Ashkenazim were a caste rather than a class, that is, they were not peasants or servants in Europe and they fostered literacy, in America they readily sought learning and aspired to the professions. While their lively demeanor and readiness to express emotion were uncouth by WASP standards, their intellectualism found favor. Liberal Christians involved with settlement houses were a small portion of Christian America, their voices and work toward ending segregation having little immediate effect against entrenched prejudice. They did weaken the barriers, in individual cases like Davidson recommending Morris Cohen and Felix Frankfurter to Harvard, and in constituting a socially prominent counter to prevailing attitudes. Class is powerful in America, but because class status and signs have never been enforced by law, "peculiar people" such as the Jews have been able to pursue opportunities their families sought in immigration.

Felix and Lucy Cohen and their friends enjoyed the fruits of their parents' struggles and their grandparents' courageous epic quest across an ocean. The generation that came of age in the 1930s, in the decade after immigration was curtailed, could become secular professionals. They were still Jews to other Americans, excluded from potential homes, resorts, colleges, employment, and recognition. The Cohens' close friend from Columbia's anthropology program, Alexander Lesser, worked hard and effectively from 1947 to 1955 to make the Association on American Indian Affairs a serious professional lobby. As the wealthy WASP Collier was public spokesman for the Indian New Deal, Collier's good friend Oliver La Farge was front man, president, for the association, signing his name to what Lesser wrote. Years later, Lesser told D'Arcy McNickle of his chagrin at continued adulation of the wealthy WASP La Farge and silence about Lesser's role (Parker 1992:114–15). Between John Collier and Felix Cohen, and Oliver La Farge and Alexander Lesser, stood America's version of Russia's Pale of Settlement, a matter not of law but of custom. Felix Cohen could be hired to write legislation but like Nathan Margold and Felix Frankfurter, custom would keep them in the background politically. It was during Franklin Roosevelt's administration, and then the horrifying disclosure of the Holocaust against Jews—witnessed by American soldiers liberating the death camps—that anti-Semitism ceased to be tolerated in America.

CHAPTER EIGHT

Felix Cohen's Awakening

On November 8, 1933, barely three weeks after being hired at the Department of the Interior to draft legislation, Felix Cohen wrote to Norman Thomas, leader of the Socialist Party in the United States, assuring him that taking employment in capitalist-dominated government did not lessen his commitment to socialism. Thomas replied quickly, agreeing that the opportunity for "real service" in the here and now could be a step toward the socialist future they worked toward (Tsuk Mitchell 2007:74, 293). Felix also wrote to Franz Boas to ask about his Nez Percé (Nimipu) student Archie Phinney, whom he anticipated hiring for the implementation stage of the Indian Reorganization Act. Lucy assisted in drafting the letter:

> Dear Professor Boas, In view of the fact that Archie Phinney is at present in Russia & not immediately available, the position we had in mind will have to be filled otherwise (for the time being).
>
> However, at the beginning of next year when the appropriation becomes available, other positions will develop, particularly work involving the drawing up of community charters and constitutions [based on a knowledge of the history—& culture of particular Indian tribes]. It is in the latter field we feel Archie Phinney, with his anthrop. training & recent work on racial Minorities in Russia, may prove of great real value.
>
> We should like to have your candid opinion of his qualifications & ability for this particular kind of work.
>
> [We understand Archie Phinney has a research fellowship at Yale for the coming year.]

We should be glad to have your suggestions from time to time on qualified individuals who might be of assistance in the work of rehabilitating Indian tribal organization & social life.[1]

A Nimipu in Leningrad, 1933–1938, in his spare time writing up his people's folklore dictated in Nimipu by his mother five years earlier, Phinney looked to be a real "red man" to promote socialism on the reservations.

Phinney (1903–1949) was hired by the Office of Indian Affairs when he returned from Russia, serving as a field agent, for example, in 1942 going to New York State to examine problems between the state and the reservations within it, and competitions between political groups on reservations. His last assignment was superintendent of the Northern Idaho Indian Agency, his home territory. Tragically, like Felix he died at the age of forty-six. Phinney is remembered principally for his leadership, shared with D'Arcy McNickle and Charles Heacock, a Lakota from Rosebud, in founding the National Congress of American Indians (NCAI) in 1944. All three were well-educated OIA employees, their goal of a national Indian organization endorsed by John Collier, yet determined to be independent of that agency. The Robert Marshall Civil Liberties Trust, established in accordance with Bob Marshall's dedication to socialism and civil liberties, helped with the NCAI's early expenses. Phinney's activism proved his deep commitment to develop effective political means to advance Indian self-governance (Cowger 1999:31–40). Although the FBI kept tabs on this traveler to Russia (Price 2004), he was no doctrinaire socialist. Indian people needed to assert their legal rights, including inherent sovereignty—the *Handbook of Federal Indian Policy* was at hand to tell them their rights—and build coalitions to counteract the multitude of encroachments.

Co-optation is said to be a common maneuver of colonial powers to nullify indigenous activism. The NCAI turned the table, creating their own counterorganization by using educated Indians brought together as employees of the OIA. Only Indians could vote or hold office in the NCAI, although non-Indians could attend its annual meetings. The initial congress in 1944 was in Denver, the second in 1945 on the Blackfeet Reservation in Montana, so it is not surprising that delegates from western and especially Plains nations predominated. It should be noted that Phinney, McNickle, and Heacock did not wait for the war to end before organizing a congress; its business of dealing with Indian people vis-à-vis the United States could not be suspended, given the momentum engendered by the IRA. Wartime did mean that men serving in the armed forces, such as Ben Reifel, an OIA employee who resigned in 1960 to win election as the first

Lakota in the US House of Representatives, would be absent at the initial meetings. The leaders' wisdom in forging ahead became evident when Roosevelt died in 1945 and his opponents attacked the New Deal.

Felix Cohen caught on quickly when for the first time he was exposed to reservation leaders at the 1934 congresses called by Collier. Prior to these trips west, he knew only the very few Indians in Boas's program at Columbia—Phinney, Ella Deloria, who had grown up in an assimilationist family off reservation, and occasional visitors recruited to dictate their languages. At the congresses, hundreds of members of Indian communities stood up, spoke oratorically or forcefully or ironically, formed into debating groups and planning huddles, told stories, and cracked jokes. Their generation often was fluent in both their indigenous language and in English. Felix saw that these people were sophisticated and frustrated. They could devise, he thought, with some legal-language guidance, constitutions or charters to give them the local powers enjoyed by municipalities. They were not going to revert to some imagined primitive socialism.

Writing the constitutions and charters was the next stage in Indian New Deal reform. The questionnaires that Lucy tabulated for the OIA helped focus Felix's work assisting tribes in formulating local governance. Add to these actions the research into facts and the give-and-take discussions Felix carried out with reservation leaders, and Felix was struck, as he said in his 1949 essay, that American Indians were oppressed much like Jews in czarist Russia. Like his grandparents there, Indians were assigned where they should and should not reside. Since the implementation of the Dawes Act around 1900, many Indians had become landless. Bureaucrats could rule autocratically and use police and jails to put down insurgency; D'Arcy McNickle quoted a 1915 report: "the Indian Superintendent is a tzar within the territorial jurisdiction prescribed for him" (1973:87). Citizens could persecute, even rape and murder, Indians almost with impunity, a situation that persisted around big western reservations into the 1970s, sparking media-attracting denouncements by militant Indians (Kehoe 2006a:77–87). Critically, American Indians and Jews struggled to retain cohesive identities separate from mainstream Christian society: they both constantly faced difficult pragmatic choices over what older practices they could let go of, and what they could take from the dominant nation without jeopardizing their heritage identities.[2]

Canadian social anthropologist Noel Dyck (1991:156) perceptively noted how landlords and managers of ostensibly public places such as hotels and restaurants acted as "gatekeepers" enforcing segregation and denying educational and economic opportunities. Or as Dyck commented on border towns, rural neighbors say, "you can spot an Indian a mile away," implying the "social distance that many of them would prefer to keep between themselves and Indians" (1983:216). Every action has an equal and opposite reaction, we learned in elementary physics. Morris Cohen saw this as the "principle of polarity"; every phenomenon exists with its negation. Indian people had their own gatekeepers, who under the oppression of federal authorities on reservations, school staffs, church missionaries, and welfare agencies, necessarily worked under the radar. Who was indeed a legitimate hereditary leader? Who truly had spiritual power from being pitied by the Almighty or its manifestation? Whose stories best represented what had been handed down through generations? What modifications could be permitted, what innovations? What could be omitted without ceasing to be Lakota or Pikuni or Nimipu? On multitribe reservations such as Fort Peck, Flathead, or Wind River, how could the separate nations coexist?

White Americans liked to label gatekeepers "full-bloods" (Sturm 2002: 56–57, 126), as if knowledge was encoded genetically. Indians know better. First Nations had and still have social classes, including aristocratic families who inculcate leadership qualities in their children regardless of whether a child may phenotypically show some European ancestry (appearance can vary even among full siblings). Men and women from leading families may have been taught more fully and deeply their language's stylistic riches, their nation's history, etiquette, and protocols, and may have been encouraged to learn priestly roles. Part of their leadership obligations would be to protect that which is precious to their nation. At the same time, First Nations, like other societies, have hoi polloi challenging aristocrats, and stories of intelligent hardworking poor kids achieving leadership are not all myths. Gatekeeping exists in First Nations, contested within and without, moving along the tide of events.

Gatekeeping internally came to a head when the Indian New Deal offered constitutions and charters. Ben Reifel remembered that on Pine Ridge many people saw no reason to change the existing tribal council of ten delegates from each of the reservation's seven districts, gathering to "express their views and to give vent to some of their feelings . . . the Indian system." These traditional leaders were generally loath to give up their status, in spite of their council's lack of power under the Indian agent. Because the IRA was the New Deal, reluctant leaders were called the Old Dealers. They were no fools. They examined the proposed constitution, noticing that it said "in practically every section 'with the approval of the Secretary of the Interior.' . . . And the Old Dealers, so-called, said,

'Well, you see, I told you. The Secretary's still going to have control. He's having control. You got to go to him'" (Reifel, quoted in Cash and Hoover 1985:112).

Rupert Costo, a Cahuilla from Southern California, spoke in blistering language from his personal experience as Cahuilla representative to Collier's 1934 Indian congress, and his researches as a historian. At the 1983 conference commemorating the fiftieth anniversary of the beginning of the Indian New Deal, Costo attacked Collier's high-handed running of the congresses (Costo's expenses were not paid because, Collier wrote to him, "you were not authorized in advance by the Commissioner of Indian Affairs as a delegate" [O'Neil 1986:45]) as well as the provisions of the IRA. Costo gave a litany of First Nations "bitterly opposed," he said, to the IRA—the Quapaw, the Yakima, thirty-seven California tribes assembled at Riverside, the Crow, the Oneida. He accused Collier of blatantly lying to Congress that nearly all the delegates and tribes favored the IRA. He said that Indian BIA employees were threatened with dismissal if they voiced opposition, that contrary to promises of self-government, the IRA gave the Secretary of the Interior more power over tribes than the office had had prior to the bill. In short, Costo proclaimed, "the Indians called it the Indian Raw Deal" (1986:86).

Damning, indeed. Costo's message bears analysis as rhetoric, regardless of its truths. Noel Dyck describes two rhetorical styles he observed used by contemporary Indian people in meetings with Indian Affairs personnel. Most striking is an "aggressive . . . implacable style of speaking . . . [from] people who were born into an all-encompassing administrative system as the inferior and subordinate party." Faced by aggrieved opponents, "the bureaucrat . . . is called upon to remain diplomatic and passive in the face of criticism that is often abrasive" (Dyck 1983:25). Diplomatic and passive John Collier was not. Dyck notes that within the aggressive speech mode, there are two tropes describing the regime: "a largely negative and critical [model] . . . of 'paternalism,' 'phony consultation' and general insincerity," and "evaluation of an individual bureaucrat . . . categorizing him [negatively] as being 'typical Indian Affairs' in the eyes of an Indian audience" (1983:267). There are, from this standpoint, two audiences being simultaneously addressed by Indian speakers in meetings with Indian Affairs officials, those to whom the speech is directed, and speakers' own community or peers who will be evaluating their performance.

Insightfully presenting "the culture of public problems," sociologist Joseph Gusfield (1981:2–3) began his book with "an apocryphal tale about the American philosopher Morris Raphael Cohen" asking students about the ethics of sacrificing people for a common good. Gusfield's thesis is that not all "social problems" are recognized as "public problems" (1981:5, 6), and institutionalization of a socially recognized problem—laws, bureaucratic authority and process, the segment of citizenry involved—tends to lock in certain possible solutions and exclude others. Speech tropes as well as terms are regularized in discourse on public problems. An example of the boxing-in effect of such discourse is the public problem of alcoholism on Indian reservations. Lakota anthropologist Beatrice Medicine bemoaned the dominant society's construction of an "alcohol problem," disregarding historic patterns of abstinence. She believed that critical attention to these patterns, in a spirit of revitalizing Indian societies, would be more effective than working at a public problem (Medicine 2001:225, 2006). Noel Dyck recounts another example, when officers of a prairie province Federation of Indian Nations went to Ottawa to meet with members of Parliament whose constituencies included that province's Indian reserves. One problem to be addressed was Indian parents' dissatisfaction with the treatment their children received in integrated public schools near the reserves. In one case, parents removed their children from the off-reserve school and demanded that Indian Affairs fund a school on the reserve. The MPs expressed concern about segregating Indian children. The federation leader told them this need not happen: "We are inviting all those [non-Indian] people surrounding the reserves to come to the educational institution on the reserve" (quoted by Dyck 1983:285).

Primed by his conviction that legal realism was key for social justice, Felix could learn from his encounters with Indian people. He wrote his father, in July 1934, on his twenty-seventh birthday, "What I'm anxious to bite into now is some accurate account of what revolutionary change looks like in a village or small town. All the accounts of revolution I know of are written from the viewpoint of the capital. I'm looking forward seriously to learning something about human nature and its capacities for quick change of patterns when I get down to work with Indian groups under our new bill" (quoted in Tsuk Mitchell 2007:117).

Such naïve optimism shouldn't surprise, considering Felix's youth. It highlights how quickly he did mature, with Margold's tutelage, into a true realist. "Transcendental Nonsense and the Functionalist Approach" was published in the second year of Felix's employment at Interior. Nowhere does it discuss American Indians. A reader would suppose that its author had been cloistered in a law library. Seen in the context of Felix's actual employment, it is a *Grundriss* laying out a legal realist's critique of conventional Anglo law and jurisprudence, setting up in their place an overriding question, "what consequences are *important*" (Cohen 1935:76, emphasis in original). Thus the ultimate question is, what is valued as important?

The IRA, so greatly reduced from his original social democratic model legislation, was set. Felix's assignment was to assist tribes with the legal language of constitutions and charters. Accustomed to anthropologists, he fully supported Collier's idea of recruiting them to inform the Bureau of existing social structures and potential fits or conflicts with the IRA version of local self-government. Disliking Boas, Collier went to the Bureau of American Ethnology in Washington to ask assistance from its staff members William Duncan Strong and Matthew Stirling, both archaeologists. Scudder Mekeel was named director of the short-lived, 1935–1937, Applied Anthropology unit in the OIA. Mekeel asserted that "fact-finding should have been started at least a year previous to actual organization work" (quoted by McNickle 1979:55). On-the-ground ethnographies of current reservations could have revealed groupings "such as full- versus mixed-blood, young versus older generation, returned student versus lesser educated, big stock-owners versus small, and so on, [that might] have fair expression and just control under a constitution" (Mekeel 1944:214–15). D'Arcy McNickle later wrote, drawing on his years in government work, that the greatest problem with writing the IRA constitutions and charters was "meeting fiscal year deadlines" (1979:55). If all the money appropriated for a project was not used before the June 30 end of a fiscal year, not only would unexpended funds revert to the Treasury, Congress would be likely to slash funds for the following year. Having no assurance that IRA funds for assisting tribes with adopting constitutions or charters would be available after 1935, Collier pushed hard for quick results. Overall, McNickle said in a 1974 conference, "the true antagonist of Collier's reform efforts was his own social insight, an inheritance which he shared with others of his class, his generation, his cultural conditioning" (quoted in Parker 1992:237). Felix, along with Lucy, Margold, Haas, and Boas, brought a considerably different cultural conditioning to the Indian New Deal.

In the back of their minds, Felix and Nathan Margold would have Morris's classic essay "Property and Sovereignty," published seven years earlier. "As a legal term property denotes not material things but certain rights," Morris declared. "Those to whom the law has accorded dominion over the things necessary for subsistence . . . [show] the character of property as sovereign power compelling service and obedience" (Cohen 1927:11–12). If Indians are to enjoy their natural rights as human beings, to life, liberty, and the pursuit of happiness, rights furthermore guaranteed to them by the bestowal of US citizenship in 1924, under Anglo law they must control property or productive labor sufficient for subsistence. Collier's rescinding of the taking of tribal lands and allotments was a step in that direction. Would it be sufficient to restore self-support to Indian people? Visiting Indian country, Felix saw that existing Indian lands, even if augmented by some buybacks, could not make all tribal members self-sufficient, especially with a growing Indian population.

Constitutions and tribal corporate charters were a step toward the natural rights sovereignty Morris Cohen advocated. Lawyers that they were, professionally, Felix and Margold, who signed as Solicitor for Interior, had to explicate the "Powers of Indian Tribes" in the document Margold issued in October 1934. Morris had opened his essay saying, "Property and sovereignty, as every student knows, belong to entirely different branches of the law" (Cohen 1927:8). Sovereignty—dominion per se, not landed property—must be clearly established. The two Jewish lawyers had by mid-1934 listened to enough Indians, in the congresses, in delegations to Washington, and on reservations, to respect them, whether sophisticated like McNickle and Phinney, or a young hothead like Costo, or, among the Pikuni Blackfeet delegation, monolingual elder Rides at the Door and experienced tribal council chairman Joe Brown.

The year 1933 was only two generations past the era when an Oxford professor of international law and diplomacy wrote, "That form of association which we call a State is a true natural growth of European and Christian civilization; a divinely ordered instrument, and in the present condition of the world an indispensable condition of human happiness and progress."[3] It elicited a comment that would strike directly, half a century later, at the heart of the Indian New Deal: "The ruling power is now so often distinguished from the true sovereignty of the State that an interference in favour of the former, although this has been the character of almost every instance in history, is repudiated and set aside as the highest injustice" ("Policy, Sociology, and Travels" 1861:548).

"Powers of Indian Tribes" revolutionized, eventually, the global field of indigenous rights. More than a legal exposition of the principle of inherent sovereignty and the enduring significance of treaties, it broke down racist legitimation of Anglo paternal governance by its presumption that Indian nations had "duly constituted organs of government." These words in the Solicitor's opinion recognize the competency that even Collier was loath to acknowledge among First Nations members. Mekeel had expostulated against the cart-before-the-horse timing of creating the Applied Anthropology Unit a year after the IRA pushed for formalizing "organs of government." Practical concerns of striking while the iron is hot, within fiscal year allocations, to immediately halt the losses of tribal lands, might excuse the haste although not the effects of the OIA once again pressuring Indian nations to do its bidding. Actions can speak louder than words. "Powers of Indian Tribes" opined that the constitutions and charters that Collier and, initially, Cohen had seen as the next step, after loss of lands was curtailed, toward idealized communes, were only pragmatic adjustments to US capitalist legal conventions.

Felix's socialism grew out of European capitalist culture, the equal and opposite reaction to exploitation of labor for employers' profit. It was formulated within modern European nation-states based on industrialization, imperialism, and agribusiness. Franz Boas's version of cultural relativism implicitly arrayed European political systems as historical particulars vis-à-vis particular systems of, say, Osage, Blackfoot, Tlingit, China, Mughal India, Samoa, and so on. For Felix, the way out of his obligation to work with tribes on their constitutions was that "tribal constitutions, after all, are not an innovation of the New Deal" (Cohen 1939:222). Assisted by Lucy's indefatigable research in libraries, Felix discovered that the "Five Civilized Tribes" labeled by Jefferson "merciless savages"—the Cherokee, Creek, Seminole, Choctaw, and Chickasaw—and the Osage had printed tribal constitutions as early as 1830. Ácoma Pueblo had one by 1908. The Iroquois Haudenosaunee League's Gayanashagowa (Great Law) is a constitution orally transmitted for several centuries.

Another line of argument Felix pursued was that "after 422 years of support for the principle of Indian self-government [by] Francisco de Vitoria in 1532 or of Pope Paul III in 1537 or of Bartholemew de las Casas in 1542 or of Chief Justice Marshall in 1832 [*Worcester v. Georgia*] . . . there is so little Indian self-government" (Cohen 1949:306). Asked ten years later to assess the effects of the IRA, Felix's friend and colleague Ted Haas wrote, "While formal tribal organization has taken many forms, some governments have been adaptations of earlier tribal organizations. Some have merged the old and new forms and provided for a modern council and at the same time invested the chieftains with some power. A few organizations like the Minnesota Chippewas are confederacies" (Haas 1947:3).

Haas and Cohen knew that government is the art of the possible. What is possible?

The Conundrum: Preserving Indian Societies with Foreign Instruments

"Indian time" is not mechanically counted, by clock or by printed calendar. "Things will happen when they happen," my Pikuni friend explained to me. Collier set calendar deadlines for voting on the IRA and then on constitutions that would have been difficult for clock-conscious urban Euro-Americans to meet—it took the US Constitutional Convention from May into September 1787, when they already had the Articles of Confederation as a base document, all delegates were fluent in English, and most of the delegates were familiar with legal language. On the reservations in 1934, many people did not speak English, few were familiar with reading legal documents, in the West they were scattered into hamlets many miles apart, and, unlike Americans in 1787, the Indians had to second-guess the reactions of a superordinate authority, the OIA. In 1787 the convention delegates had freed themselves of the onerous yoke of Britain; in 1934 the Secretary of the Interior quite explicitly insisted upon final say over Indian tribes.

Given the very limited power to be gained by an IRA constitution, why should a tribe bother with the exercise? Answer: access to the Revolving Loan Fund was given only to tribes that had voted for the IRA (Biolsi 1992:141; Fowler 2002:108; Rosier 2001:90, 92). Indians were accustomed to high-sounding rhetoric cloaking the usual pressures to assimilate. Because access to loans was a carrot, a stick was assumed to be in the bureau's other hand. Collier's enormous pressure to sign up—the massive Plains congress at Rapid City and the eight other regional congresses, his deployment of personnel to proselytize for votes for the IRA and for constitutions—and the short time frame to decide on what should be a major organization of a tribe, were bound to cause suspicion that the IRA was another encroachment upon First Nations. Even so, in the depths of the Depression, plus for Plains nations the Dust Bowl drought, the lure of loans was powerful. Bear in mind that, generally, Indians could not raise capital using land for collateral because Indian land was in trust status.

To outsiders, debates within tribes over accepting the IRA and then over constitutions and charters seemed to be conflicts between older full-bloods and younger mixed-bloods. OIA anthropologist Scudder Mekeel, for example, wrote, "two of the earliest constitutions drawn up [were] Flathead and Blackfoot. On these two reservations the conflict has mainly concerned relative representation of mixed- and full-blooded Indians. This might well have been obviated if representation had been by natural community groupings" (1944:214). Flathead, now called Confederated Salish and Kootenai Nations Reservation, was complex, officially combining Kutenai (Ktunaxa), once living on both sides of the Rocky Mountains continental divide until the Blackfoot drove them over to the west side valley, and the Pend d'Oreille Salish living in intermontane valleys of western Montana. In 1819, a group of Catholic Iroquois families emigrated west to escape Anglo domination, settling in the valley and in 1839 inviting the first Catholic priest to come to minister to their community. Not only did the United States fix the two native groups speaking wholly independent languages on one valley reservation and ignore the Iroquois, the valley had been a place where fur traders retired with their families (Métis) throughout the nineteenth century, and after the unsuccessful 1885 Riel Rebellion of Canadian Métis, but many of these families and Cree who feared the Canadian police moved into the Flathead valley as refugees. Who were "the full-bloods" here? Salish? Ktunaxa? Iroquois? Cree not officially recognized? Did the Métis fit the stereotype of "mixed-bloods" being younger, educated? Not necessarily.

Over on the east side of the mountains, the Blackfeet Reservation was somewhat less heterogeneous. Even so, there were refugee Cree from the Riel Rebellion and Cree who came early in the twentieth century to earn money working on the irrigation ditches the Bureau ordered for the reservation. There were inmarried Gros Ventres and traders. One prominent family, originally named Sandoval, is descended from "a Mexican" who came with the pioneer Missouri River fur trader Manuel Lisa from New Orleans and may have been Creole like him. Around 1900, this family, their name anglicized to Sanderville probably at Carlisle Indian School, lived in the southwest of the reservation at the edge of the foothills, with one sister near the agency town of Browning. Anthropologist Clark Wissler's collaborator David Duvall lived in the southwest village with his Pikuni Blackfoot mother after the death of his "French Canadian" (Métis?) trading post employee father. A Sanderville, called Tom Kyaiao ("Bear"), was the religious leader of the community; he generously dictated to Duvall detailed rituals that Wissler published in New York in the American Museum of Natural History Anthropological Papers. Was Tom Kyaiao a mixed-blood because he had a Creole grandfather? Or full-blood because he had mastered Pikuni religious knowledge and led his community in its practices? By the 1930s, Kyaiao's village was characterized as "conservative full-bloods," apparently because its location so close to the mountains was less suited to ranching than the rest of the reservation, therefore its residents neither developed ranches themselves nor had their allotments leased to outside ranchers. Their tendency to oppose economic and political measures favored by Pikuni ranching on the wide grasslands east and north of their village reflected the principle, "What's in it for me?" (Wissler and Kehoe 2012:158).

Mekeel's suggestion that "natural community groupings" would have averted some conflicts in reservation politics sounds reasonable. In fact, most reservations did and still do have natural communities in addition to headquarter agency towns. On the Plains, band leaders selected their allotment and the families who camped with them usually chose allotments nearby, making a band into a neighborhood. Less nomadic nations tried to retain preconquest communities when, as usually happened, they were displaced from their best lands and moved to marginal country, or farther as when eastern nations were forced on the Trail of Tears to Oklahoma. Cherokee, Creek, and other exiled nations then reproduced their villages there. Migrant harvester camps, for example for sugar beets and hops, drew groups traveling together from communities on reservations. It has been the natural communities, that is, the settled bands, of the Montana Blackfeet Reservation that have caused the more intractable conflicts between tribal council members elected by geographical districts representing initial settlements by band communities. Sturm's (2002:121) observation among Cherokees that language is a marker of full-blood status, regardless of ancestry or appearance, was true of Pikuni until the 1970s. Fluency in English signaled mixed-blood and correlated with relative prosperity; monolingual Blackfoot signaled full-blood, inability or disinterest in commercial ranching, and poverty. Such a neat dichotomy of course often failed. On the Montana Blackfeet Reservation as early as around 1900, Robert Hamilton, a Carlisle-educated trader's son by a Pikuni woman, began championing full-bloods' (monolingual Blackfoot) interests against those of bilingual ranchers and their non-Indian business associates (See figure 7.1, page 127) (Wissler and Kehoe 2012:157).

At the 1983 conference evaluating the IRA fifty years later, Onondaga leader Oren Lyons said, "The values in our system and in the system of the United States government are too diverse for us to put them together in one place" (1986:100). Robert Burnette of the Lakota insisted, "The Indian Reorganization Act was a suppressive kind of government" (1986:106). Earl Old Person of the Montana Blackfeet testified, "Many of my people have wanted to do away with the IRA. But government officials told them, 'You must come up with a program or something that will replace the IRA. . . . We cannot do away with it because it is not working right for you.' We can see that we were not really given self-government" (1986:107–8). LaDonna Harris, speaking for her Comanche people, recalled, "The Comanche said, 'Well, we are going to pass this constitution to get white people off our back. Who needs it? We will not use it anyway'" (1986:108).

A consensus among Indian people that the IRA constitutions were disconforming impositions upon First Nations should not surprise us. Formal legal written constitutions patterned on Anglo law blatantly contradicted the promise Collier held out for self-government. True, the Wheeler-

Howard Act as passed distorted and emasculated Cohen's lengthy original draft legislation. That said, the way Collier pushed the foreign instrument upon the tribes, linking it to economic opportunities for desperately impoverished communities, reveals his paternalistic ideology. Felix Cohen was a young, newly hired assistant solicitor in 1934. The next two years, traveling to reservations and talking and corresponding with Indians as he complied with his assignment to assist them with writing constitutions and charters, awakened his understanding of colonialism and of the depth of injustice suffered by our First Nations. He had written to Franz Boas at the beginning of the assignment that it would be "work involving the drawing up of community charters and constitutions (based on a knowledge of the history & culture of particular Indian tribes)" but after two years, he knew the promise of "history & culture of particular Indian tribes . . . [and] rehabilitating Indian tribal organization & social life" was not to be fulfilled (Cohen n.d.).

CHAPTER NINE

Of Counsel to Tribes

Felix Cohen resigned from the Department of the Interior on December 15, 1947, two years after John Collier's resignation, a year after Harold Ickes resigned, and, strangely, the day before Nathan Margold unexpectedly died. Cohen's Indian Claims Commission Act had been signed by President Truman in August 1946. Half a year later, the president appointed the three commissioners the act required; disregarding the recommendation from then Secretary of the Interior Julius Krug and Commissioner of Indian Affairs William Brophy to name Felix Cohen chief commissioner, Truman passed him over entirely. He also passed over the other highly recommended attorney, Napoleon B. Johnson, an Oklahoma Cherokee who was president of the National Congress of American Indians (NCAI). Instead, Truman put in three political appointees inexperienced or, in the case of the attorney general of Wyoming, Louis O'Marr, likely biased against Indians. Anthropologists were left out.

Lucy Kramer Cohen, now a mother of two, took temporary jobs at the UN Food and Agriculture Organization, the Non-ferrous Metals Commission, and the Bureau of Labor Statistics. Her dedication to justice prompted her into economics research for liberal congresswoman Helen Gahagan Douglas. In a campaign for the Senate in 1950, Douglas lost to Richard Nixon. Lucy finally found her niche after she was widowed, working for the US Public Health Service, 1958–1989, where her anthropologist's understanding of cultural context enriched her mastery of statistics. The agency recognized her with a Public Health Service Superior Service

Award in 1976, a Health Resources Administrator's Special Citation, 1980, and, as she neared retirement in 1988, an Administrator's Award for Excellence, "For dedication to duty and outstanding service to PHS during a noteworthy career."[1]

Offers to teach at CCNY and Yale Law School gratified Felix after he left federal employment. He agreed to teach one day a week at each institution, while working as an associate of his cousin Henry Cohen's law firm, Curry, Bingham, and Cohen. Curry was James Curry, the same age as Felix, already legal counsel to the NCAI. Between 1936 and 1938, he was one of Indian Affairs's attorneys; from 1938 to 1942 he continued in Interior, working on Puerto Rico projects and with the Consumers' Counsel Division (for which Felix applied to be director, January 1941), until in 1945 he left for private practice. James and his wife Alma were socialists, active in the ACLU and other, farther left, groups: "Jim Curry . . . once general counsel to the Central States Cooperative League and is now counsel to the Puerto Rico Reconstruction Administration. He is a member of the National Lawyers guild's committee on consumer problems. In my opinion his training and his activities in the cooperative movement will make him a most valuable man to take charge of the Union's legislative program. . . . Fraternally, Felix S. Cohen."[2]

Alma told Lucy, August 9, 1937, "For 2 months now, Jim & I have been 'doing' Oklahoma—in temperatures that are almost unbearable. . . . Jim has been driving away at the formation of co-ops, and results are beginning to appear" (figure 9.1). A December 12, 1937, letter revealed disappointment: "It seems a shame that we have both given ourselves to this gov't work where neither of us had any great hopes of the work being useful." She looked forward to moving to Chicago in February and teaching "progressive education" in the Dante School in the slums.[3] In January 1945, Felix tried to save Curry's Puerto Rico work: "I believe I am engaged in a very exciting, perhaps quixotic, battle to save the public purpose corporations of the Puerto Rico New Deal, set up by Munoz Marin and Jim Curry."[4]

Jim Curry and Felix both worked for the rights of Tlingit and Haida communities in the Tongass National Forest in southeastern Alaska. The crux of the issues was the communities' right to cut and sell timber on their "immemorial" lands. Behind the timber rights issue loomed the fundamental question of Indian title. One would suppose that Margold and Cohen's 1934 memorandum "Powers of Indian Tribes" would have made clear the Indian plaintiffs' right to use the timber on their ancestral and still-occupied land:

Figure 9.1. Jim Curry in Oklahoma, probably 1937. Photo from Felix S. and Lucy Kramer Cohen Photograph Collection.

Opinions of the Solicitor, October 25, 1934:
I assume, finally, that any ambiguity in the phrase which I am asked to interpret ought to be resolved in accordance with the general rule that statutes passed for the benefit of dependent Indian tribes or communities are to be liberally construed, doubtful expressions being resolved in favor of the Indians. Alaska Pacific Fisheries v. United States (248 U.S. 78, 89).

And see, to the same effect, Seufert Bros. Co. v. United States (249 U.S. 194); Choate v. Trapp (224 U.S. 665); Jones v. Meehan (175 U.S. 1). . . .

The statutes of Congress, then, must be examined to determine the limitations of tribal sovereignty rather than to determine its sources or its positive content. What is not expressly limited remains within the domain of tribal sovereignty, and therefore properly falls within the statutory category, "powers vested in any Indian tribe or tribal council by existing law."

The acts of Congress which appear to limit the powers of an Indian tribe are not to be unduly extended by doubtful inference.[5]

Still under Collier's program in 1946, Ted Haas and anthropologist Walter Goldschmidt had worked in the field with Tlingit schoolteacher Joe Kahklen to document Tlingit occupation for their villages. They recommended that Congress and the Department of the Interior recognize Indians' rights to their territories—"possessory rights." This conflicted, in the eyes of Secretary Krug and many members of Congress, with the postwar push for capitalist businesses to develop Alaska's resources. Japan's wartime threat to invade via the Aleutians and Alaska had stimulated the federal government's interest in the territory, which was not yet a state. Tlingits' salmon fisheries, competing against lower-forty-eight–owned canneries near Tlingit and Haida villages, were a prize, in addition to timber rights. Cohen, still working in Interior, compromised in the fall of 1947 with a plan to have the Forest Service (an Interior agency) manage Tongass timber exploitation, with royalties to Indian communities, until possessory rights were determined. In November, the NCAI, with James Curry their attorney, assisted two villages, Kake and Kasaan, to sign contracts for timber harvesting. Kake and Kasaan had asked to be included in an Indian reservation to be expanded from the one established in 1943 for the Town of Hydaburg, as part of the Indian New Deal extended to Alaska. Cohen, as an employee of Interior, was caught between his work obligations, his sympathies for Indian people, and his socialist ideals.

Then an anonymous letter arrived warning Felix that he had ignored a conflict of interest when he constructed the compromise to harvest timber, with royalties to the Tlingit communities, before possessory rights were decided. His personal integrity was not impugned, only his proposal of an income-generating scheme for Tlingits in advance of in-process negotiations for including Kake and Kasaan in an expanded Hydaburg reservation. Interior had granted that in October, then very quickly rescinded it when its Department of Agriculture objected. An anonymous letter—he had opponents that low. Felix was not obliged to suffer such below-the-belt blows. Curry, Bingham, and Cohen had seemed an appropriate law firm to join, with Henry Cohen his cousin and James Curry a colleague he had already worked with.

It was not the good choice it appeared. Curry and Felix could not get along. Curry aggressively sought to represent as many tribes as he could persuade to engage him, at the same time as he was general counsel to the NCAI. His strategy was to garner contracts and subcontract other attorneys to do the detail work. Being counsel to the NCAI of course provided him access to many tribes' leaders. Cohen had expected that by joining Curry,

Bingham, and Cohen he would be able to draw a salary to support his family while building an infrastructure to recruit capable law firms for Indian claims cases for the new Indian Claims Commission. Legal ethics prohibited Felix from working with Claims Commission plaintiffs for two years after leaving Interior. A Joint Efforts Group of law firms interested in Indian claims would facilitate needed research, reducing duplication of effort. Riegelman, Strasser, Schwarz, and Spiegelberg was one of the firms; Felix decided to affiliate with it, remaining in Washington on a salary and research funds subsidized by the Joint Research Group. Henry Cohen ceased contributing to Curry's expenses, and the firm Curry, Bingham, and Cohen dissolved in mid-1948.

Curry's resentment blew up early in 1949 when Felix invited him to partake of the Joint Reseach Group's resources, for which he would owe a percentage of fees from claims awards. Curry retaliated against this perceived insult from the man he considered his rival by getting the NCAI to ask the US attorney general to investigate whether the Joint Research Group of twenty law firms was a syndicate organized to pursue billions of dollars in fees, and whether Cohen was working on claims cases before the two-year ban ended. The Justice Department determined that no felonies appeared to have been committed. Curry's anger over competition fed into Commissioner of Indian Affairs Dillon Myer's crusade to terminate the special status of Indian tribes, in which Myer was following Congress's wishes. Myer insisted on his office exercising full power over tribes' relations with attorneys, deciding whether or not they should hire any, whom they could hire, what the contracts and fees would be, and—a mortal blow to James Curry—discouraging attorneys from taking multiple claims cases and subcontracting.

Outcry initially came from the Joint Research Group, the ACLU (represented by Ted Haas), NAACP, NCAI, Association on American Indian Affairs, of which Felix was general counsel, and other groups defending civil liberties. The brief from these protesters pointed out that Section 16 of the IRA specified that tribes could hire attorneys and negotiate fees, although Collier's paternalism had made these actions subject to the Secretary of the Interior's approval. Oscar Chapman, Secretary of the Interior 1950–1953, did not curb Myer, leading to a challenge in 1951 by the American Bar Association. Myer and his boss, Secretary Chapman, were attempting to curtail one of the most basic and precious rights of American citizens, the right to an attorney of one's choice. Indians are citizens. Opposed by the American Bar Association, Chapman and Myer could not prevail.

Reversing the Indian New Deal

Meanwhile, Tlingit were still fighting for their timber and fishery rights, and, as it developed, their land itself. According to legal scholar (and Lumbee Indian) Robert Williams Jr., Congress decided to test the issue of "possessory rights" in Alaska through a joint resolution in August 1947 to authorize the federal government to contract for selling Tongass National Forest timber, depositing proceeds in a special account pending final court judgment on possessory rights. It was this congressional resolution that Lucy Kramer Cohen recalled to have so disheartened her husband (Tsuk Mitchell 2007:249). The case selected for the test was the claim of Teeyhittaan — spelled Tee-Hit-Ton in court documents — Tlingit for timber rights around their village. It went all the way to the Supreme Court, whose justices decided 6–3 against the plaintiffs in *Tee-Hit-Ton Indians v. United States* (348 US 272, February 1955). Attorney for the plaintiffs was William Paul, himself a Teeyhittaan Tlingit and a founder of the Alaskan Native Brotherhood, principal organization of Alaskan First Nations defending their rights. The basis for the case was the Teeyhittaans' invocation of their Fifth Amendment protection, the "takings clause": "No person shall be ... deprived of life, liberty, or property, without due process of law; nor shall private property be taken for public use, without just compensation."

Congress, in its backlash against the Indian New Deal, wanted to deny that Indian land had been private property. Without arguing directly that the natives had been conquered and were thereby unable to hold their property, a position difficult to uphold in the case of Alaska where there had been no campaigns of conquest, the Court majority held that private property simply had not existed prior to the United States' purchase of Alaska. Where Paul argued that his Tlingit people were and had been civilized, with substantial timber houses, commercial-scale fisheries, private and corporate property (in crests and titles, and extended household ownership of resources), organized religion, and trading enterprises, the Court saw the situation otherwise:

> The Court of Claims had before it the testimony of a single witness who was offered by plaintiff. He stated that he was the chief of the Tee-Hit-Ton tribe.
>
> The witness pointed out that their claim of ownership was based on possession and use. The use that was made of the controverted area was for the location in winter of villages in sheltered spots, and in summer

along fishing streams and/or bays. The ownership was not individual, but tribal. As the witness stated,

> "Any member of the tribe may use any portion of the land that he wishes, and, as long as he uses it, that is his, for his own enjoyment, and is not to be trespassed upon by anybody else, but, the minute he stops using it, then any other member of the tribe can come in and use that area."

When the Russians first came to the Tlingit territory, the most important of the chiefs moved the people to what is now the location of the town of Wrangell. Each tribe took a portion of Wrangell harbor, and the chief gave permission to the Russians to build a house on the shore.

The witness learned the alleged boundaries of the Tee-Hit-Ton area from hunting and fishing with his uncle after his return from Carlisle Indian School about 1904. From the knowledge so obtained, he outlined in red on the map, which petitioner filed as an exhibit, the territory claimed by the Tee-Hit-Tons. Use by other tribal members is sketchily asserted. This is the same 350,000 acres claimed by the petition. On it, he marked six places to show the Indians' use of the land: (1) his great uncle was buried here, (2) a town, (3) his uncle's house, (4) a town, (5) his mother's house, (6) smokehouse. He also pointed out the uses of this tract for fishing salmon and for hunting beaver, deer, and mink.

The testimony further shows that, while membership in the tribe, and therefore ownership in the common property, descended only through the female line, the various tribes of the Tlingits allowed one another to use their lands. Before power boats, the Indians would put their shelters for hunting and fishing away from villages. With the power boats, they used them as living quarters.

In addition to this verbal testimony, exhibits were introduced by both sides as to the land use. These exhibits are secondary authorities but they bear out the general proposition that land claims among the Tlingits, and likewise of their smaller group, the Tee-Hit-Tons, was wholly tribal. It was more a claim of sovereignty than of ownership. The articles presented to the Court of Claims by those who have studied and written of the tribal groups agree with the above testimony. There were scattered shelters and villages moved from place to place as game or fish became scarce. There was recognition of tribal rights to hunt and fish on certain general areas, with claims to that effect carved on totem poles. From all that was presented, the Court of Claims concluded, and we agree, that the Tee-Hit-Tons were in a hunting and fishing stage of civilization, with shelters fitted to their environment, and claims to rights to use identified territory for these activities, as well as the gathering of wild products of the earth. We think this evidence introduced by both sides confirms the Court of Claims' conclusion that the petitioner's use of its lands was like the use of the nomadic tribes of the States Indians.

The line of cases adjudicating Indian rights on American soil leads to the conclusion that Indian occupancy, not specifically recognized as ownership by action authorized by Congress, may be extinguished by the Government without compensation. Every American schoolboy knows that the savage tribes of this continent were deprived of their ancestral ranges by force and that, even when the Indians ceded millions of acres by treaty in return for blankets, food, and trinkets, it was not a sale, but the conquerors' will that deprived them of their land. (US Supreme Court 1955:248–90)

"Every American schoolboy" is the ultimate authority here for six justices of the Supreme Court.

Tee-Hit-Ton was a trumpet fanfare for the resurgence of Jeffersonian Indian policy, or perhaps we should see it as capitalism redux, the underlying situation being a postwar push to exploit Alaska's minerals, timber, and fisheries. Robert Williams notes that part of the case was an argument by the defendant's lawyers, that is, Department of Justice attorneys, that if those Indians were found to have possessory rights that had been taken, many similar pending cases would be recognized, leading to claims totaling $1 billion in compensation and an astonishing $8 billion in accrued interest (Williams 2005:89–90; Wildenthal 2003:61). Figures like these spurred politicians to rein in Indian claims. Every lawyer who expressed interest in litigating an Indian claim was suspected of having dollar signs for eyes, looking for huge contingency fees.

For Felix Cohen, the Joint Research Group was a means to keep down lawyers' expenses in the claims cases, and for him personally to obtain a living for his family while keeping freedom to work with tribes against the tide of reversals swept in by the government's termination policy. He opened a Washington office for Riegelman, Strasser, Schwarz, and Spiegelberg in 1949, its first branch outside New York City, which quickly grew to cover other fields of practice in addition to Felix's specialty in Indian claims. Thirteen years of working within government had enlightened and toughened Felix. Racism and xenophobia encompassing First Nations within America joined with hard-nosed economic powers to force back the limited Western-style self-government recognized tribes had been allowed under their IRA constitutions and charters. Only about half of the number of recognized tribes had adopted IRA-type constitutions, and somewhat fewer created chartered corporations. Cohen had written and Margold had ruled that Indian nations retain inherent sovereignty except powers explicitly delegated to Congress in treaties, that Congress does not have plenary power to unilaterally abrogate treaties. When the Truman administration and its Commissioner of Indian Affairs, Dillon Myer, sought to take the idea of ending OIA power over Indians down a road not built by Cohen and Margold, to termination of federal relationships with tribes—that is, abrogation of treaties—Felix felt righteous anger at this betrayal of his country's moral obligations. He also felt angry at the challenge to him personally, the implicit denigration of his legal accomplishments with his trilogy of IRA, *Handbook*, and Indian Claims Commission Act.

Montana's Blackfeet Tribe was one of several retaining Felix Cohen as legal counsel. The Blackfeet Tribal Business Council offered him a $5,000 per year retainer but Cohen would accept only $3,600 (Rosier 2001:324, nn. 95, 97). Commissioner Myer saw Cohen and Jim Curry as adversaries. Myer's OIA had reverted to the pre-Margold position that Interior and the Department of Justice defended the United States against grievances and claims by its Indians, never mind the trust relationship (McMillen 2007: 127–28, 172). Myer promulgated, in October 1950, a set of regulations detailing OIA power over tribes seeking justice under law. Myer forbade tribes to hire attorneys on their own, to pay retainers for legal counsel, and to employ any but local attorneys. Clearly, he intended to cripple Cohen and Curry (Philp 1999:112). Neither lawyer would accept OIA despotism for their clients. Without waiting for the many civil rights and American Bar Association protests to hobble Myer, Cohen and Curry persisted in their work for tribal clients, including, for Cohen, the Montana Blackfeet's assertion of the right to choose agency superintendents and OIA operations on their reservation.

Southernmost of the Blackfoot alliance, the Amskapi Pikuni ("Blackfeet") held off invasions of their territory following Meriwether Lewis's killing of two of their youths in 1806 during the return journey of the US Corps of Discovery. Pikunis' first treaty with the United States was at a September 1853 council with Isaac Stevens, sent out to explore routes for a transcontinental railroad to the Pacific. Low Horn, principal Pikuni leader, agreed to peace between his nation and Stevens's, publicly calling upon his young men to abstain from warring. At this time, Pikuni were recognized to hold about fifty thousand square miles between the Canadian border and the Missouri River, from the Milk River on the east to the

Rockies on the west. The other three Blackfoot groups occupied southern Alberta north of the border. Two years later, Stevens returned to make a formal treaty with the Blackfoot, including those north of the Canadian border. Lame Bull of the Amskapi Pikuni led the Blackfoot at the council. The treaty was ratified by Congress in April 1856, and an Army officer, Major Vaughan, sent out as agent.

Vaughn encouraged a Jesuit mission to settle in Pikuni territory in 1859, and the next year set up a farm on the Sun River for his agency and another, smaller farm was prepared for Little Dog, a Pikuni leader willing to try agriculture. Floods in 1862 and 1864 ruined most of the farm fields, convincing Little Dog to go back to hunting bison. Another kind of flood also hit Blackfoot territory in 1864—a flood of thirty thousand non-Indians questing for gold, or, in the case of the more astute, profits to be made by selling food and supplies to the gold miners. Montana was quickly made a territory of the United States. Placer gold was exhausted by 1870, with some miners moving on while others homesteaded under Congress's 1862 Homestead Act, which specifically excluded Indians. Ranching being the only agricultural enterprise suited to the high plains of Blackfoot territory, cattle were imported by the thousands and left to graze open range. Inevitably, they impinged on Pikuni wintering and hunting grounds.

Lame Bull's treaty was to expire in ten years, so in 1865 a new treaty was negotiated with the Pikuni. It stipulated "acknowledgment to be made by the Indians of their dependence upon the United States, and obligation to obey . . . the direction of the superintendent or agent" (Wissler and Kehoe 2012:83). Whether this clause rendered the agreement invalid in the eyes of the Pikuni has not been recorded; no matter, the 1865 document was not submitted to Congress, and the Pikuni announced in 1866 that they would not permit any American incursions or settlement. Again in 1868, a council of Blackfoot signed a treaty with the United States, and again Congress failed to ratify. Killings of Indians by settlers and of settlers and whiskey traders by Indians continued through 1869. On January 23, 1870, a company of US cavalry massacred a Pikuni camp in retaliation for Pikuni killing a settler who had married a Pikuni woman and abused her, quarreling with her brothers who told him to stop. The official count on that bitter winter morning was 173 Pikuni dead, most being women and children. More than a hundred women were captured but "turned loose," the official report stated, because Colonel Baker had no wagons to take them to the agency built the year before. Struggling on foot through deep snow to reach Canada, most of these women died; Baker's troops had seized their band's three hundred horses.

There would be no next treaty with the Blackfoot, because in 1871, Congress declared it would no longer make treaties with Indian tribes. Instead, in 1873, the President used an executive order to create an Indian reservation for several tribes together, encompassing all of northeastern Montana from Fort Union at the confluence of the Missouri and Yellowstone Rivers, west to the Rockies, and north of the Missouri to Canada. Outcry from settlers reached Congress's ears, which were deaf to Indians' pleas, and it cut up the reservation into parcels separated by public lands open to settlement. Pikuni ended up with a reservation insufficient to maintain enough bison for their sustenance. Wild herds were rapidly being depleted by commercial slaughter for hides used for industrial belting, and no more free-roaming bison were seen after 1884. Technically, the Montana Blackfeet had no treaty, nor had they means of subsistence.

The Dawes Act to allot tribal lands in severalty reached the Montana Blackfeet Reservation in 1907. A detailed census was prepared, with each tribal person's parents and grandparents as well as spouse and children, to determine who qualified as Indians to be given allotments. The process of allotting took several years. By 1914, it was done, leaving approximately half the reservation as "surplus" that could be sold off. This of course provoked controversy, some of the already successful mixed-blood ranchers wanting to either buy land to expand their own properties, or to sell surplus land to bring in money for tribal enterprises or to provide welfare for the less successful full-bloods. Opposed to selling any reservation land were most of the full-bloods—those who could not or would not speak English—and a good number of mixed-bloods (bilingual and generally literate Indians).

The Montana Blackfeet had a General Council operating in the traditional manner as a gathering of band leaders to discuss, negotiate, or adjudicate common concerns. It did have formal officers and maintained a Tribal Business Committee that in 1915 reorganized as the Blackfeet Tribal Business Council and became the governance organ of the tribe. Accepting an IRA constitution thus did not introduce a new type of governance to the Blackfeet; they had evolved such a council through formal education and interactions with non-Indian businesspeople and ranchers, some of whom married into the nation. Throughout the twentieth century, continuing conflicts wracked the Tribal Council as its members, elected under its IRA constitution from geographic districts, struggled to build and maintain a sustainable economy in the face of OIA paternalism and often inept or even venal agency superintendents. Until late in the century, conflicts tended to be labeled "poor full-bloods" versus "successful mixed-bloods," a trope that played well before Congress and OIA top

Figure 9.2. Blackfeet participants in a 1932 program teaching crafts and painting: Tom Dog Gun, Aloysius Evans, and Sam Calf Robe, at Heart Butte (community) Round Hall. Photo from Blackfeet Tribal Historic Preservation Office; identifications by William Farr.

officials and obfuscated the serious difficulties of earning income from economically marginal land subject to strangers' bureaucratic plans and decrees. John Collier's Indian Arts and Crafts Board facilitated selling local art and handicrafts (figure 9.2), cooperation with state extension instructors taught home economics to women (figure 9.3), and for some of the "full-bloods," their picturesque quality earned occasional fees as movie extras (figure 9.4) or posing for tourists at Glacier Park hotels.

During World War II, Congress limited tribes' access to their own funds deposited in Treasury accounts—Congress wanted Treasury reserves for war expenditures. A lump sum was permitted to the OIA to disburse as needed for tribal welfare programs, forcing the bureau to decide which tribes were most needy. Because the Blackfeet tribe had some income from oil and gas extraction, it was told it must support its impoverished members out of local tribal funds, and could not draw its own funds from Treasury. War or no war, Senator Burton Wheeler continued his efforts to get the Wheeler-Howard Act repealed, holding a hearing about it on the Blackfeet Reservation in August 1943. "Full-blood leader" Charles Reevis, whose father was a "mountain man" trapper settled on the reservation with his Pikuni wife, argued that full-bloods could never understand nor want to work with so foreign an instrument as an IRA constitution. Wheeler took that as support for repeal, although Montana congressman James

Figure 9.3. Blackfeet women in WPA Sewing Club, Two Medicine community: Mrs. Calf Looking, Mae Williamson, unidentified teacher, Nora Spanish, Louise Pepion, Tiny Racine, Anna Potts, Rosy Big Beaver. Photo from Blackfeet Tribal Historic Preservation Office; identifications by William Farr.

O'Connor, accompanying Wheeler, admitted under questioning about alternatives, "I do not believe that anybody has thought through on the matter and has figured out something to take its place" (quoted in Rosier 2001:197).

When the war ended, the Blackfeet Tribal Business Council, led by Joe Brown since the late 1920s, continued its efforts to build an economy under its own control. Brown, like most of his councilmen, was the son of a white settler who married a Pikuni, in this case Sarah, daughter of Melting Marrow and Bird Sailing This Way. Like many of the councilmen, his family ranched on the north side of the reservation, whereas many of the full-bloods lived in the southwest sector closer to the foothills, their allotments less suited to ranching. Full-blood families in consequence depended more on per capita payments from tribal funds and welfare. Not having been raised by white businessmen fathers, they customarily spoke Blackfoot rather than English, fully participated in days-long celebrations and rituals in Montana and Canada, and espoused the traditional ethos

Figure 9.4. Blackfeet at train depot, 1939, to travel to participate in the film *Suzanne and the Mounties*: Tom Many Guns, with child; Mrs. Many Guns; Josephine Turtle; Turtle; Victor Chief Coward (?) and wife; Insima (sister of Richard Sanderville) and husband Yellow Kidney; couple on right unidentified. Photo from Blackfeet Tribal Historic Preservation Office; identifications by William Farr.

expecting band leaders to generously disperse whatever food and goods they might amass. Such "traditional full-bloods" were increasingly a minority on the reservation. I use quotes for this group because biologically, some had fathers or grandfathers who were white but had not endeavored to establish themselves in ranching and other business enterprises. Joe Brown, deeply respecting his Pikuni mother's family, struggled to be generous to the elderly as befitted a Pikuni leader, while constrained by US laws, the OIA, and the tribe's IRA constitution.

Late in April 1945, Joe Brown brought Ted Haas to Browning to speak to a constitutional convention convened by the Tribal Business Council. Haas urged investment rather than distributions of tribal funds, suggesting not only bonds but land and livestock as investment choices (Rosier 2001: 201). Another matter deliberated was the number of council members — five, nine, or the existing thirteen — and the effect of popular election. To mollify the traditional full-bloods, the council appointed full-bloods to a committee to set enrollment criteria; they decided on one-sixteenth Blackfoot ancestry and added that to receive benefits, enrolled members must live on, or regularly come to, the reservation. Obtaining this critical power did not satisfy the full-bloods' anxiety over mixed-bloods' dominance of the council. Reevis and four others went to Chicago, the OIA's wartime headquarters, to talk with William Brophy, who had just replaced Collier as Commissioner, Walter Woehlke, D'Arcy McNickle, and Felix Cohen.

Postwar conditions did not resolve tribal conflicts, even as the generation that had been born before the reservation was dying off. "Socioeco-
nomic full-bloods," to use historian Paul Rosier's insightful term, continued to be the minority of Blackfeet choosing to live traditionally, as if that
were possible without subsisting on free-range bison. The Tribal Business
Council pursued the vision they glimpsed within their IRA constitution of
managing their nation without OIA control. Denial of the use of their own
money deposited in the US Treasury did not end with the termination of
war. Blackfeet saw their money held in Washington being, apparently, dis-
bursed to Europeans under the Marshall Plan: "The Blackfeet Nation is
poorer than any nation of Europe aided by the Marshall Plan, poorer than
any of the nations that our boys helped to free from dictatorship. . . . We
ask . . . the right to expend our own funds."[6] Paradoxically, in that period
of congressional policy to terminate federal involvement with Indian
tribes, the Blackfeet council's persisting efforts to implement their IRA
promise of tribal independence found no favor with the OIA.

Felix Cohen became tribal attorney to the Blackfeet Tribe in autumn
1949. Three years later, he used his experiences in this position to write "A
Case Study in Bureaucracy" for the *Yale Law Journal* (Cohen 1953). It is
actually an indictment against Dillon Myer's conduct of the OIA, beginning in May 1950. Cohen organized his indictment under three headings,
"Restrictions upon Indian Freedom," "Restrictions upon Indian Control
of Indian Property," and "Indian Bureau Organization."

Under the first heading, Cohen described the BIA's circulation of articles attacking candidates for June 1950 elections to the Blackfeet Tribal
Business Council, and its insistence on holding a May 1952 referendum
on fiscal controls, rather than allowing the Council and other Blackfeet to
work out reform. That vote was particularly blatantly orchestrated by the
agency superintendent, who in the same month had sent a tribal police-
man to order people to stop playing the stick game by six p.m. Cohen detailed the Myer regime's attempts to prevent tribes from engaging their
own choice of legal counsel. He went on to tell how Myer had linked repeal of laws prohibiting Indians from purchasing alcohol or ammunition
to Myer's desire to abolish tribal courts and police. Discrimination against
Indians within OIA hiring and in reservation economics had escalated, for
example, by charging Blackfeet $5.22 per head to run sheep, while non-
Indian agribusiness operators were charged $2.65 per animal.

Under the second heading, Cohen himself won in 1951 an invalidation
of OIA control over Blackfeet and other Indian livestock operators, and
over leasing Indian land without owners' or tribal consent. In 1950, Myer's

administration had ordered the Blackfeet Tribal Business Council to re-
move its funds in excess of $5,000 from the local bank in Browning and
deposit the monies instead at the Blackfeet agency under the superintendent's control, a policy applied that year to many other tribes as well. Myer's OIA insisted it retained ownership, and thereby control, over agency
buildings built with tribal monies, and over 1930s drought-weakened cattle shipped to graze on Blackfeet range, for which the Blackfeet had completed payment at high interest. Attempting to wrest control of their funds
from the OIA, the Blackfeet in 1952 persuaded Montana's two senators
and their congressional representative to introduce bills to allow the tribe
to pay in full its debts to the federal government and then be free to manage its own credit, measures that should have ensued under the IRA constitution but were opposed by the OIA.

Cohen's third heading, "Indian Bureau Organization," described the
shift of control from local agencies to regional offices outside reservations.
This section concluded with a list of OIA employees dismissed by Myer,
"men who were thoroughly familiar with the intricacies of Indian administration, the commitments of the Federal Government, and the feelings
of nearly half a million Indians": Assistant Commissioner Zimmerman;
Walter Woehlke, special assistant to the commissioner; Joseph McCaskill
and John Provinse, also assistant commissioners (Provinse an anthropologist); Willard Beatty, chief of the Branch of Education; D'Arcy McNickle;
and Chief Counsel Theodore Haas (Cohen 1953:383). Altogether, Cohen
saw in Myer an effort to end tribal consent to measures proposed by the
federal government—"We must proceed even though Indian cooperation
may be lacking in certain cases," Myer directed (Cohen 1953:376).

On a larger screen, Cohen worked to accommodate Indian values
within US domination. Felix wrote to his clients the Blackfeet Tribal Business Council in June 1950 that "white officials" oppose "the generosity
that Blackfeet Indians and their tribal leaders have always shown towards
those of their own people who are in need or distress. We have a hard job
ahead of us, in trying to combine Blackfeet generosity and white man's
business practices" (quoted in Rosier 2001:241). "This success at cooperation is now the target of the Indian Bureau's most intense attack," he stated
in his *Yale Law Journal* article (Cohen 1953:363). Through the years, the
Indian ethos of leaders assisting members of their band infused the Tribal
Business Council. Because council members were elected by and represented geographic districts on the reservation, their constituencies were for
the most part originally bands whose members took allotments near one
another and their band chief, perpetuating the older ethos of leaders (now

councilmen) helping their kin, neighbors, and themselves to prosper that they might personally be generous. Charges of nepotism, favoritism, and improper loans were easily brought, by competing candidates for council positions and their supporters, and by the OIA. Cohen countered OIA intrusions upon council decisions by advising on its rights and jurisdictions under its constitution and federal Indian law. Council chairman George Pambrun wrote to the OIA area director in August 1950 that they would "insist on respect for the existing legal powers of the Blackfeet Tribe" (quoted in Rosier 2001:246), prompting OIA officials to suspect Cohen authored the letter, a role he denied. His actual role is pictured in a photo taken in April 1951, when he stood to one side watching as a No Trespassing sign was posted on a Blackfeet agency building claimed by the tribe, challenged by the OIA. Tribal council chairman George Pambrun and councilwoman Cora Irgens stand closer to the workman attaching the sign (Philp 1999: photo 23).

So far as records go, Felix Cohen's work with the Blackfeet Tribe of Montana was part of his legal practice. It happens that the Blackfeet Reservation borders the Bob Marshall Wilderness, a pristine memorial to Felix and Lucy Cohen's friend the forestry expert who died so young in 1939. Felix and the Marshall brothers, Bob and George, were New York Jews whose passion for social justice carried them far from the city. The Bob Marshall Wilderness, with its mountain grandeur, thick forests, grizzly bears, and mountain lions, preserves the vision that invigorated Bob Marshall the man. For Felix Cohen, no monumental preserve perpetuates what never was pristine. During his years with the OIA, Cohen learned that his early socialist good intentions had to be transmogrified under the variety of existing and abrogated First Nations societies. Reinforced by the Boasian anthropology he absorbed through Lucy, Felix became the most effective advocate for Indian sovereign self-determination. Only the cancer that killed him in 1953 had the power to still his unrelenting drive to force his own government to respect its moral and legal obligations to its encapsulated indigenous communities.

CHAPTER TEN

Sovereignty

Not So Simple

The Indian New Deal was the turning point in colonialism. Margold and Cohen's pronouncement on inherent sovereignty, supported by Felix's assertion in the *Handbook of Federal Indian Law* that treaties with Indian nations remain in force, counteracted the long-standing European position that military conquest overrides diplomatic treaties. Legal opinion does not, in the case of First Nations' continuing sovereignties, comport easily with the observation that might makes right. The termination policy of the 1950s opened the postwar era of tides of battle between the brute fact of white America's power and the struggles of other constituencies to gain their legitimate status and opportunities.

Colonialism and its conjoined twin, racism, will not die easily. Overtly granting overseas colonies political independence when administering them seems too costly, and pushing for individuals' assimilation and tribal terminations to end expenditures for internal colonies were mid-twentieth-century policy choices for most European empires and the United States and Canada. Surrogate wars in third world countries such as Vietnam, Guatemala, and Afghanistan allowed imperial nations to contest power without jeopardizing citizens at home. Unrestrained global capitalism moved jobs to populations that could be exploited with wages, hours, and working conditions not tolerated in those imperial nations. Sovereignty seems fungible for third world nations, even relatively Europeanized ones such as Chile (as when, in 1970–1973, the United States fomented the assault on socialist president Salvador Allende that resulted in his death).

How much more vulnerable are encapsulated fourth world nations, tiny percentages of the voting populations of major powers?

The Indian New Deal's troika of Indian Reorganization Act, *Handbook of Federal Indian Law*, and Indian Claims Commission framed but did not provoke postwar Indian activism. Earl Old Person, Blackfeet Tribal Business Council leader for half a century, explained,

> In the 1960s, the reservation was seeing its first high school graduates attend college. The BIA had again reorganized its educational programs, this time allowing for equal opportunities to go to college or vocational school. It was during this time that the young people who chose to attend colleges or vocational schools became active in the Red Power and the American Indian Movement, also known as AIM.
>
> At that time, Indian life expectancy was just forty-four years, one-third less than that of the typical American. Deaths caused by pneumonia, hepatitis, dysentery, strep throat, diabetes, tuberculosis, alcoholism, suicide, and homicide were two to sixty times higher than among the whole United States population (US Digital History 2006). Many Blackfeet families lived in unsanitary, dilapidated dwellings, many in tents. The young Blackfeet became more aware of their reservation surroundings when they went off to college.
>
> They began to realize that conditions on their own reservation were not unlike those found in underdeveloped countries. Many of the homes they left had no running water, some had no electricity, they used outdoor toilets, and woodburning stoves for heat. Some of the poorest homes were located on the south side of Browning, called "Moccasin Flat." It was during the late 1960s that young Blackfeet who left the reservation began to revolt against such conditions. It was the same group of young Blackfeet that continued their education and graduated from such prestigious colleges as Berkeley, Harvard, and others.
>
> On the home front, Chief [Earl] Old Person and other tribal leaders were mounting their own rebellion against conditions that Native Americans faced. In 1969, Chief Old Person was elected president of the National Congress of American Indians. During his tenure as NCAI president the United States Government continued to discuss termination of reservations. In a speech given to members of the National Congress of American Indians, Chief Old Person spoke of termination in these terms:
>
> "Again, I say, 'Let's forget termination and try a policy that has never been tried before—development of the Indian reservations for Indians

and development of Indians as human beings with a personality and a soul and dreams for a bright future.'" (Old Person 2012:178–79)

During Old Person's administration, the Blackfeet Council supported Elouise Cobell's work to build Blackfeet National Bank to serve the reservation, then its expansion to other reservations as Native American Bancorporation and its offshoot, Native American Community Development Corporation. Cobell's culminating work was as lead plaintiff in the Indian Trust Monies lawsuit, 1996–2011, against the Department of the Interior for its failure to fulfill its fiduciary responsibilities under treaties.

Old Person served on Nixon's Indian Self-Determination Task Force, 1968–1970. Nixon's 1970 proclamation of "self-determination" for tribes meant, said Old Person, "From that time on, the Blackfeet realized that they were in charge of their own destiny" (2012:179). This certainly was the message Felix Cohen meant to convey. Against that is the harsh reality of a reservation fit only for ranching, constrained by an agreement between the United States and Canada to divert reservation river water essential for hay crops to Alberta and then past the reservation to eastern Montana. The push for irrigation water came from a Mormon colony in the St. Mary River valley in Alberta, a colony sent out of Utah when the Mormon Church formally accepted an end to polygyny (Morris 2006:175). Negotiations from 1904 to 1909 did not include Blackfoot, on either side of the border cutting through their homeland, and the international agreement crippled Montana Blackfeet ranching. A pencil factory using the tribe's timber from the foothills along its western border was the principal economic innovation, in 1972, following Nixon's policy announcement. Its products prized by pencil connoisseurs, the factory itself was sold in 1992 and ceased operations a few years afterward, unable to compete with products from the National Institute for the Blind.

Sovereignty and self-determination are a struggle in the marginal territories the United States left to its First Nations (AILTP 1988:ix). Getches, Wilkinson, and Williams, in their 1993 casebook on federal Indian law, warn, "One broad point remains strikingly apparent. From *Worcester v. Georgia* over one and one-half centuries ago to the cases decided most recently by the [Supreme] Court, the central issue in Indian law has changed hardly a whit: who governs the land, the resources, and the people in Indian country?" (Getches, Wilkinson, and Williams 1993:460).

Treaty abrogations by the United States primarily were dispossessions of land, that is, reduction of the territorial extent of an Indian nation's sovereignty. Outright seizure of resources, such as taking the Black Hills from the Lakota for the Hills' gold, in the twentieth century morphed into the OIA's failure to negotiate and receive fair royalties for tribal land resources such as oil and range land, and its further failure to transfer to tribes and allotment owners what royalties and lease fees it did collect. Who governs the people became complex in 1924 when the United States unilaterally made its native-born Indian residents citizens of the United States. Before that act, Indian members of Indian tribes did not have constitutional rights because they were not under the jurisdiction of the US Constitution. In 1968, the Indian Civil Rights Act proposed by Senator Sam Ervin of North Carolina spelled out rights parallel to those in the US Bill of Rights, not to be denied by tribal governments. Unquestionably, the Indian Civil Rights Act is an infringement upon tribal sovereignties, and it was so interpreted in 1978 by the Supreme Court in denying membership in Santa Clara Pueblo to the children of Mrs. Julia Martinez, a Santa Clara woman married to a Navajo man. Santa Clara decided to admit only children of male members to enrollment, regardless of their mothers' membership, their birth in the pueblo, or their continued residence in it.[1] The Court upheld the Pueblos' sovereignty over membership.

Charles Wilkinson, in his 1987 classic *American Indians, Time, and the Law*, contrasts sixteenth-century European understanding of sovereignty as absolute, undivided, and unlimited in the Crown by divine mandate, with later structures making monarchies constitutional and sharing power with parliaments, or combining states' limited sovereignties with constitutional powers of a federal government. This latter model accommodates First Nations on a parallel with states and provinces, in Canada quite literally, with the Chief of the Assembly of First Nations sitting with the premiers of the provinces in Canada's federal government. The United States lacks a comparable national leader representing its First Nations (tribes). Such a lack relates each US tribe directly to the federal government through the Department of the Interior, in one sense preserving each Indian nation's sovereignty while at the same time weakening it politically. The NCAI was formed to strengthen the political voice of the US First Nations, but unlike Canada's Assembly, it has no position within the federal government.

The Postwar Chicago Indian Conference

A generation after Margold and Cohen's efforts on the IRA, another American Ashkenazi Jew felt he must employ his talents to help American

Indians fight the injustices they still suffered. Sol Tax was born, like the Cohens, in 1907 to immigrant parents in America (figure 10.1). He launched, in 1961, an American Indian Conference that could affiliate tribes and other Indian communities into a pan-Indian organization and lobby reaching beyond the NCAI.

Figure 10.1. Sol Tax. Photo from Marianna Tax Choldin.

A Midwesterner who grew up in socialist-governed Milwaukee, Tax was a professor of anthropology at the University of Chicago. He had led a graduate student project beginning in 1948 to study the Mesquakie (Fox) community in Tama, Iowa. Seeing the effects of the federal termination policy for the Mesquakie, including an unwelcome busing of their children to off-reservation schools, Tax felt a mitzvah to advocate for the Indian community, dubbing the effort, in a 1951 presentation, "action anthropology." Tax summed up his commitment to action anthropology, declaring that as an anthropologist he would be "taking upon himself the ultimate responsibility for satisfying his conscience in terms of the obligations he feels toward his colleagues and toward his fellow men" (Tax 1964:255, quoted by Bennett 1996:S30).

This very Jewish principle reflects Tax's realization that although he did not consider himself religious or obliged to fulfill all the minutiae of his parents' orthodoxy, he was a Jew. His first experience outside the United States was as a student on a Beloit College archaeological project in Algeria, where a Passover seder with a local Jewish family felt like home, even though the conversation was in French, contrasted with the difference he felt from the other American students in the camp, all Gentiles. At the Algerians' table, he enjoyed "the same quickness . . . the same eagerness" and "above all, there were the same premises—premises which all but the two exceptional members of our expedition [John Gillin and Lauriston Sharp] utterly lacked—that my Jewish friends at home have, the fundamental belief in Social Justice as the necessary goal, and the ultimate perfection of mankind as the desired end" (quoted in Stocking 2000:226). That Algerian seder provided another reinforcement of Tax's Jewish identity, the perception that Jews and, he would see later, American Indians, "against impossible odds" had survived as communities with much of their "basic religion and world view intact" (quoted in Stocking 2000:230).

Action anthropology began, in 1948, at the request of the University of Chicago Department of Anthropology that Tax, just established as a professor there, lead an ethnographic field project for graduate students. Fieldwork for students on Indian reservations had been a staple of American university graduate programs in anthropology, interrupted by World War II's enlistment of anthropologists in the war effort. War work, following employment of anthropologists in a range of New Deal agencies, stimulated organization in 1941 of the Society for Applied Anthropology. "Applied" anthropology was considered of lower status than academic teaching; purportedly, real-world projects lacked theory. Academics looked upon these projects as case studies from which to illustrate theories (Weaver

2012). Sol Tax was drawn to interacting with grassroots communities, rather than to ivory-tower intellectualisms.

As Tax had written his dissertation in 1935 about fieldwork, in 1932 and 1934, with Mesquakie (Fox) in Tama, Iowa, returning to Tama with half a dozen students seemed feasible. World War II and Hiroshima had intervened, spurring the mature Tax to realize his mitzvah. The students, too, were politically concerned, feeling a noblesse oblige to help the Indians (Stocking 2000:191). Three years of relative immersion in the Tama Mesquakie community clarified the principle of action anthropology, that it should illuminate a community's various needs and values, sharing the knowledge within it and with outside agencies to assist in overcoming hindrances (Stocking 2000:193; see Bennett 1996; Stapp 2012). The Fox Project went on for several more years with Tax as advisor. Students raised money for college scholarships for Mesquakies, organized a crafts business (that was subsequently taken over by non-Indian Tama businessmen), and tried to get Mesquakies into recreation projects supposed to build greater community spirit. When their projects petered out, the students judged the community dysfunctional (Foley 1995:156). A generation later, an anthropologist reared in Tama went back to do an ethnography of the town and the Mesquakies, concluding that the Indian community retained a strong component of traditional culture that included a political mode of apparent factional disagreements better seen as explorations of consequences, leading to adaptational "fusions" of newer needs with older ways (Foley 1995:159). Indians do not generally show the "quickness . . . the eagerness" characteristic of Jewish dialogues—usually more value is given to listening to a speaker, even refraining from rejoinder in order to allow more time for letting issues work themselves out—so Tax may have been discouraged, as certainly the students were. Their project, after all, took place during the heyday of termination. The anthropologists could no more halt the juggernaut of that racist policy than could Indians.

Primed by growing up a Jew in a city led by "sewer socialists," Sol Tax combined dedication to bettering daily life in oppressed communities with curiosity to discover how such communities—be they Jews or Mesquakie—could persist in the face of powerful pressure to dissolve. Technically, Jews before the establishment of Israel in 1948 had no sovereignty although they cooperated in maintaining ghetto communities, while US Indians had limited sovereignties, according to Cohen's *Handbook.* From Jefferson's presidency at the beginning of the nineteenth century, Indians were to assimilate into American society or disappear. During the 1930s, American anthropologists focused on Indians' "acculturation," implicitly leading to assimilation. Tax and his Cherokee student Robert K. Thomas spoke out, denying that assimilation was inevitable.

Tax and Thomas saw, and Thomas published, that the United States was a imperial power, its reservations so many colonies. Obvious as this was, most American anthropologists could not see this relationship, naïvely assuming that a democratic republic would not have colonies. It was easy to marginalize Bob Thomas because he was Indian; the same racism contributed to marginalizing the Jew, Tax, colleagues claiming that he was no theoretician, only an ineffective applied anthropologist. His later outstanding successes in carrying off the 1973 International Congress of Anthropological and Ethnological Sciences and building a premier journal, *Current Anthropology*, were attributed to his Jewish instinct for business, which even a Chicago PhD had not expunged.

Where Sol Tax stands as successor to Felix Cohen in forcing the United States to acknowledge First Nations' sovereignties is in the watershed American Indian Conference he organized in 1961. At first named American Indian Charter Convention, its venue led to its being known as the American Indian Chicago Conference. Its beginning was in summer workshops in Indian affairs that Tax had worked on organizing, since 1956, to prepare Indian college students to deal with governmental issues. Locking this generation into the proposed large conference, he arranged that the 1961 workshop would start in Chicago alongside the conference, before moving to the University of Colorado for formal workshop studies. Out of the workshop came the National Indian Youth Council, a parallel to the NCAI founded in 1944. The young men and women who had continued in Boulder to learn about Indian Affairs—the bureau—and Indian affairs—the state of Indian country—had their consciousness raised by Bob Thomas, on colonialism, and Robert Rietz, another University of Chicago alumnus from the Fox Project, who had worked at Fort Berthold on action anthropology to halt Garrison Dam displacing the Mandan, Hidatsa, and Arikara from their river valley homes and fields. Rietz was in 1961 employed as director of Chicago's American Indian Center, founded in 1953 with assistance from the American Friends Service Committee (Quakers) to help Indians settled in the big city as part of the federal relocation program.[2] Those summer workshops on Indian affairs created an assertive postwar cohort of young, formally educated Indians savvy about US history, policies, bureaucracy, and economics.

More attention is usually directed to Tax's crowning moment in action anthropology, the 1961 Chicago Conference with nearly a thousand participants—467 delegates representing ninety tribes, many more from the

Chicago Indian community, and some 150 non-Indians allowed to listen. Preparing for the conference, Tax and his graduate student assistants worked with NCAI leaders to set up nine regional meetings across the country to discuss issues and select delegates, sending D'Arcy McNickle's draft "New Frontier in Indian Affairs" to five thousand possible partici-pants.[3] Both the regional meetings and the mailings were similar to Col-lier's nine congresses to discuss the IRA, and Nancy Lurie, the project's principal assistant, confirms that Tax was familiar with the IRA legislation and the congresses. Collier had used the regional congresses and the mail correspondence with hundreds of Indians to sell his ideas to the constitu-ency; Tax would invert that, providing structure for Indians to articulate their ideas to the dominant society (Nancy O. Lurie, personal communi-cation, January 7, 2013).

Lurie, a Milwaukee native, remembers the Midwest regional meeting hosted at the Milwaukee Public Museum by its director, anthropologist Stefan Borhegyi, and that at least one of its attendees was inspired to start working with her tribe toward its own governance (Lurie, personal com-munication, June 20, 2012). Rules of order promulgated for the regional and Chicago conferences were seldom enforced, the emphasis being in-stead on a more Indian mode of courteous listening aiming toward con-sensus. Discussion groups of about fifty persons reported to plenary ses-sions of the whole that produced a Declaration of Indian Purpose detailing major issues faced by Indian communities. An Oklahoma Cherokee at-torney objected to lack of a formal declaration of loyalty to the United States, so one was added to the beginning of the official final declaration. At the opposite pole, William Rickard, a Tuscarora familiar with a half century of Iroquois efforts to insist on sovereignty, proclaimed the confer-ence and its declaration no advance, their frame of reference still the con-straints of "domestic dependent nations" (Cobb 2008:51).

Chicago conference participants had hoped that John Kennedy's cam-paign promises to listen to Indian grievances would be fulfilled. They in-vited his administration to send a representative to listen and to receive their Declaration of Indian Purpose. As Rickard would have expected, no one was officially sent. Undaunted, Tax persuaded the Carnegie Corpora-tion to support *Indian Voices*, a newspaper to be sent to the American In-dian Chicago Conference mailing list, and a five-year action anthropology project with Bob Thomas's people, the Oklahoma Cherokee. Appointed to the 1966 White House Task Force on Indian Affairs, Tax protested the absence of Indian members and circulated the AICC Declaration of In-dian Purpose. The same year, Tax served on an advisory committee to the

National Study of American Indian Education, and by 1974 succeeded in the establishment in Chicago of Native American Educational Services, Inc. under Indian leadership, offering college courses and a BA degree (Stapp 2012:9). In all these enterprises, Tax received recognition as a social sciences professor working with, but not within, the power structure, as his daughter put it (Freeman 2012:73).

The issue of who qualifies as an Indian became a bone of contention in the conference. Tax insisted, over and over, that "self-identified" Indians be included as well as those enrolled in federally recognized tribes. He strongly supported Rickard's recognition of representatives from many federally unrecognized eastern First Nations, ranging from Maine's Penobscot and Passamaquoddy through the Middle Atlantic Shinnecock, Wampanoag, Narragansett, Pequot, and Mohegan, to southern Lumbee, Pamunkey, Mattaponi, Catawba, and Tunica-Biloxi (Hauptman and Campisi 1988:318–22). When a party from the Chicago conference finally presented its Declaration of Indian Purpose to President Kennedy at the White House, in August 1962, nine of the thirty-two Indians in the party were from federally unrecognized nations (Hauptman and Campisi 1988:329). Without question, Tax's inclusiveness in 1961 was a factor in the push for more federal recognition beginning in the 1970s. If federal recognition seems retrograde in regard to sovereignty, it does acknowledge the status of the appellant groups to nationhood (Den Ouden and O'Brien 2013).

Who Is an Indian?

Roger Echo-Hawk, a Pawnee Confederacy citizen, announced, "I used to be an Indian" (2010:14). "I am not an Indian and I have never been an Indian. It is true that I once thought I was an Indian. I used to believe in race because it believed in me. In those days I thought that race came from somewhere in my genes" (Echo-Hawk 2007a:6). "We weren't always Pawnee Indians. Our ancestors didn't have race. They weren't Indians" (2007a:5). He states, "Practitioners of federal Indian law assume that the political status of Indian tribes is a matter of historical sovereignty, not a matter of race. There is a historical truth here, of course, but it is impossible to reasonably define 'Indian tribe' without reference to race" (2007a:112). He points out that Texas could enter the federal union as a state, "but this option was never available to racially defined Indian tribes.

Unlike states, Indian tribes would be sovereigns that lacked representation in the US federal system" (Echo-Hawk 2007b:3).

Legal scholar Robert A. Williams Jr. (2005:23), a Lumbee, concurs, explaining that racism in jurisprudence rests on the principle of stare decisis, "to stand by" judicial decisions based on precedent decisions. While in 1790 when the commerce clause in the Constitution referred to Indian nations that in realpolitik were unquestionably territorial sovereign nations with their own soldiers ("warriors"), by the time of Justice John Marshall's 1823 ruling in *Johnson v. M'Intosh*, the United States' success in the War of 1812 and its breaching of the Appalachian divide between Indian nations and colonists changed the balance of power east of the Mississippi. Jefferson's language in the Declaration of Independence, that his First Nations neighbors were "merciless savages," could be reinforced by Marshall writing that "the tribes of Indians inhabiting this country were fierce savages, whose occupation was war, and whose subsistence was drawn chiefly from the forest" (quoted in Williams 2005:54). Similarly racist in the two subsequent landmark cases in the trilogy, Marshall ignored the fact that the Cherokee Nation opposed to the State of Georgia's takeover had numerous prosperous farms and plantations, earning it the sobriquet "Civilized Tribe." By enshrining Indian law in Jefferson and Marshall's racist stereotype, under stare decisis the courts would again and again affirm that Indian people are "in need of pupilage" imposed by the European-descended colonial power (Williams 2005:61).

Felix Cohen addressed racism in the *Handbook*:

> Clear thinking on the subject has been sacrificed in the effort to find ambiguous terms which will permit us, by appropriate juggling, to maintain three basic propositions:
>
>> (1) that Indians are human beings;
>> (2) that all human beings are created equal, with certain inalienable rights; and
>> (3) that Indians are an "inferior" class not entitled to these "inalienable rights." (1942:152)

A recent affirmation of the racist divide between the United States and its Indians came in *United States v. Lara* (2004), the Supreme Court ruling that Indian tribes had criminal jurisdiction over all Indians on their reservations, whether or not the Indian in question was a member of the tribe exercising jurisdiction over the alleged crime. The Court deliberately did not discuss whether nonmember Indians, who since 1924 would be US citizens, could appeal their cases to the US Constitution's equal protection and due process clauses (Williams 2005:156). In 2001, in *Nevada v. Hicks*, the Court had upheld the legality of a non-Indian state officer trespassing on the Fallon Paiute-Shoshone Reservation in search of evidence that Hicks, a tribal member, had killed an animal on the federal endangered species list. The Fallon tribal police and court might exercise jurisdiction over Indians, Paiute, Shoshone, or others, but were adjudicated powerless over a trespassing State of Nevada non-Indian (Williams 2005:138–41).

Collier's Indian congresses, the NCAI, and particularly the American Indian Chicago Conference fostered pan-Indianism, a consciousness that in Anglo America, "Indians" form a caste determined by birth. Privileges and restrictions different from those of other US and Canadian citizens unite Indians in common causes. Seeing hundreds of articulate, sophisticated Indians in these meetings encouraged them to organize to work in tandem. In numbers there is strength. Disparate histories and customs could be submerged under the banner of Indian Country. Pan-Indianism is also furthered by the many marriages between men and women enrolled in different tribes, giving their children multiple First Nation affiliations. Intermarriage and even fostering of children to strengthen international friendships occurred before European invasions, were prodded by displacements and alliances against colonial encroachment, were encouraged in the Indian residential schools, and facilitated among Indians in cities, where pan-Indian powwows and celebrations take the place of older First Nations' various rituals and gatherings.

An unanticipated effect of pan-Indian public activism, beginning in the 1960s and peaking in the 1970s, has been renewed efforts by eastern nations to assert their continued existence. Generally without treaties because they were invaded and their displacement negotiated a century or more before the establishment of the United States, smaller nations became local communities marginalized by the dominant settlers. Intermarriage with Euro-Americans and African-Americans was reflected in physical appearance, enabling some descendants to pass as whites and subjecting others (sometimes in the same family) to discrimination as "colored." At the same time, the Indian communities, especially in the South, fought against being lumped with blacks under Jim Crow segregation. The United South and Eastern Tribes, founded in 1969 by the Eastern Band of Cherokees, Mississippi Band of Choctaws, and Miccosukee and Seminole Tribes of Florida, and the Coalition of Eastern Native Americans, founded in 1972 under guidance from the Native American Rights Fund work with some eastern and southern communities for federal recognition, and with member tribes toward political and economic strength.

The upsurge in Indian visibility during the activist 1970s, coupled with the potential unleashed by the 1975 Indian Self-Determination Act, prompted greater efforts by federally unrecognized Indian communities to gain official status. To handle these claims, the OIA in 1978 created a Branch of Acknowledgment and Research (BAR). A study of federal recognition petitions in the era of casinos states that the BAR staff endeavors to be guided by "the so-called Cohen Criteria, in use informally since Felix Cohen's tenure at the BIA" (Cramer 2005:37; she refers to Section 19 of the IRA, defining "Indian" through membership in a tribe, descent from a member, or one-half or more blood quantum). Claimants could alternately petition Congress for acknowledgment, obviously a procedure steeped in politics (Cramer 2005:45). Federal acknowledgment became contentious when Indian casinos sprouted in the 1980s. Both of the largest Indian casinos, the Mashantucket Pequots' Foxwoods and the nearby Mohegan Sun, are run by initially small, federally unrecognized Indian communities in eastern Connecticut. African ancestry evident in some of the Pequots has been targeted as indication of fraudulent claims to being Indian in order to get rich quick (Eisler 2000:153, 236).

"Tribes," not individual persons, are officially recognized as Indian by the federal government. A person must show genealogical descent from someone documented as a member of a "nation, tribe, or band . . . regarded as an Indian entity" (*Dobbs v. United States* 1898). The Court of Claims in 1898 ruled that treaties would be the principal means of establishing that a group is "an Indian entity." If there was no treaty, "officers of the Government whose duty it was to deal with and report the condition of Indians to the executive branch" might be held to have documented "an Indian entity." Where a recognized Indian "tribe or band" subdivided, the divisions could be accepted as Indian entities (Strickland et al. 1982:11) (figure 10.2, the Winnebago moved to Nebraska subdivided from Hochunk [Winnebago] in Wisconsin homeland). Soon after *Dobbs*, the Supreme Court declared in *Montoya v. United States* (1901), that a tribe is "a body of Indians of the same or similar race, united in a community under one leadership or government, and inhabiting a particular though sometimes ill-defined territory," while a "band" is usually an offshoot of a tribe acting independently under its own leadership (Strickland et al. 1982:11). Between *Dobbs* and *Montoya*, "nation" was elided from legal definition of "an Indian entity." "Tribe" is the term preferred: it connotes a lesser sovereignty than "nation."

Figure 10.2. Winnebago Agency, Nebraska, 1935, Indians gathered with Felix and Lucy Cohen. (1) Mr. Alfred (farm agent, Omaha). (3) Superintendent Parker. (5) Henry Roe Cloud (Winnebago, noted educator, first Yale Indian graduate, 1910). (6) Mrs. Merrick (land clerk). (7) Frank Beaver, chairman, Winnebago Council. (8) Felix Cohen (back row). (9) Ed Cline, former chairman, Omaha Council. (10) Lucy Kramer Cohen (front row, center). (11) Fred H. Daiker. (13) Lillian. (14) Elwood Harlan, chairman, Omaha Council. (15) Joe Penuska, chairman, Ponca Council. (16) Isaak Red Owl, Santee. (17) Joe Jennings. (18) Dave Frazer, chairman, Santee Council. (19) Mr. Brewer, farm agent, Niobara. Photo from Yale Collection of Western Americana, Beinecke Rare Book and Manuscript Library. Photo and identifications by Charlotte Tuttle Walkup.

Morton Fried, an anthropologist who was a CCNY graduate a genera-tion younger than Felix Cohen, critiqued the term "tribe" in 1975, when the Indian Claims Commission had raised the issue of recognizing tribes. Fried surveyed historical and anthropological examples of the term's us-age. Whether referring to the "tribes" beyond the borders of the Roman and Chinese empires, those of sub-Saharan Africa, or those of North America, "tribes" invariably existed in conjunction with states. Fried's con-clusion was unequivocal: "tribe [is] a secondary sociopolitical phenome-non, brought about by the intercession of more complexly ordered socie-ties, states in particular" (1975:114). Used by the interceding state to label those it was subjugating, the term "tribe" has a "pejorative shading" (Fried 1975:7), as does "chiefdom," an academic word used for "tribes" (Kehoe

1998:182–84). A. L. Kroeber remarked, in one of the first issues of the journal *Ethnohistory*, "The more we review aboriginal America, the less certain [is] . . . our usual conventional concept of tribe; and the more largely does this concept appear to be a White man's creation of convenience for talking about Indians, negotiating with them, administering them—and finally impressed upon their own thinking by our sheer weight" (1955:313). Realizing this, we can see how "nation" came to be elided when Americans talked about their territorial predecessors. Federal recognition of Indian tribes remains a colonial encroachment upon the continent's First Nations (Bruyneel 2012).

Cohen had worked his way through the accumulation of cases and legislation pertaining to Indians in the United States, arriving at the Secretary of the Interior's November 1935, Indian Law and Order Regulations: "For the purpose of the enforcement of the regulations . . . an Indian shall be deemed to be any person of Indian descent who is a member of any recognized Indian tribe now under Federal jurisdiction." That means, wrote Cohen, "in dealing with Indians the Federal Government is dealing primarily not with a particular race as such but with members of certain social-political groups toward which the Federal Government has assumed special responsibilities" (1942:5). In light of the United States' "basic proposition" he listed on page 152, that Indians are an "inferior race," this is a bold, Boasian coup against Americans' prevailing equation of Indian status with "race."

The *Handbook* notwithstanding, "blood quantum" continues to be the sine qua non of Indian status. Tribes have the power to set membership criteria, but they tend to base it on percentage of "Indian blood," a European concept at odds with most First Nations' willingness, in the past, to accept refugees (e.g., the Tewa among the Hopi) and to allow young men or families from other nations to reside in their communities (Sharrock 1974). A century ago, Franz Boas declared, in his iconoclastic *Mind of Primitive Man*, that "an attempt to correlate the numerous classifications that have been proposed shows clearly a condition of utter confusion and contradiction; so that we are led to the conclusion that type ["race"], language, and type of culture, may not be closely and permanently connected" (1911:127). That statement highlights the question of what enrollment in a federally recognized tribe is supposed to signify. Heirship of property documented in a treaty? Genealogy provides the evidence for this, and it is inappropriate to say "blood quantum" when what is meant is the number of forebears documented in a treaty-derived entity. Sovereignty is derived from treaties, legally inheres through treaty statuses, and is dependent in the final analysis upon European constructions of admissible statuses and enforceable rights.

Cultures and Sovereignties

American First Nations are in jeopardy of losing their cultures and languages, because they have no reservoirs, as it were, in overseas continents. If an American language is no longer spoken, if a ritual is abandoned and its details forgotten, if ecological knowledge is no longer actively practiced, if a worldview is replaced by conventional Western mythology and metaphysics, then they are likely lost forever. Reconstructions based on classic ethnographies and the memories of elders generations removed from preconquest independent nations may serve to revitalize a sense of nation. In turn, culture can be proferred to assert sovereignty (Frank and Goldberg 2010:introduction).

Looking to culture to distinguish contemporary Indians from other Americans ignores that performing culture is voluntary, contrasted with birth legal status as US and tribal citizen. Reenactors carefully perform obsolete tasks in public view, a popular hobby, without thereby becoming heirs of the people they imitate. Conversely, if horse nomadism was the foundation of historic Plains Indian culture, living a sedentary life without a horse does not disqualify a twenty-first-century descendant from claiming to be Blackfoot or Lakota—although as icons of traditional wealth, it may explain the ubiquity of horses on the landscapes of Plains reservations (Wissler and Kehoe 2012:221). Displaying a culture in a museum and doing performances make an ethnicity tangible. They further support claims under NAGPRA and the sovereignty that implies.[4] It also makes imitation easy.

Tribal museums in the United States range from local community centers housed in preserved historic buildings to the large exhibit and research museum the Mashantucket Pequots built with Foxwoods Casino profits, to the National Museum of the American Indian on the Mall in Washington, DC, with its series of alcoves crammed with particular First Nations artifacts and nuggets of history. Disconcertingly, facing the wall of small alcoves is a massive center display case of the guns that won the West—and not for the Indians. Each alcove was prepared in consultation with representatives of the tribe portrayed, meaning each became a compromise between what the tribal representatives wanted shown and what was feasible in the space and nonconfrontational to the public. The Canadian

Museum of Civilizations across the river from Ottawa is another take on displaying First Nations, in this case in a very large hall entered from a high glass-walled lobby with totem poles. Exhibits in the First Nations section run curvilinearily with waist-high cases of text and artifacts in front of murals and wall-mounted objects. Testimonies from contemporary First Nations citizens are embedded, making clear the continued existence of these nations within the Canadian mosaic. The Canadian Museum of Civilizations housing under one roof displays of all the country's principal ethnic groups in a real mosaic, contrasts with the United States' policy of separating its Indian tribes from its National Museum of American History "devoted to the scientific, cultural, social, technological, and political development of the United States" and memorialized in George Washington's army uniform, the flag that inspired Francis Scott Key's anthem, Jefferson's lap desk, and "Dorothy's" ruby slippers worn in *The Wizard of Oz*.[5] Older exhibits of American First Nations artifacts remain on view in the Museum of Natural History, along with the beasts, plants, and rocks of the continent.

Illustrative of embedded conflicts faced by federally funded museums is the Museum of the Plains Indian in Browning, Montana, in the agency town of the Blackfeet Reservation. Built by Works Progress Administration funds during the Depression and operated by the Indian Arts and Crafts Board, this nice brick two-story building with attached cottage for a curator originally had a lobby featuring murals by Blackfeet artist Victor Pepion somewhat in the style of painted bison robes. A hall to the visitor's right is U-shaped, routing visitors past dozens of wall cases exhibiting fine examples of mostly Blackfoot articles, from a children's sled made of bison ribs to an exquisite small quill-embroidered tobacco case. The majority of this collection was donated by Louis Hill of the Great Northern Railway, operator of luxury hotels in Glacier National Park, which was cut out of the reservation's western strip. Opposite this wing in the museum is one with several rooms in which were miniature dioramas prepared by Smithsonian Institution craftsmen in Washington under the direction of the museum's first director, John C. Ewers, a Yale PhD in anthropology. The third wing, opposite the entrance, held a large shop affiliated with the Blackfeet Arts and Crafts Association.

After the 1960s, it became difficult to attract a qualified museum director to this remote stepchild of the Department of the Interior. A local Blackfeet caretaker curator oversaw the building and its contents for years, annually begging Montana's congressional representatives to intervene to keep funding for basic operations. Finally, at the turn of the twenty-first century, this person retired and was replaced by a local Blackfeet artist who brought in exhibits of Indian artists' work and wanted to promote the museum to tourists journeying to nearby Glacier National Park. A retired anthropologist experienced in museum management agreed to form a Friends of the Museum of the Plains Indian nonprofit, reaching out for local, state, and national funding and to the Blackfeet Tribe. For the tribe to take over the museum was not economically possible; its small casino in a state that allows non-Indian casinos to proliferate could not provide for that. The tribe did take over a large wooden building near the museum that had been built as a wildlife museum by a prominent, non-Indian taxidermist and Western bronzes artist. It renovated this building to showcase and sell Indian art and jewelry, the museum shop having long ago moved into a smaller room to leave the larger hall for showing videos. There would seem no point in the tribe undertaking its own museum of Amskapi Pikuni (Montana Blackfeet) culture when the federal government maintains the Museum of the Plains Indian, predominantly Blackfoot, on the reservation by the main highway junction. Yet from its beginning as a federal regional museum, the Museum of the Plains Indian does not, and cannot, identify with the Blackfeet Tribe exclusively, nor can it be dictated to by the Tribal Business Council or any other tribal agency. The separation is maintained on the ground with the museum on one side of its parking lot and the tribe's fenced powwow grounds, ritual arbor, and a historic former OIA agency log building, on the other side of the parking lot. Adjacent on another side is the tribe's casino and racetrack. These are under tribal sovereignty, while the museum with its cultural displays is not.

Along with revisionism in historical pictures of America's past, and postmodernism's insistence on soul-searching reflection upon one's biases, NAGPRA pushed museums to balance displays of settler achievements with testimonies to First Nations' and African-Americans' active roles in US history. Historian Patricia Galloway recounts the Mississippi state historial society museum's unprecedented outreach to representatives of the latter two constituencies, as well as descendant French and Spanish communities, in its 1990s revamping of exhibits for the period 1500–1800. To the surprise of the professionals, she reports, the contacted communities eagerly participated in planning and offered videos and objects for display. Visitors now can hear Chickasaw, Choctaw, and Tunica spoken in videos, in addition to local French, Spanish, and English. They must realize that Indians have not vanished. Galloway (2006:377–87) writes of the interplay of the First Nations, Europeans, and Africans in the colonial period, presented as three groups engaged in living in what became the territory of Mississippi, these more dynamic stories replacing the earlier museum exhibits extolling the triumphs of the Europeans. Mississippi's state museum displays half a dozen "cultural sovereignties" coexisting within the sovereignties of the state and federal governments.

Chickasaw museums as signs of sovereignty are the focus of an innovative study by Joshua Gorman (2011). History here tells that the Chickasaw Nation officially ceased to exist, in the view of the United States, in 1907 when Oklahoma became a state. Chickasaws are one of the Five Civilized Tribes of the Southeast, along with Cherokee, Creek, Choctaw, and Seminole, so called on account of their relatively large town-based populations dependent on agriculture. Traders who married into the nations assisted in organizing opposition to Anglo colonizing. Literacy, including literacy in their own syllabary among the Cherokee, was common, with formal governmental structure written in documents. In 1837, the Chickasaw Nation living in northern Mississippi sold—not ceded—their homeland to the United States, placing the sale money into a trust to be used to pay for their removal from Mississippi to new national territory in Oklahoma, purchased from the Choctaw Nation that had already settled there.

After a decade of adjustment, with some Chickasaws building commercial agricultural enterprises and others depending on subsistence farming, the Chickasaws negotiated political independence from the Choctaw Nation, accepted in 1855 by the United States. A log cabin council house was soon superseded by a brick building, and eventually by a granite courthouse. In spite of Oklahoma statehood in 1907 legally dissolving the Chickasaw Nation within the state, Chickasaws continued to recognize their own governor of the Chickasaw Nation and a council. A 1990s exhibit label for a restored original log council house states, "From this small Council House came the reemergence of our sovereign nation" (Gorman 2011:62). Chickasaws in Oklahoma, along with their relatives in Mississippi whose forebears resisted removal in 1837, in the 1990s used the authority assumed in state historical society museums to publicly assert sovereign status and insist it had been unbroken from precontact times. Casino profits underwrote new exhibits in the Council House Museum and Chickasaw Cultural Center and, by 2010, a third Chickasaw culture museum called Hayochi ("Discover") was established where the labels are bilingual—Chickasaw first followed by English—and details of the Chickasaw nation's history is left out, to present to visitors a timeless Chickasaw culture, a national essence, "an expression of sovereignty" (Gorman 2011:159).

Who Can Be an Indian?

Felix Cohen worked to restore to Indian people the power of their fore-bears to act independently of the conquering invader. He was impelled not by Indian ancestry but by the mitzvah inherent in his own heritage, in the words of Rabbi Hillel (see Buxbaum 1994) two thousand years ago:

> If I am not for myself, who will be for me?
> If I am not for others, what am I?
> And if not now, when?

Secular Jew though he was, proudly a modern American, Felix was very aware of the Zionist movement identifying his people with the land they had removed from, still named in their prayers. The question of who is a Jew was, and is, much debated. Hitler used the one-drop-of-blood racist rule that still tends to be popularly accepted in the United States. Countering the "biological" definition that ignores actual genomes is the argument that the culture in which one is raised makes one a Jew, or an Indian.

Section 16 of the IRA aimed at the "tribe," not "Indians," stating that "any Indian tribe, or tribes, residing on the same reservation" could "organize for its common welfare," and ratification of a constitution and bylaws required majority vote of "the adult members of the tribe, or of the adult Indians residing on such reservation." Collier's crusade was to reverse the dissolution of tribal lands, by which he meant Indian lands, his vision essentializing "the Indian" as a "tribal person" betrayed by American land grabbing. The IRA wording exposed the issue of which should predominate, the physical community in a designated place, or the kin community that includes dispersed members. Tribal membership rules came to embrace dispersed kin, inevitably as populations outgrew reservation resources. In turn, that meant that some enrolled tribal members who were raised off the reservation were ignorant of their heritage and the contemporary culture practiced on their tribe's reservation. One might term them "secular Indians."

Annual tribal powwows proliferated after World War II as a kind of family reunion, a weekend to bring in dispersed families to see their homeland again and participate in cultural events. Being social affairs, tribal powwows don't check ID cards to see who's enrolled, while at the same time, people ask, "Who are you related to?," informally identifying tribespeople. Great numbers of Americans who are Indian may in this way resolve the technical problem of being related through parents and grandparents to more than one tribe, not uncommonly to four or five tribes, plus Europeans. Those who do live on the reservation maintain a local government similar to a municipality. On the fringe of being Indian are those who casually mention Indian ancestry without attending to any Indian community. Harvard Law School professor Elizabeth Warren, while running for the Senate in 2012, said she had let the law school identify her as Indian when it was attempting to prove it was diversifying its faculty. Her alleged, single Indian forebear is a Cherokee great-great-great-grandmother, quite plausible for a family in her home state of Oklahoma.

Felix and Lucy didn't spend much time discussing in what way were they Jews. Overt anti-Semitism took care of defining them. Experiencing this outsiders' designation of their "race" heightened Felix's sophistication in constructing federal Indian law. He deeply understood that federal law must be the instrument to free Indian citizens from unjust denial of their inalienable rights. Fortunately for First Nations, Felix Cohen was a legal realist who saw beyond stare decisis, and a brilliant rhetorician who could write the *Handbook* convincingly establishing their inherent sovereignties recognized in treaties.

CHAPTER ELEVEN

Jewish Science, Philosophy, and Jurisprudence

Hitler famously damned "Jewish science." His goal of eliminating Jewish scientists drove out many of Germany's best, including Einstein. What nonsense. How can theoretical physics be "Jewish"? Or is there something in growing up Jewish that fosters talent in science? Maybe just intellectual talent?

A simple answer is that spending all day every weekday indoors in school, *cheder* or secular, instead of roughhousing outdoors, fostered intellectualism. The heroes of Jewish boys were the great rabbis of the Talmud. In America, Jewish boys like Morris Cohen were in school and working indoors after school. Their limited exercise was walking to school and work and games of stickball on the street. Morris confided to his scraps-of-paper diary on June 6, 1897, "I would like to go out and play ball with the gang but M[amma] would not allow me to go away on Sunday." He continued, "If I treat myself in the right way I could develop myself into a genius. To my opinion the mind is the most (pliable should I call it) easily worked on by everyday influences." The next Sunday he wondered, "I don't know whether I should continue to delight in books and theories or try and turn practical" (Rosenfield 1962:13). His niggling, in his private diary, over a phrase, "easily worked on" or "pliable," sounds like the rabbis niggling over each word in Scripture and then over each other's opinions.

Rabbi Geoffrey Mitelman (2011) explained, in his online blog, this Judaic culture:

Judaism as it is practiced today is not biblical, it's rabbinic. . . . The Rabbis [read] . . . through the lenses of fairness, of common sense, of other verses in the Torah, and of the best legal knowledge they had at that time. . . . [The Bible is] a source of study and exploration for the questions of our time. The point of the creation story is really to challenge us with questions like, "How should we treat people if everyone is created in the image of God? What are our responsibilities to this world if God has called it 'good'?" . . . The Rabbis always had to explain their reasoning. And if there was a choice between believing something because of a divine miracle or believing something because of thoughtful and reasoned arguments, there was no question which one the Rabbis would accept—reason and logic would always win. . . . Critical thinking, an essential aspect of science, is deeply rooted in Jewish tradition.

Rabbi Mitelman concludes, "Judaism is about how we act to improve this world, here and now."

In marked contrast to Jewish tradition, America's Boston Brahmins, led by their Unitarian clergy, highly valued "mental calm. . . . For them, difficulties might be ignored; doubts were waste of thought. . . . Dogma, metaphysics, and abstract philosophy were not worth knowing" (Adams 1918:34–35; see Lears 1981:288–90 for discussion). At the beginning of the twentieth century, deviants from this bloodless calm could be found among WASPs in Chicago, New York, and even Harvard. Morris Cohen met William James, Josiah Royce, and Charles Peirce there, men who would not abide by canons of gentility. John Dewey moved from Chicago to Columbia University, working on pragmatism that would materialize in Chicago's Laboratory School for children and New York's New School for Social Research. These men could engage with Morris in the life of the mind. Much of his discourse seemed adversarial (Hollinger 1975:89); perhaps it was more rabbinic, in that Morris insisted personal feelings and psychological factors should be divorced from a cutthroat logic aimed to expose falsity (Klingenstein 1998:73, 77–78).

During the New Deal heyday of employing Jews in government, *Time* magazine carried this under the heading "Science":

Abraham Aron Roback, thoughtful and erudite Jewish psychology professor at Boston's Institute of Advertising, onetime instructor at Harvard. To the current issue of Character and Personality Dr. Roback contributed a report on characteristics of Jewish habits of thought and modes of expression. "Paradoxical though it be," says Dr. Roback, "most of the major Jewish philosophers of the present day are not willing to own up to any Jewish influence." Henri Bergson stoutly denied that either his style or his ideas revealed any Semitic traits. Lucien Levy-Bruhl, distinguished anthropologist, thought his work was typically French. But the question, Dr. Roback thought, was not likely to be settled by comparing the work of known authors. He hit on the idea of trying to sort Jews from non-Jews in the writings of unknown persons. Accordingly he persuaded a colleague to let him have sixty-four examination papers, with names removed, from psychology classes at Harvard and Radcliffe. On forty-three of these papers he correctly spotted the students as Jewish or non-Jewish. In twenty-one cases he missed. A mathematician showed him that the probability of this performance having resulted from pure chance was only 3 in 1,000.

Dr. Roback concluded that, in written examinations, Jewish students:

Generally chose, where an option was permitted, broad historical topics in preference to technical and restricted questions.

Were more "expansive" (not necessarily more verbose), more prone to illustrate from personal experience, less matter-of-fact.

Were more likely to intrude personal points of view.

Had more flexibility or elasticity of style.

Wrote simpler and more legible hands. (*Time* 26(14):39, September 30, 1935)

Morris Cohen's writings somewhat reflect these tendencies (except that his handwriting was hard to decipher). While adhering to standards of objective tone, his publications are less narrowly technical than many from other philosophers. Morris Cohen cared passionately about grand broad topics, the meaning of existence, dedication to truth, justice.

Would Roback have spotted Felix as a Jew? Probably. Felix's legal training on top of his philosophy degree masked the personal point of view in his writings. Other than that, he, too, had these tendencies. Underlying Roback's characterization of Jewish psychology students' writing is what may be termed a humanities outlook, contrasting to a technician's. Scholars in the yeshivas might seem to be niggling over tiny esoteric points, but cosmology was their real concern. When a bar mitzvah boy came to the Torah, he touched the embodiment of the cosmos. And there was no rigid hierarchy in Judaism. Every boy should be bar mitzvah and from that day could take full part in worship. Morris's father did so daily. Morris and

Felix, nonbelievers in Jewish (or any) theological doctrine, were in every sense humanitarians. That deep engagement with the human world did have its roots in Judaism (Tsuk 2001:209; Gimbel 2012:168).

Jurisprudence

> Keep ye justice, and do righteousness. Happy is the man that doeth this. (Isaiah 56:1)

Writing about Charles Peirce and his influence, philosopher Roberta Kevelson remarked, "Morris Cohen saw his self-appointed mission of relating philosophical pragmatism to an evolving, open-ended legal dynamics as a privilege to which he devoted most of his life" (1996:88). It will be recalled that Morris compiled and edited Peirce's papers after his death (chapter 4). To be just is a compelling mitzvah. Both Cohens, father and son, made justice central to their lives, searching to understand and to do it (figure 11.1). Jurisprudence is the real-world domain where justice is pursued. The Cohens' quest focused on the principle of legal realism, that law is not a collection of fossils but living in society, malleable, adapting, yet somehow

Figure 11.1. Morris and Felix Cohen at a mountain lake. Photo from Felix S. and Lucy Kramer Cohen Photograph Collection.

compatible with ideals of mercy and justice. In "Jews and Legal Realists," Morton Horwitz summed up the realists' goal, "to combine a pre-modern, prophetic and essentialist moralistic passion for social justice with a critical modernist sense of the socially constructed character of social categories and institutions" (unpublished manuscript quoted by Tsuk Mitchell 2007:47).

Felix carried on the quest through a series of major articles on legal realism and ethics and law. As of February 2012, his article "Transcendental Nonsense and the Functional Approach" (1935), had been cited 1,743 times in scholarly publications, and other articles a total of 1,983 times, two having more than 300 citations.[1] Agreeing with his father that the scientific method, *sensu lato*, should lead jurists into distinguishing custom from principle, Felix pursued the use of the functionalist approach in the social sciences during the 1930s. It helped that one of his professors at Columbia Law School, Karl Llewellyn, led legal realists in comparing legal systems, culminating in *The Cheyenne Way*, coauthored with anthropologist E. Adamson Hoebel. Llewellyn's efforts echo Felix's 1934 statement, "The moral basis of law is not a set of moral dogmas but a method of testing all legal doctrines in terms of their effects upon human life. . . . Law is a social tool" (Cohen 1934:29, 30).

"Their effects upon human life" suggests an empirical, scientific method for understanding how law develops and how laws could be evaluated for practical, social, and for moral considerations. Along with Felix's youthful vision was his father's flow of critiques. A professor of philosophy and law at Duke University said, more than thirty years after his death, that Morris's "work . . . was much admired by Holmes, [Roscoe] Pound, and Cardozo. Cohen's articles are scholarly, deep, and acute; they range over the entire field; and he was a masterful, if sometimes overly harsh, critic. In my opinion these articles are still worth reading. . . . Principles and maxims, he showed, often mask unanalyzed philosophical assumptions about economics and political order" (Golding 1980:464). Jews in an era of arrant anti-Semitism were well aware of legal opinions' masking power, gentleman's agreements, as it were.

Pragmatic functionalism contrasted with judgments of elegance and logic that judges and lawyers reveled in. "Justice, thus conceived as something apart from the concrete values of human life, becomes a special type of beauty [*elegantia juris*]. . . . The false slant which this craftsman's approach gives to much legal thinking can be removed only by a more conscious sense of the diverse human values which impinge upon any legal case" (Cohen 1934:30–31). Having thus disposed of the seduction of a well-crafted legal opinion, Felix zeroes in on Blackstone, whose *Commentaries on the Laws of England* (1765–1769) served as the ultimate reference to English common law. Blackstone, according to Felix, mixed the unconformable opinions of Hobbes and Coke on the source of law: "Hobbes, the grandfather of realistic jurisprudence, . . . a tough-minded cynic," saw law to be the dictates of the power vested in a state by citizens desiring security from unrestrained violence, while Edward Coke's *Institutes of the Lawes of England* (1628–1644) taught that law is "the perfection of reason, . . . commanding what is right and prohibiting what is wrong" (Cohen 1935:63–64; see Boorstin 1941, another American Jew with a similar opinion on Blackstone; Boorstin's father assisted in the legal defense of Leo Frank). Grandson of families driven to emigrate by a czar's unjust laws, Felix could not espouse Brahmins' rosy belief that law dispassionately strives toward perfect reason. His whole experience, and Ashkenazi heritage, drove him to Hobbes's cynicism and a well-founded fear of the power of the state.

After his years of government service, in 1949, Felix could see that words made for intractable problems in justice. "Double-talk is not always a sign of hypocrisy. Probably the easiest way of maintaining consistency in our principles is to have a second-string substitute vocabulary to use in describing any facts that do not fit into the vocabulary of our professed principles" (F. Cohen 1949:308). "Indian self-government" was the principle that provoked him. He recalled, "when we were helping Indians draft the constitutions and charters which were supposed to be the vehicles of self-government under the Wheeler-Howard Act, all of the Indian Bureau officials were very strongly in favor of self-government, and in favor of allowing all tribes to exercise to the full extent their inherent legal rights" (F. Cohen 1949:309). When push came to shove, letting duly constituted tribal councils control reservation land management, policing, schools, and so on, each bureau division protested that its expert knowledge had to override self-government. Superintendents on the reservations similarly declared that they could not jeopardize their wards by allowing tribal councils freedom to govern. To a lawyer, it was especially troubling that the Commissioner of Indian Affairs and many superintendents insisted tribes must not independently hire attorneys. Their double-talk about "liberty," to the effect, "Mine I will defend to the death—I am American! But of course the red men don't understand, aren't competent," disgusted him. Indian Affairs highlighted the "perennial conflict between democratic self-government and the various modern forms of aristocracy, or government by experts. . . . We have a vital concern with Indian self-government because the Indian is to America what the Jew was to the Russian Czars and Hitler's Germany" (F. Cohen 1949:313; the next sentence is the often-quoted "the Indian tribe is the miners' canary").

Tough-minded cynic was the stance Morris Cohen adopted in class, forcing his students to realize how much they took on faith. Felix saw his father batter double-talk, hammering at word substitutions masking injustice. He also directly witnessed the deep respect Morris enjoyed from leading philosophers, legal scholars, and jurists, notably including Supreme Court justices Holmes, Cardozo, Brandeis, and Frankfurter.

Felix was no clone of his father. He saw himself as a lawyer and Morris, as he himself realized already in adolescence, was a teacher (Rosenfield 1962:15). Felix's Harvard dissertation, "Ethical Systems and Legal Ideals," addressed the hard question of unmasking judicial decisions. Moving on quickly to "Ethics for Lawyers and Judges" (in "Modern Ethics and the Law," 1934), he opened his essay, "The term 'ethics' to many lawyers and judges, carries the flavor of a trade code. The precepts of 'legal ethics,' like the precepts of those moral codes drawn up, from time to time, by dentists or real estate dealers, treat of the common questions that arise in the course of a tradesman's dealings" (Cohen 1934:17). Ouch! It gets worse:

> Judges want their conduct to be free not only from their own doubts, but also from the doubts of others. . . . The slot machine doctrine of the judge's function, which teaches that judgments emerge from judges as gum comes forth from a vending machine, implies that a judge's beliefs about ethics have nothing to do with his work on the bench. . . . There is no use in kicking at a slot machine. Complaints must be referred to the owners . . . the proper law making bodies of state or nation or . . . to the Founding Fathers. (Cohen 1934:18–19)

Becoming more serious in tone toward the end of his next major article, Felix makes his functionalist statement: "A truly realistic theory of judicial decisions must conceive every decision as something more than an expression of individual personality, as concomitantly and even more importantly a function of social forces, that is to say, as a product of social determinants and an index of social consequences. A judicial decision is a social event . . . an intersection of social forces" (Cohen 1935:70–71). Felix concludes, "It is through the union of objective legal science and a critical theory of social values that our understanding of the human significance of law will be enriched" (Cohen 1934:76).

Scientific Method for Understanding Law

To the ordinary citizen, urging the use of scientific method to study juris-prudence and the functions of law is a strange notion. Doesn't law belong in the humanities, and science to physical things? Both Cohens reiterate over and over in many writings that laws and judicial decisions are observ-able things. They can be collected, classified, dissected. Roscoe Pound, dean of Harvard Law School, friend of Frankfurter and interlocutor of the Cohens, interestingly took all three of his degrees in botany, from the University of Nebraska. The things of law and governance are phenomena for which, once a field of inquiry is demarcated, a logic of relationships can be constructed and tested against additional phenomena. Cohen père ex-plicated how logic should be employed in scientifically studying social phenomena; Cohen fils insisted, "the tracing of consequences of conduct is a proper domain of science. . . . Observations are subject to correction and refinement as we learn how to separate what is actually perceived from the conceptual mass that the observer brings to the relation of obser-vation. . . . Our observations, in ethics as in physics, are fallible and cor-rectible" (Cohen 1946:402).

Historian Dorothy Ross (1991:396–400) places such a conviction, that social phenomena are amenable to science, in the crisis of liberalism in the twentieth century's second decade when conservative politics over-whelmed the Progressive Party and faith in progress fell under the horrors of world war. Ross's book deals with the professions of economics, political science, sociology, history, and the social sciences, concluding with their embrace of scientism. Anthropology and, not surprisingly, jurisprudence are omitted, the former likely because Boas in his lifetime guarded it from scientism, the latter because it was supposed to be, ideally, outside politics, economics, and history. Morris Cohen's continuing work on clarifying how, and why, the scientific method could and should extend to social phenomena responded to the great shift Ross describes from prewar opti-mism about progress to postwar disillusionment.

Felix Cohen thrust jurisprudence and governance into the newer mind-set, with a very important distinction. Those postwar American econo-mists, political scientists, sociologists, and historians examined by Ross re-acted to the cruel realities of their world by determining to discover, scientifically, the laws of human behavior and use the discoveries to con-trol it. In this they were bankrolled by the Rockefeller Foundation (Ross 1991:400–403; Berman 1983; Fisher 1993; Richardson and Fisher 1999).

It is truly chilling to read, over and over, the open announcement by Rockefeller grantees that they sought means to predict and control the behavior of Americans. As late as 1952, mainstream sociologist Bernard Barber published a popular book on scientific work on understanding and predicting "the social order," including within Germany and Russia. That predicting and controlling citizens' behavior is incompatible with democracy did not seem to occur to the enthusiasts for social science (Ross 1991:452–57). Felix found this repugnant. In "Modern Ethics and the Law," he says, "Dr. John B. Watson, who regards ethics as an outworn fetish, offers us, in the name of science, many moral rules as to how we ought to bring up our children." Watson's cold, sterile prescriptions for babies, Felix says, "do not *describe* human conduct, but rather *prescribe* moral rules as to how we ought to behave. . . . The law faces ethics in a hundred guises when it deals with any of the current problems of the social order" (Cohen 1934:23–24, emphasis in original).

Clearly, the Cohens realized that popular acceptance of a sort of Platonic ideal of philosopher-kings, now to be scientist-kings, manipulating humankind was naïve, sure to fail in discovering those laws of behavior it needed. Rockefeller millions could not buy, in America, the overt fascist control displayed in Nazi Germany, Stalinist Russia, or Mussolini's Italy. Democracy here was far more imperiled by racism and capitalist greed, embedded in American laws, jurisprudence, and politics. Morris's orientation toward a realistic appraisal of the doable guided his students, such as Nathan Margold, as well as his son. Margold's strategy paper for the NAACP, prepared before he left for his Interior position, called for unceasing legal challenges to inequality of education for African-Americans, a strategy taken up, with some narrowing toward the most vulnerable targets, postgraduate professional schools, by Charles Houston, Thurgood Marshall, and their associates. Ultimately, they won in 1954's *Brown v. Board of Education*. Thurgood Marshall was a year younger than Felix.

In hindsight, Rockefeller Foundation millions for WASP men to study how to predict and control the American people, fascist style, is shocking in a decade when lynchings were commonplace and Jim Crow kept African-Americans ignorant, impoverished, and in servitude. Rockefeller initially had, beginning in 1902, a fund to assist black people, primarily for manual training schools in the South, and the Laura Spelman Rockefeller Memorial of the 1920s sponsored research on African-American problems and interracial relations, but expenditures for African-Americans fizzled out after 1928 (Nielsen 1972:338–42). By contrast, Sears Roebuck magnate

Julius Rosenwald, from an immigrant Jewish family, created the Rosenwald Fund in 1910 to spend his millions to expose and combat segregation of African-Americans and the suffering it imposed upon them. Vastly richer, the Rockefeller Foundation with its WASP leaders was a strong conservative power, veiling the crying need to ameliorate suffering by its "transcendental nonsense" promotion of would-be scientist-rulers.

Against this background of favored elite control, the Cohens' persistence in their version of scientific study of social phenomena, specifically the laws and jurisprudence that directly impinged on millions of human lives, was marginal to America's hegemonic culture. Against the scientism touting statistics to reveal hidden truths about nature, societies, and behavior, the Cohens remained steadfast and sophisticated realists. Strikingly, many of Morris's associates compared him to Spinoza—the CCNY philosophy department chairman in 1911, Harry Overstreet, told Morris's daughter that when he reluctantly agreed to interview the "pushy Jew" teaching mathematics in CCNY's secondary school, "it suddenly flashed on me: *This was Spinoza sitting in front of me! I was to have Spinoza in my department!*" (Rosenfield 1962:93, emphasis in original). At Morris's 1947 memorial services, Columbia philosophy professor Irwin Edman recalled that "the philosophy that he admired above all was Spinoza's . . . and Morris Cohen himself exemplified in his point of view at once detachment and a passionate faith in reason" (quoted in Rosenfield 1962:167), qualities prominent in Spinoza's life and works. Spinoza, a man revered for his stainless moral character and a secular Jew, was a philosopher Morris Cohen wished to emulate. He was Albert Einstein's favorite philosopher, too (Gimbel 2012:27–28). Morris and Felix could model their scientific method and their commitment to ethical issues in law and governance on their honored Jewish predecessor.

Scientific method in the sense the Cohens used it is, in Felix's words, "to throw light upon the real meaning of legal rules by tracing their effects throughout the social order." Studies of effects of legal rules are scientific insofar as they do not "appraise or value these effects," for that is the task of ethics (Cohen 1934:27). "Effects [in] the social order" are observable; the observations are replicable; they can be amassed, classified in various ways, explanations inferred, and tested with further data. Like the Talmud and Midrash, scientific method applied to the study of law and jurisprudence engages real-world events, messy as they are and recalcitrant to neat final statements. WASP-dominated "social sciences," Dorothy Ross wrote, "desired 'a certain disengagement from the contemporary scene' and developed a taste for 'nonvulgar instruments' that displayed rigor, elegance, and special technique" (Ross 1991:176, quoting in part from George Stigler's 1972 book). *Elegantia juris* would be the legal criterion for rigor and elegance, the "craftsman's" goal that Felix denounced. Nonreligious as they were, the Cohens practiced Jewish science contrasted with the science of pallid rigor, engrossed with technique, distant from human suffering, carried on by many of their Gentile contemporaries and promoted by the Rockefeller Foundation in the 1930s.

Felix Cohen was imbued with the liberal Judaism of his parents, friends, and CCNY fellow alumni. Like them, he felt a mitzvah to do justice. Like them, he felt justice might best be realized through social democratic governance principles. The call from Nathan Margold to come to Washington in 1933 was an opportunity to fulfill a mitzvah. He and Lucy brought to Washington sharp and well-schooled minds, warm personalities that drew people to them, energy and gratification in work, and above all, passion for the true and just carried down through two millennia of rabbinic disputation. Felix and Lucy took their marching orders from Hillel: "If I am only for myself, then what am I? And if not now, when?"

CHAPTER TWELVE

The White Man, the Jew, and the Indian

Let us picture a small town near the border of a western reservation. A white man, a Jew, and an Indian walk into a bar. . . . The white man settles onto a stool, relaxed; it's his culture, his country, his solid right to be there. The Jew stands, uncertain—he doesn't usually go into small-town bars. The bartender too is uncertain—what do Jews drink? The Indian barely steps into the bar. The bartender's stare makes it clear that Indians aren't served there. There's an Indian bar on a back street.

Racism is ingrained into Anglo culture. Second-generation Jews' push into the professions undermined the nineteenth-century idea that Jews are a race. American born, well nourished, active outdoors, Jewish Americans were less distinctive than their immigrant parents. Still, they were outsiders, not routinely hired by the better law firms, discriminated against in medicine and universities. World War II broke down overt barriers against American Jews as they served in the armed forces alongside white Christians, while African-American troops were still segregated in Negro regiments. American Indians also served in white regiments, usually singled out by being called "Chief," a stereotype but not a derogatory one. Perhaps the postwar benefits given to the nation's defenders, the GI Bill and housing assistance in Levittowns, were the strongest forces against customary racism, moving millions of young adults out of the lower class. Elite colleges dropped their Jewish quotas and the new suburbs melted veterans' families into a mass-produced middle class. Jews among them joined Reform temples resembling large liberal Protestant churches. They became white folks, in anthropologist Karen Brodkin's (1998:2) felicitous phrase.

Philosopher Steven Gimbel (2012:211) sees the mid-twentieth-century secular Jew as an icon of modern cosmopolitanism. Albert Einstein, in Gimbel's view, exemplifed this, his rumpled person and enjoyment of jokes embodying the freer spirit of modernism, as his forced emigration from Nazi Germany reflected its dark authoritarian opposition. His theory of the relativity of time and space rejected Newton's laws supposedly set by God, the Final Cause. The universe was freed to expand. As with the popular entertainers Jack Benny and Danny Kaye, Einstein being Jewish did not seem to matter in modern America.

The Indian New Deal was radically antimodern for John Collier, a powerful push to save primitive, earthy, soulful communities from the horrors of twentieth-century warmongering capitalism (Jenkins 2004:88–89). For Harold Ickes, it was Progressive, fulfilling principles of social justice his party saw promised in American democracy. Nathan Margold and Felix Cohen felt injustices to Indians as sons of Jews who similarly suffered dispossession, massacres, and their religion banned. Unlike their families in Europe who were denied citizens' rights, Margold and Cohen were legally full citizens of the United States of America, and so were the Indians, since 1924. Law was an instrument they were entitled to use to gain equality in practice, as it stood in principle. Young Cohen innocently went along with Collier's paternalism when he was hired in 1933, inexperienced with the lives of Indians except for the few working with Boas at Columbia. Those Indian congresses Collier held preliminary to the Indian Reorganization Act opened Cohen's eyes to that paternalism, to the stranglehold it maintained over First Nations. With his philosophical inclination to legal realism, Felix saw his mitzvah was to find a lawful foundation to free Indian citizens from Anglo domination. Working as a civil servant in 1930s Washington, he knew that as a Jew, he had to be circumspect. The *Handbook of Federal Indian Law*'s assertion of the principle of inherent sovereignty is a stunning challenge to four centuries of Anglo arrogance brooking no brake upon its drive for supremacy.

"Settler sovereignty" is the term historian Lisa Ford uses for the claims of British settlers in the American and Australian colonies. Closely analyzing the histories of Georgia in the United States and of New South Wales in Australia, she shows that colonizers in both regions initially respected indigenous communities' jurisdiction over the persons of their members when defining and dealing with crimes, as reciprocally, settlers assumed the right to deal with their own people. In other words, jurisdiction was phrased in terms of persons, not territory. Increase in numbers of invading settlers, their farms and towns, changed the landscape. When colonists in

Georgia could look around and see their kind filling the land, by 1802 (Ford 2010:196), they presumed to hold jurisdiction over the territory they had settled, and over the persons residing in it. Court cases culminating in Marshall's trilogy had two sources, states' rights versus federal power and contestation between First Nations and intruders. Indians' removal beyond the Mississippi resolved both issues for settlers, taking First Nations' right to occupancy of their lands, acknowledged by Marshall, to be a right not to original territory but to acreage needed for subsistence, therefore tenable in Oklahoma when denied in Georgia.

Surveying historians' discussions of states and sovereignty, James Sheehan noted, "Initially [in Europe], sovereign boundaries were jurisdictional and personal, marking the extent of sovereigns' authority over their subjects. Over time, these boundaries became increasingly spatial, marking the territorial limits within which sovereign power could be exercised" (2006:3). Georgia versus the Cherokee Nation in the early nineteenth century is not solely a question of settler sovereignty; the contest was part of the long transition from feudal to modern government.

Realizing that colonization of North America was taking place over the same centuries when modern nation-states evolved in Europe makes Justice Marshall's struggles to figure out Indians' and settlers' competing claims more than quieting Georgia belligerence and Cherokee retribution. The United States was a pioneer in constructing a federal union of states, before Switzerland (1848), Italy (1861), or Germany (1871). Nazi expansion was a throwback to earlier Europe when raw military power overrode legitimate governments (Sheehan 2006:12). Sovereignty is an ideal of a *super regnum*, and it is never stable because power is never equitably distributed among all residents of a territory. Thus for Margold and Cohen to state that Indian nations retain "inherent sovereignty" was to boldly appeal to an ideal only imperfectly manifest in any political entity.

Sophisticated and well versed in legal history and jurisprudence, Margold and Cohen were arguing in a fallible human world for an ideal they knew was beyond their reach. Margold, the senior, staked the position for rejecting paternalism, and Cohen soon gained enough experience in Washington to craft the revolution. Their mode of claiming, of making points for, the ideal of inherent sovereignty in full cognizance of opponents' arguments is a Jewish exercise in the sense of philosopher Gimbel's Jewish science exemplified by Einstein. Even CCNY's best and brightest cannot command the totality of knowledge in God's universe; we can only discuss together what we perceive and what we have been taught, to illuminate how we may live righteously. Gimbel (2012:213) proposes that the

Talmudic or Jewish style centers on accepting that there are "different frames of reference"—hence, for example, a general theory of relativity—each of which has some validity in illuminating the search for knowledge. Granting this, it is still incumbent upon us to endeavor to discover which ideas seem more likely to fulfill our basic mitzvah so clearly spoken by Rabbi Hillel. Brodkin agrees: "To do good works (however understood) for a community larger than one's family and self is still at the center of Jewishness as a this-worldly system of meaning" (1998:186). For Margold and Cohen, whose parents emigrated to a land promising life, liberty, and the pursuit of happiness to everyone, the glaring oppression of Indian people called for them, the fruit of their parents' quest, to use their gifts to relieve that injustice.

Inherent Sovereignty?

So, inherent sovereignty is an ideal; it is not a material object like a constitution. The new United States held a Constitutional Convention to produce a thing, a document, to materialize its sovereignty. Looked at from this perspective, Cohen's labor to steer Indian tribes into writing constitutions and charters was perhaps not naïve. To the contrary, he knew, realist that he was, that holding an actual legal constitution document physically manifested sovereignty. From one standpoint, on behalf of the First Nations he was beating the Man at his own game, playing by the white man's rules to win a degree of real sovereignty. This was not paternalism, although it appealed as such to John Collier's sense of noblesse oblige. Those constitutions and business corporation charters of the IRA were not simple socialist models, and farther yet from Collier's romantic primordial communalism. They were instruments formally construed to combat OIA domination, however hamstrung by Collier's insistence on Interior veto power.

Entrenched power may seem to be dammed, as by the 1934 Wheeler-Howard Act, only to surge out again in backlash, as in Burton Wheeler's effort to rescind his act. *United States v. Lara* (2004) is one of a series of recent Supreme Court cases revealing the morass on which First Nations sovereignty rests. As befits a capitalist nation built on Locke's elevation of private property, these cases debate lawsuits about jurisdiction, civil as well as criminal, over non-Indians on tribal lands. The issue in *Lara* was whether Billy Lara, a Turtle Mountain Chippewa living on his wife's reservation, could be prosecuted by her tribe for assaulting a federal police officer on her reservation. Complicating the issue was whether the federal government could then prosecute Lara for the same crime. Double jeopardy? No, said the Court, because the two prosecutions were by "separate sovereigns." Two sovereigns; logically, that would invalidate Congress's plenary power over Indian tribes. Justice Clarence Thomas wrote a concurrent opinion in *Lara*, stating flatly, "tribes either are or are not separate sovereigns, and our federal Indian law cases untenably hold both positions simultaneously" (quoted in Williams 2005:159). Thomas held that unlike states, Indian tribes' powers are not spelled out in the US Constitution, and therefore they are not protected as are states' rights. Justice Thomas holds a frame of reference different from Felix Cohen's. A libertarian would go beyond both to claim that every individual person has inherent sovereignty not to be impinged upon.

Felix Cohen invoked a metaphysical ideal to frame the structure he built in the *Handbook of Federal Indian Law*. Before that, he wrote legislation pulling Indian nations into the paradigm under which the United States operates, governance under constitutions and business under corporate charters. Justice Thomas astutely pointed out that we really can't have it both ways, First Nations as sovereigns and federally recognized Indian tribes under congressional jurisdiction. Richard Nixon moved toward the libertarian pole in explicitly choosing "self-determination" as the principle of a revised Indian policy. Although as illusory as "inherent sovereignty," "self-determination" avoids the head-on clash of jurisdictions. It also continues Cohen's realist construction in that the "selves" it means to address are corporations.

The continuing force of treaties between Indian nations and the United States and the principle of inherent sovereignty found also in states' rights under federalism are the pillars upon which rest federal Indian law after Cohen. Both are attacked by controversies over Congress's plenary powers. Different frames of reference held by politicians, jurists, political scientists, First Nations leaders, and ordinary Americans in and near reservations or in regions with few Indians, hold off any final resolution of issues. Felix Cohen constructed a frame of reference based on Social Democrat ideals of community and of revolution through the ballot box, infused by Franz Boas's deconstruction of racism. He left federal employment when the conservative backlash unleashed by Roosevelt's death showed him that litigating as counsel to tribes would help them more than continuing as a relatively low-level civil servant. His tragic early death left the arena more open to other frames of reference.

Back to that bar in a reservation border town. Does the Jew put his hand on the Indian's shoulder and tell the bartender to give each of them a beer? Does he stalk out of the bar and walk with the Indian over to the Indian bar on the scruffy side street? What would Rabbi Hillel say? Perhaps our Jew should consult with the Native American Rights Fund, headed by a cousin of Roger Echo-Hawk, to see whether they are pursuing legal action against the blatant racism in those border towns. If Felix Cohen had lived, he likely would have offered his remarkable talents to these Indian lawyers, whose cases included Elouise Cobell's class-action lawsuit for billions of dollars withheld from Indian people by the federal government. And Lucy Kramer Cohen? Never remarrying, she found her niche in the US Public Health Bureau as a wise and humane economist, statistician, and editor, becoming a beloved and honored senior problem solver—Boas's legacy.

Notes

Acknowledgments

1. Stultifying bureaucracy sapped expectations of the "Indian New Deal." For example, a Klallam community on Puget Sound, Washington, eagerly planned small homes and farms on land restored to them in 1936. White settlers from whom the land was purchased used a private electric power line they had cooperated to build. They were willing to sell the utility to the Klallam for $2,643. The Klallam's agent applied to the Office of Indian Affairs for the money, explaining that electricity was necessary to bring the families out of the squalor they had endured. The Office of Indian Affairs replied,

> It does not appear that funds appropriated for the purchase of lands under the provisions of the Indian Reorganization Act of June 18, 1934, are applicable to the purchase of power transmission lines or telephone lines, inasmuch as the authority contained therein extends only to the purchase of lands, interest in lands, water right and surface rights. It is possible that revolving credit funds could be used to finance the Indians . . . once the Indians have completed organization and incorporation under the Indian Reorganization Act. Until that time it will apparently be necessary that each Indian needing electrical energy or telephone connections will have to arrange to pay the existing company its going rates. (quoted in Boyd 2009:16)

Chapter 1

1. Beinecke Library, Lucy Kramer Cohen (LMK) Papers, box 3, folder "Membership Cards"; box 1, folder 2, "Correspondence, courses, conferences, causes, jobs, personal 1937–1939."

2. "Hillel the Elder," Wikiquote, http://en.wikiquote.org/wiki/Hillel_the_Elder;

"Hillel the Elder," Wikipedia, http://en.wikipedia.org/wiki/Rabbi_Hillel, accessed January 3, 2011.

3. Felix Cohen to Joe Lash, December 10, 1943, Beinecke Library, LMK Papers, box 3, folder "Felix S. Cohen Personal correspondence 1942."

4. The phrase is from Chief Justice John Marshall, in *Cherokee Nation v. Georgia*, 1831. Marshall used the word "nation" rather than "tribe," and I follow his usage, now official in Canada as "First Nations," in this book.

5. Grant's program echoes the words of Augustine, Bishop of Hippo, in *City of God*, book 19, chapter 12, 426 AD. See my *Militant Christianity: An Anthropological History* (Kehoe 2012:27).

6. Readers may recall Laura Ingalls Wilder's series of "Little House" books, and the television series, describing her childhood on the homesteading frontier. Her father, "Pa" Ingalls, never fulfilled the ideal of establishing his family upon a homestead by decades of steady improvements upon the farm. Small farms were not the panacea for a perfect republic.

Chapter 2

1. Most of the larger eastern First Nations had been forced to Oklahoma Territory by the 1830 Indian Removal Act. These included those conventionally termed the "Five Civilized Tribes" (Creek [Muskogee], Cherokee, Choctaw, Chickasaw, and Seminole). Others in Oklahoma included the Osage, who had purchased the land they lived on when they were dispossessed of their homeland on the Missouri River.

Chapter 3

1. Lyndon LaRouche Watch, http://lyndonlarouchewatch.org/larouche0british7A .pdf, accessed March 2, 2011, site now discontinued; Lyndon LaRouche Watch, "Jews and the Constitution and Courts," http.//www.lyndonlarouche.org/larouche-british7A .pdf, accessed October 25, 2013; "How the Jews Forced America into World War II," http://lyndonlarouche.org/larouche-british12.pdf, accessed October 25, 2013.

2. Wilson had considered Brandeis for his cabinet in 1913.

3. Oliver Wendell Holmes Sr., father of the Supreme Court justice, used the phrase "Boston Brahmins" in an 1861 novel, *Elsie Venner*, referring to the castelike exclusivity of the Puritan-descended leading families of Boston and Cambridge.

4. "List of Jewish Political Milestones in the United States," Wikipedia, http:// en.wikipedia.org/wiki/List_of_Jewish_political_milestones_in_the_United_States, accessed March 22, 2011.

5. Pound 1908, quoted in "Judicial Discretion in the Law of Torts," *Harvard Law Review* 35: 68–70.

6. Beinecke Library, LMK Papers, WA MSS S-2635, box 3, folder "1934–1959"; WA MSS S-2635, box 1, folder 2.

7. Letters from Felix Cohen to Norman Thomas, November 8, 1933, and reply from Thomas, November 14, 1933, Joseph P. Lash Papers, box 50, folder 9, Franklin D. Roosevelt Library, quoted in Tsuk 2001:206, 210.

Chapter 4

1. Beinecke Library, LMK Papers, box 1, folder 1, "Correspondence 1937–1939," letter March 31, 1937, from Katherine S. Doty, Barnard.
2. Beinecke Library, LMK Papers, box 1, folder 2, "Correspondence. Courses, conferences, causes, jobs, personal 1937–1939."
3. Beinecke Library, LMK Papers, box 1, folder "Correspondence 1928–1932."
4. Beinecke Library, LMK Papers, box 1, folder 4, "Correspondence 1935–1936," letter from Irving [Kahn], October 7, 1936.
5. Beinecke Library, LMK Papers, box 1, folder 1, box 12, folder, "Job search circa 1947."
6. Beinecke Library, LMK Papers, box 1, folder 2, letters from Joseph Herzstein, MD, and Mollie (no surname).
7. Beinecke Library, LMK Papers, box 1, folder "Correspondence, misc.—important 1931–1932."
8. See Katz 2012:202–3 on the New York Rebel Arts socialist arts group. Beinecke Library, LMK Papers, box 2, folder "Cohen, Francis S. [*sic*] & Lucy K. Activities 1930s"; box 1, folder 3, "Correspondence. Courses, conferences, causes, jobs, personal 1937–1939."
9. IRG members listed in 1933: Felix S. Cohen, PhD, LLB; Elizabeth Dublin, BA; Mary Dublin, BA; Maurice Goldbloom, MA; Theodore Haas, BA, LLB; Jerome R. Hellerstein, MA, LLB; Dora Horn, BA; Irving Kahn; Ruth Perl Kahn, BA; Lucy M. Kramer, MA; Joseph P. Lash, BA; George Marsall, PhD; Florence Mishnun, BA; Inez Pollak, BA; David Ryshpan, BA; Ruth Schechter, BA; J. J. Stone, BA, LLB; Morton Yohalem, BA, LLB. George Marshall, with a PhD in economics, was a son of Louis Marshall, a highly successful civil rights lawyer whose own father had emigrated from Germany after the revolutions of 1848, and a brother of Collier's forestry chief, Bob Marshall. Elizabeth Dublin married George Marshall, and the couple, like the Cohens, went to Washington in 1934 to work in the New Deal. Advisors to the group are listed as: Dean [of Duke University Law School] Justin Miller, professors Evelyn Burns, Morris R. Cohen, David Saposs, Paul F. Brissenden, Theresa Wolfson, Miss Grace Hutchins, and Mr. Solon De Leon (Beinecke Library, LMK Papers, box 1, folder 4, "1933–1934").
10. Beinecke Library, LMK Papers, box 12, folder "Job search circa 1947."
11. Beinecke Library, LMK Papers, box 12, folder "Job search circa 1947."
12. Beinecke Library, LMK Papers, box 12, folder "Job search circa 1947."
13. Beinecke Library, LMK Papers, box 12, folder "printed material and research notes on Indians 1935–1938."
14. Lucy Kramer Cohen, "A Survey of Social Problems in the Production and Consumption of Foods—an Analysis of Fields for Research," Social Sciences Research Council, November 1934.
15. Beinecke Library, LMK Papers, box 3, folder "Industrial Research Group Files, proposed constitutions, charters, by-laws," letter November 12, 1934.
16. Beinecke Library, LMK Papers, box 12, folder "printed material and research notes on Indians 1935–1938."
17. Beinecke Library, LMK Papers, box 11, folder "Correspondence and writing related to Indian work 1930s."

18. Beinecke Library, LMK Papers, box 11, folder "Correspondence and writing related to Indian work 1930s," Collier letter March 12, 1938, to Civil Service Commission.

19. Beinecke Library, LMK Papers, box 11, folder "Correspondence and writing related to Indian work 1930s," undated handwritten letter draft. Phinney was hired by the BIA as a field agent after he returned from Leningrad; he completed assignments in Minneapolis, Albuquerque, Denver, the Navajo Reservation, and, finally, for five years before his untimely death at age forty-six, as superintendent at his home agency in Idaho. A special issue of *Journal of Northwest Anthropology* 38(1), Spring 2004, memorializes Phinney with a biographical article by William Willard and other articles based on his research with his own Numipu people.

20. Beinecke Library, LMK Papers, box 1, folder "1933–1934," three pages from 3 × 5 notepad.

21. Beinecke Library, LMK Papers, box 11, folder "Papers from collaboration with Felix S. Cohen on Indian affairs. 1930s," emphasis in original.

22. Beinecke Library, LMK Papers, box 1, folder 4, letter from Schechter July 11, 1934.

23. In an interview with the author, December 3, 2007, Charlotte Tuttle Westwood Walkup remarked that Cohen hired women law graduates because women at the top of their law classes were less likely than men to be offered desirable law firm positions and were willing to work for the government at relatively lower salaries than male classmates.

24. Beinecke Library, LMK Papers, box 1, folder 3 of "Correspondence, courses, conferences, causes, jobs, personal 1937–1939," and Lucy's telegram box 2, folder "Misc. from Lucy Kramer Cohen's desk top drawer 1935–1937."

25. Beinecke Library, LMK Papers, box 1, folder "Correspondence 1928–1932," letter misplaced in this folder.

26. Beinecke Library, LMK Papers, box 12, folder "printed material and research notes on Indians 1935–1938."

27. Ella Deloria to Franz Boas, letter, August 25, 1935, Boas Papers, American Philosophical Society.

28. Beinecke Library, LMK Papers, box 2, folder "Misc. from Lucy Kramer Cohen's desk top drawer 1935–1937."

29. Beinecke Library, LMK Papers, box 1, folder 2, "Correspondence, courses, conferences, jobs, personal 1937–1939."

30. Beinecke Library, LMK Papers, box 12, folder "correspondence, research notes on Indian history, culture, and language circa 1935," letter dated July 18, 1936.

31. Beinecke Library, LMK Papers, box 11, folder "Correspondence and writing related to Indian work 1930s."

32. In 2007 Michael Chabon published a novel, *The Yiddish Policemen's Union*, describing the Jewish colony in Alaska that might have existed had Ickes's proposal been successful.

33. Transcription from the original in the Beinecke Library by Yonatan Moss; I am grateful to Mr. Moss for taking time from his own research to transcribe and translate this smudged pencil document for me. This transcription working from a scan of Felix's page, and this translation are by Ben Sadock and Joshua Snider (personal communication January 26, 2014); they also searched for identification of the poem and with the assistance of Professor Dov-Ber Kerler of Indiana University, found a song, "Jacob's Voice," with the same first line in the catalog of the National Library of Israel

Music Library: "Yiddish folk text . . . English, Babette Deutsch, music Artur Wolf, © Dec. 7, 1939." Deutsch (1895–1982) was a poet in New York. Tracking down the song, Mr. Sadock found it is similar to, but not the same as, the poem Felix Cohen hastily wrote down, perhaps before late 1939.   I am very grateful to Joshua Snider and Ben Sadock for many hours of work on the text and translation, and assiduously pursuing the quest for the source of the poem.

Felix and Lucy were living at 401 Twenty-Third St. in October 1935.

34. Beinecke Library, LMK Papers, box 1, folder "Correspondence, courses, conferences, causes, jobs, personal 1937–1939."

Chapter 5

1. Felix Cohen himself made the link between Jews and American Indians: "The Indian plays much the same role in our American society that the Jews played in Germany" (1953:389).

2. Declaration of Independence, 1776, twenty-seventh "Fact": "He has excited domestic insurrections amongst us, and has endeavoured to bring on the inhabitants of our frontiers, the merciless Indian Savages whose known rule of warfare, is an undistinguished destruction of all ages, sexes and conditions."

Chapter 6

1. Historian Francis Paul Prucha remarked in 1984, "Paternalism seems abiding" (1986:402).

Chapter 7

1. Felix Cohen, letter to M. Anderson, October 27, 1944, Beinecke Library, LMK Papers, box 3, folder "Felix S. Cohen Personal Correspondence 1941."

2. Felix Cohen, "The Social and Economic Consequences of Exclusionary Immigration Laws," *National Lawyers Guild Quarterly* (October 1939), reprinted and now online at www.lexisnexis.com/

3. Felix Cohen to M. Anderson, October 27, 1944.

4. Margold to Cohen, July 7, 1941, in Beinecke Library, LMK Papers, box 3, folder "Felix S. Cohen Correspondence Personal—1941," his emphasis.

5. Margold to Cohen, August 11, 1941, in Beinecke Library, LMK Papers, box 3, folder "Felix S. Cohen Correspondence Personal—1941," his emphasis.

Chapter 8

1. Felix Cohen and Lucy Cohen, Beinecke Library, LMK Papers, draft, box 11, folder "Correspondence and writing related to Indian work 1930s," Cohens' brackets.

2. Albert Wahrhaftig recounts how, during his participation in the 1963–1966 Carnegie Corporation Cross-Cultural Education Project among eastern Oklahoma Cherokee, he was asked to serve as note-taking secretary to the Original Cherokee Community Organization. Only Cherokee were to be allowed into the group's meetings; they were to be kept secret from whites. Members discussed whether that excluded Wahrhaftig. Finally, the Cherokee decided that "Jews are not white people but rather are like 'a tribe of Indians from the other side of the water'" (Wahrhaftig 2012: 37 n. 2).

3. Mountague Bernard, "On the Principle of Non-Intervention" (Oxford: J. H. and Jas. Parker, 1860), quoted in "Policy, Sociology, and Travels" 1861:548.

Chapter 9

1. Beinecke Library, LMK Papers, box 27, box 34. Lucy Kramer (the name she used professionally) deserves her own biography. Her niece Nancy Kramer Bickel (2012) did prepare a biographical DVD, "A Twentieth Century Woman: Lucy Kramer Cohen 1907–2007," available from Bickel at http://lucykramercohen.com/index.aspx. Lucy worked for the UN Food and Agriculture Organization, the Bureau of Labor Statistics, and the Non-ferrous Metals Commission, 1945–1947 and 1949; for Congresswoman Helen Gahagan Douglas in 1948 and 1950; at the Department of Labor's Bureau of Labor Statistics as an economist, then in the Mexican Farm Labor Program, 1950–1953; and as the editor of the country studies at the Washington Human Relations Area Files (WaHRAF, written for US Army use), 1955–1957, when they were declassified and transferred to Yale as HRAF under George P. Murdock. She was employed 1956–1957 on the President's Commission on Scientists and Engineers, National Science Foundation, then in 1958 found permanent employment with the US Public Health Service, retiring in 1989 amid many acclamations. While with Public Health, her assignments included work as economist, statistician, editor, and project manager; the citation with her 1988 Administrator's Award for Excellence describes her as "Technical Publications Writer-Editor, Office of Data Analysis and Management, Rockville, Maryland" (Karen Cohen Holmes, personal communication, June 11, 2013). For recreation, Lucy painted watercolors and was active in the Washington arts community. She continued involvement with national American Indian issues as a member of the board of directors of the Association on American Indian Affairs, from 1954 until, forty years later, the association decided that only Indians should serve on the board. Lucy, her two daughters, and their families treasured the family vacation home on Lake Clear in the Adirondacks, where the love of canoeing and hiking she had shared with Felix continued. Lucy died in her Washington home in 2007, not quite one hundred (information supplied by Nancy Kramer Bickel, http://lucykramer cohen.com/aboutlucy.aspx, accessed January 10, 2012).

2. Felix Cohen, letter to UFWA, Local 50 members, November 4, 1938, Beinecke Library, LMK Papers, box 1, folder "Industrial Research Group Files, proposed constitutions, charters, by-laws."

3. Alma Curry letters, Beinecke Library, LMK Papers, box 1, folder 3, "Correspondence, courses, conferences, causes, jobs, personal 1937–1939."

4. Felix Cohen, letter to Ted Haas, Beinecke Library, LMK Papers, box 3, folder 1, "Felix S. Cohen Personal correspondence 1942."

5. Nathan Margold, Department of the Interior, August 9, 1934, in *Opinions of the Solicitor of the Department of the Interior Relating to Indian Affairs 1917–1974* (Washington, DC: Government Printing Office), University of Oklahoma Law Center, http://thorpe.ou.edu/sol_opinions/p426-450.html.

6. Tribal Business Council to Commissioner Zimmerman, letter, April 1949, quoted in Rosier 2001:228.

Chapter 10

1. Ironically, the Navajo Nation enrolls only children of female members. The Martinez children were doubly denied.

2. Rietz continued as director of the American Indian Center until his death following surgery in 1971, at age fifty-six.

3. President Kennedy had announced his New Frontier program in 1960.

4. Native American Graves Protection and Repatriation Act, 1990.

5. National Museum of American History, http://americanhistory.si.edu, accessed June 30, 2012.

Chapter 11

1. Google Scholar, February 7, 2012; this count excludes citations to *The Handbook of Federal Indian Law.*

Sources by Chapter

Dedication: Kelly, William 1954
Acknowledgments: Boyd, Colleen 2009
Introduction: Gluckman, Max 1961; Kehoe, Alice 2006b; Roth, Cecil (1932) 1966; Uchmany, Eva Alexandra 2001; Wiessner, Siegfried 2008; Wilson, Woodrow 1918

Chapter 1. The Indian New Deal

Beinecke Library, Lucy Kramer Cohen Papers WA MSS S-2635; Bourdieu, Pierre 1977; Fischer, David Hackett, and James C. Kelly 2000; Gates, Paul Wallace 1973; Hietala, Thomas R. 1997; Ickes, Harold L. 1943; Jacobs, Margaret D. 1999; Kehoe, Alice Beck 2012; Lears, T. J. Jackson 1981; Miller, Robert J. 2008; "National Affairs" 1934; Prucha, Francis Paul 1986; Quinton, Amelia S. 1894; Robertson, Lindsay G. 2005; Taylor, M. Scott 2007; Wallace, Anthony F. C. 1999; Watkins, T. H. 1990; Williams, Robert A., Jr. 1999; Wissler, Clark [1938] 1971

Chapter 2. The Indian Reorganization Act

Biolsi, Thomas 1992; Clarke, Jeanne Nienaber 1996; Cohen, Felix S. 1942; Collier, John 1922; Deloria, Vine, Jr. 2002; Deloria, Vine, Jr., and Clifford Lytle 1984; Dunn, Susan 2010; Dyck, Noel 1991; Fisher, Donald 1993; French, Laurence Armand 2007; Goldman, Irving 1937; Hauptman, Laurence M. 1981; Holm, Tom 2005; Ickes, Harold L. 1943; Kelly, Lawrence C. 1983; Lear, Linda J. 1981; McLerran, Jennifer 2009; Mead, Margaret, ed. 1937; Parker, Alex et al. 1976; Pfister, Joel 2004; Philp, Kenneth R. 1977, 1986; Pommersheim, Frank 1995; Prucha, Francis Paul 1986, 1994; Rosier, Paul C. 2009; Smith, Jane F., and Robert M. Kvasnicka, eds. 1972; Soyer, Daniel 2012; Strong, John A. 2011; Taylor, Graham D. 1980; Turner, Charles C. 2005; Watkins, T. H. 1990; Wenger, Tisa 2009; White, Graham, and John Maze 1985

Chapter 3. "Frankfurter's Jewish Cabal"

Alexander, Michael 2001; Baker, Leonard 1984; Bickel, Nancy Kramer 2000; Bowen, Catherine Drinker 1943; Brodkin, Karen 1998; Bronitsky, Gordon 1990; Burt, Robert A. 1988; Crockett, Sam 1961; Frankfurter, Felix 1960; Howe, Irving 1976; Konvitz, Milton R. 2000; Lipset, Seymour Martin, and David Riesman 1975; McMillen, Christian W. 2007; Murphy, Bruce Allen 1982; "National Affairs: Jobs and Jews" 1934; Nye, Russel B. 1951; Pound, Roscoe 1908; Seidler, Murray B. 1961; Shuldiner, David P. 1999; Spyer, Daniel 2012; Spiro, Jonathan Peter 2009; Soyer, Daniel 2012; Tsuk, Dalia 2001; Tsuk Mitchell, Dalia 2007; "12 in 'Brain Trust' Called Socialists" 1934; Woeste, Victoria Saker 2012; Zeidler, Frank P. 2006

Chapter 4. Felix and Lucy

Bickel, Nancy K. 2000, 2011; Carpenter, Cari M. 2005; Cohen, Felix S. 1937; Cohen, Morris Raphael 1949; Collier, John 1954; Deloria, Vine, Jr., ed. 2002; Ewers, John C. 1978; Haas, Theodore H. 1947; Katz, Daniel 2012; Kramer Cohen, Lucy 1986; Rusco, Elmer R. 2000; Tsuk Mitchell, Dalia 2007; van Willigen, John 2002; Warren, Dave 1986; White, Richard 1983; Willard, William, and J. Diane Pearson, eds. 2004

Chapter 5. *The Handbook of Federal Indian Law*

Boas, Franz 1911; Clark, Blue 1994; Cohen, Felix S. 1942, 1953; Culhane, Dara 1998; Dyck, Noel 1991; Garry, Joseph R. 1954; Getches, David H., Charles F. Wilkinson, and Robert A. Williams, Jr. 1993; Goldschmidt, Walter Rochs, and Theodore H. Haas 1946; Haas, Theodore H. 1954; Laurence, Robert 1988; Martin, Jill E. 1995; Newton, Nell 2005; Price, Monroe E. 1973; Prucha, Francis Paul 1994; Reed, Stanley Forman 1955; Robertson, Lindsay G. 2005; Strickland, Rennard, et al.; Charles F. Wilkinson, Reid Peyton Chambers, Richard B. Collins, Carole E. Goldberg-Ambrose, Robert N. Clinton, David H. Getches, and Ralph W. Johnson, eds. 1982; Wilkinson, Charles 2005; Williams, Robert A., Jr. 1986

Chapter 6. The Indian Claims Commission

Bernardini, Wesley 2005; Cohen, Felix S. 1942, 1953; Cohen, Morris Raphael 1927; Cowger, Thomas W. 1999; Crum, Steven J. 1994; Farmer, Malcolm F. 2006, 2007; Getches, David H., Charles F. Wilkinson, and Robert A. Williams, Jr. 1993;

Jennings, Jesse D. 1973; Katz, Daniel 2012; Kerns, Virginia 2003; Krech, Shepard, III 2012; Locke, John 2003; Lurie, Nancy O. 1956; McMillen, Christian W. 2007; Metcalf, R. Warren 2002: Price, Monroe E. 1973; Prucha, Francis Paul 1986; Ray, Arthur J. 2006, 2008, 2010, 2012; Ronaasen, Sheree, Richard O. Clemmer, and Mary Elizabeth Rudden 1999; Rosenthal, Harvey D. 1990; Steward, Julian H. 1938; Strickland, Rennard, et al. eds. 1982; Tsuk Mitchell, Dalia 2007; Vansina, Jan 1985; Wilkinson, Charles 2005; Williams, Robert A., Jr. 1992; Yates, Frances A. 1966

Chapter 7. The Consequences of Being Jewish

Bentley, Matthew 2012; Beyer, William 1991; Cohen, Morris Raphael 1949; Dubrovsky, Gertrude Wishnick 1992; Feldstein, Stanley 1978; Fuchs, Lawrence H. 1958; Gilman, Sander L. 1996; Glazer, Nathan 1958; Gregory, Brad S. 2012; Haley, Bruce 1978; Halperin, Edward C. 2001; Hollinger, David A. 1996, 2002; Howe, Irving 1976; Hurtado, Albert L. 2012; Kaplan, Jeffrey 2000; Kobrin, Rebecca 2012; Lipset, Seymour Martin, and Everett Carl Ladd Jr. 1971; Merton, Robert K. 1994; Miller, Abraham H., and Euphemia V. Hall 1984; Parker, Dorothy R. 1992; Rosenfield, Leonora Cohen 1962; Sklare, Marshall 1971; Smith, Carol 2011; Veblen, Thorstein [1919] 1993; Wenger, Beth 1996

Chapter 8. Felix Cohen's Awakening

Biolsi, Thomas 1992; Burnette, Robert 1986; Cash, Joseph H., and Herbert T. Hoover 1985; Cohen, Felix 1935, 1939, 1949, n.d.; Cohen, Morris R. 1927; Costo, Rupert 1986; Cowger, Thomas W. 1999; Dyck, Noel 1983, 1991; Fowler, Loretta 2002; Gusfield, Joseph R. 1981; Haas, Theodore H. 1947; Harris, LaDonna 1986; Kehoe, Alice Beck 2006; Lyons, Oren 1986; McNickle, D'Arcy 1973, 1979; Medicine, Beatrice 2001, 2006; Mekeel, Scudder 1944; Old Person, Earl 1986; O'Neil, Floyd A. 1986; Parker, Dorothy R. 1992; "Policy, Sociology, and Travels" 1861; Price, David H. 2004; Rosier, Paul C. 2001; Sturm, Circe 2002; Tsuk Mitchell, Daria 2007; Wahrhaftig, Albert L. 2012; Wissler, Clark, and Alice Beck Kehoe 2012

Chapter 9. Of Counsel to Tribes

Bickel, Nancy Kramer, www.lucykramercohen.com, website developed by Nancy Kramer Bickel 2012; Cohen, Felix S. 1953; Fried, Frank, Harris, Shriver & Jacobson Company Profile; McMillen, Christopher 2007; Philp, Kenneth R. 1999; Rosier, Paul C. 2001; Tsuk Mitchell, Dalia 2007; US Supreme Court 1955; Wildenthal, Bryan H. 2003; Williams, Robert A., Jr. 2005; Wissler, Clark, and Alice Beck Kehoe 2012

Chapter 10. Sovereignty: Not So Simple

AILTP (American Indian Lawyer Training Program) 1988; Bennett, John W. 1996; Boas, Franz 1911; Bruyneel, Kevin 2012; Cobb, Daniel M. 2008; Cohen, Felix S. 1942; Cramer, Renée Ann 2005; Echo-Hawk, Roger 2007a, 2007b, 2010; Eisler, Kim Isaac 2000; Foley, Douglas E. 1995; Fried, Morton H. 1975; Galloway, Patricia 2006; Getches, David H., Charles F. Wilkinson, and Robert A. Williams Jr. 1993; Gorman, Joshua M. 2011; Hauptman, Laurence M., and Jack Campisi 1988; Kehoe, Alice Beck 1998; Kroeber, Alfred L. 1955; Lurie, Nancy O. 1961, 2012, 2013; Morris, Peter S. 2006; Old Person, Earl 2012; Sharrock, Susan R. 1974; Smith, Joshua 2010; Stapp, Darby C. 2012; Stocking, George W., Jr. 2000; Strickland, et al. 1982; Tax, Sol 1964; Washington, Jesse 2012; Weaver, Thomas 2012; Wilkinson, Charles F. 1987; Williams, Robert A., Jr. 2005; Wissler, Clark, and Alice Beck Kehoe 2012

Chapter 11. Jewish Science, Philosophy, and Jurisprudence

Adams, Henry 1918; Barber, Bernard 1952; Berman, Edward H. 1983; Boorstin, Daniel J. 1941; Cohen, Felix S. 1934, 1935, 1946, 1949; Fisher, Donald 1993; Gimbel, Steven 2012; Golding, Martin P. 1980; Hollinger, David A. 1975; Kevelson, Roberta 1996; Klingenstein, Susanne 1998; Lears, T. J. Jackson 1981; Mitelman, Geoffrey A. 2011; Nielsen, Waldemar A. 1972; Richardson, Theresa and Fisher, Donald, eds. 1999; Roback, Abraham Aron 1935; Rosenfield, Leonora Cohen 1962; Ross, Dorothy 1991; Tsuk, Dalia 2001; Tsuk Mitchell, Dalia 2007

Chapter 12. The White Man, the Jew, and the Indian

Brodkin, Karen 1998; Ford, Lisa 2010; Gimbel, Steven 2012; Jenkins, Philip 2004; Sheehan, James J. 2006; Williams Robert A., Jr. 2005

Bibliographic Essay

Sources for This Book

Focusing a study of the Indian New Deal on its lesser-known contributors, the New York Jews Nathan Margold, Felix Cohen, and Lucy Kramer Cohen, brings in two substantial research fields, American Indian ethnohistory and Jewish studies. Behind the immediate sources are my years of living with Indian friends and colleagues and even more years of living as an American Jew. I've tried to provide citations for my statements here, but some are what I know from experience. The writing style is anthropological rather than historiographical, citations in text rather than in long endnotes.

One spur to this book was the availability of Lucy Kramer Cohen's papers, deposited in Yale's Beinecke Library. Lucy lived nearly a hundred years, until 2007. She had put her husband's personal papers in the Beinecke years before. Her own joined them and were opened to researchers in 2010. For a few years before that, her niece, Nancy Kramer Bickel, worked through the papers, held by the family, to create a DVD biography, *A Twentieth Century Woman: Lucy Kramer Cohen 1907–2007*. Bickel generously shared her film transcripts and photos, answered my queries, and brought her cousins, Gene Cohen Tweraser and Karen Cohen Holmes, Felix and Lucy's daughters, into the discussions. These rounds of e-mails and Bickel's film illuminated much in the Beinecke boxes of Lucy's papers. Complementing the Cohen-Kramer cousins' knowledge has been Dalia Tsuk (Mitchell), biographer of Felix Cohen: *Architect of Justice: Felix S. Cohen and the Founding of American Legal Pluralism* (Cornell University Press, 2007). Rounding out sources on Felix Cohen is his widow's compendium of a selection of his principal papers: *The Legal Conscience: Selected Papers of Felix S. Cohen*, edited by Lucy Kramer Cohen (Yale University Press, 1960).

The foundation for analyzing the Indian New Deal is a combination of American First Nations ethnohistory and historical studies of US Indian policy. For the ethnohistory, I would refer readers to my textbook, *North American Indians: A Comprehensive Account* (Prentice-Hall, three editions, 1981, 1992, 2006). It includes bibliographies for each culture area and for contemporary affairs. For US Indian policy, there is Francis

Paul Prucha's *The Great Father: The United States Government and the American Indians* (University of Nebraska Press, two-volume full publication 1984, paperback without the full documentation 1986). It has been my great fortune to know Fr. Prucha as a colleague at Marquette University, to be able to ask him to clarify confusing events and documents (which abound in Indian policy records) and to test my interpretations by asking his opinions. Similarly, it has been my good fortune that Milwaukee is also the home of another outstanding student of American Indian affairs, anthropologist Nancy Oestrich Lurie. Like Fr. Prucha, Dr. Lurie has been a sounding board and source of facts and clarifications. Regarding the Indian New Deal, her report, as Sol Tax's principal assistant, on the American Indian Chicago Conference, "The Voice of the American Indian: Report on the American Indian Chicago Conference," *Current Anthropology* 2(5):478–500 (1961), and, equally drawn from participant observation, "The Indian Claims Commission," *Annals of the American Academy of Political and Social Science* 436:97–110 (1978), are essential sources.

Leading up to the Indian New Deal was more than a century of US policy of dispossessing American First Nations. Anthony Wallace's *Jefferson and the Indians: The Tragic Fate of the First Americans* (Belknap, 1999), Robert J. Miller's *Native America, Discovered and Conquered: Thomas Jefferson, Lewis and Clark, and Manifest Destiny* (University of Nebraska Press, 2008), Lindsay Robertson's *Conquest by Law: How the Discovery of America Dispossessed Indigenous Peoples of Their Lands* (Oxford University Press, 2005), and Lisa Ford's *Settler Sovereignty: Jurisdiction and Indigenous People in America and Australia, 1788–1836* (Harvard University Press, 2010) are good sources on the policy of dispossession. Robert A. Williams Jr.'s *The American Indian in Western Legal Thought: The Discourses of Conquest* (Oxford University Press, 1992) places US policy and language in the broad frame of European concepts of conquest.

The Indian New Deal itself had several phases. First was the 1920s shift away from dispossession, marked by the United States unilaterally bestowing citizenship in 1924 upon US-born Indians. Tisa Wenger's *We Have a Religion: The 1920s Pueblo Indian Dance Controversy and American Religious Freedom* (University of North Carolina Press, 2009), Jane F. Smith and Robert M. Kvasnicka, eds., *Indian-White Relations: A Persistent Paradox* (Howard University Press, 1972), and Tom Holm's *The Great Confusion in Indian Affairs: Native Americans and Whites in the Progressive Era* (University of Texas Press, 2005) cover this period. Next came the Indian Reorganization Act of 1934, for which the documents are reprinted in Vine Deloria Jr.'s *The Indian Reorganization Act, Congresses and Bills* (University of Oklahoma Press, 2002). Lawrence C. Kelly's *The Assault on Assimilation: John Collier and the Origins of Indian Policy Reform* (University of New Mexico Press, 1983) remains the best discussion of John Collier's crusade for an Indian New Deal. Collier's rejection of unrecognized East Coast tribes is discussed in John A. Strong's *The Unkechaug Indians of Eastern Long Island* (University of Oklahoma Press, 2011). Elmer Rusco's *A Fateful Time: The Background and Legislative History of the Indian Reorganization Act* (University of Nevada Press, 2000) details the act's history. After the IRA passed, Felix Cohen, backed by Harold Ickes and Nathan Margold, created the *Handbook of Federal Indian Law*, of which the first (1942) and subsequent versions are available in law libraries, and a facsimile 1942 edition may be purchased from University of Michigan Libraries. Getches, Wilkinson, and Williams Jr., *Cases and Materials on Federal Indian Law*, a series of editions, complements the *Handbook*. The landmark case in which the United States defended

Indians, at Margold's insistence, is in Christian McMillen's *Making Indian Law: The Hualapai Case and the Birth of Ethnohistory* (Yale University Press, 2007). Thomas Cowger's *The National Congress of American Indians: The Founding Years* (University of Nebraska Press, 1999) presents the educated, federally employed men who organized a counterweight to federal management of Indians, and Harvey Rosenthal's *Their Day in Court: A History of the Indian Claims Commission* (Garland, 1990) describes the Indian Claims segment of the Indian New Deal. A series by Kenneth Philp covers much of the Indian New Deal: *John Collier's Crusade for Indian Reform, 1920–1954* (University of Arizona Press, 1977), *Indian Self-Rule: First-Hand Accounts of Indian-White Relations from Roosevelt to Reagan* (Howe, 1986), and *Termination Revisited: American Indians on the Trail to Self-Determination, 1933–1953* (University of Nebraska Press, 1999).

A spin-off from the Indian Claims Commission was development of the academic field of ethnohistory. For a volume of essays on postwar anthropology, I solicited an overview of ethnohistory from one of its leading practitioners, Shepard Krech: "Thinking Big and Thinking Small: Ethnohistory in the 1970s," in *Expanding American Anthropology, 1945–1980: A Generation Reflects*, edited by Alice Beck Kehoe and Paul L. Doughty (University of Alabama Press, 2012). McMillen's book on the Hulapai case includes the stimulus to ethnohistory from such court hearings, and so do essays by Arthur Ray, a prominent practitioner, in *Pedagogies of the Global*, edited by Arif Dirlik (Paradigm, 2006), and in *Aboriginal Title and Indigenous Peoples*, edited by Louis Knafla and Haijo Westra (University of British Columbia Press, 2010). Ray's *Telling It to the Judge: Taking Native History to Court* (McGill-Queen's University Press, 2011) uses Canadian cases but is applicable to US court issues as well.

In spite of the Indian New Deal and the more revolutionary 1975 American Indian Self-Determination and Education Act, American First Nations continue on a rocky road. Robert Williams's *Like a Loaded Weapon: The Rehnquist Court, Indian Rights, and the Legal History of Racism in America* (University of Minnesota Press, 2005) is a hard-hitting exposé of regressive rulings. Bryan Wildenthal's *Native American Sovereignty on Trial* (ABC-Clio, 2003), Daniel Cobb's *Native Activism in Cold War America: The Struggle for Sovereignty* (University Press of Kansas, 2008), Renée Cramer's *Cash, Color, and Colonialism: The Politics of Tribal Acknowledgment* (University of Oklahoma Press, 2005), and Amy Den Ouden and Jean O'Brien's *Recognition, Sovereignty Struggles, and Indigenous Rights in the United States* (University of North Carolina Press, 2013), Charles Wilkinson's *American Indians, Time, and the Law* (Yale University Press, 1987), Circe Sturm's *Blood Politics: Race, Culture, and Identity in the Cherokee Nation of Oklahoma* (University of California Press, 2002), and Charles Turner's *The Politics of Minor Concerns: American Indian Policy and Congressional Dynamics* (University Press of America, 2005) describe contemporary legal and political issues.

Jewish studies is the other set of sources for this book. I've been a Jew since conception, raised in the liberal secular Social Democrat culture that Felix and Lucy Cohen represent, occasionally reading a book or article on my heritage. It was my own experience that sensitized me to the unacknowledged influence of this culture and, more narrowly, Franz Boas's influence on the Indian New Deal. I do not presume to be expert in Jewish studies—there's more than enough to keep up with in my bread-and-butter field of anthropology and American Indian studies—but I'll list some of the publications I found particularly enlightening or useful. Steven Gimbel's *Einstein's*

Jewish Science: Physics at the Intersection of Politics and Religion (Johns Hopkins University Press, 2012) gave me just the argument I needed: what specifically is Jewish in us liberal secular science-minded American Jews? Professor Gimbel generously sent me several chapters before publication and e-mailed stimulating discussion. Karen Brodkin's *How Jews Became White Folks: And What That Says About Race in America* (Rutgers University Press, 1998), as the title puts it, says it all. Robert Burt's *Two Jewish Justices: Outcasts in the Promised Land* (University of California Press, 1988) is one of several studies of Supreme Court justices Brandeis and Frankfurter. Frankfurter's own as-told-to autobiography, *Felix Frankfurter Reminisces* (Reynal, 1960) was sitting on my own bookshelf, legacy of my attorney father who admired that epitome of the successful American Jew. Morris Raphael Cohen was even more extraordinary; his autobiography, *A Dreamer's Journey* (Beacon, 1949) reads like a Yiddish fairy tale. Very odd, but telling, that such a man, famous for his cutting rationality, thought of himself as a dreamer. Several books by or edited by Marshall Sklare, *America's Jews* (1971), *The Jews: Social Patterns of an American Group* (1958), and *The Jew in American Society* (1974), cover the early- and mid-twentieth-century period of the Cohens' lives. Rebecca Kobrin's edited *Chosen Capital: The Jewish Encounter with American Capitalism* (Rutgers University Press, 2012) is especially relevant both to Jews and American Indians and to the socialism and Social Democrat activities of the Cohens' milieu.

Bibliography

Adams, Henry. 1918. *The Education of Henry Adams*. Boston: Houghton Mifflin.

AILTP (American Indian Lawyer Training Program). 1988. *Indian Tribes as Sovereign Governments*. Oakland, CA: American Indian Lawyer Training Program.

Alexander, Michael. 2001. *Jazz Age Jews*. Princeton, NJ: Princeton University Press.

Baker, Leonard. 1984. *Brandeis and Frankfurter: A Dual Biography*. New York: Harper and Row.

Barber, Bernard. 1952. *Science and the Social Order*. Glencoe, IL: Free Press.

Beinecke Library, Lucy Kramer Cohen (LMK) Papers WA MSS S-2635. New Haven, CT: Yale University.

Bennett, John W. 1996. "Applied and Action Anthropology." *Current Anthropology* 36 (Supplement): S23–S53.

Bentley, Matthew. 2012. "'Kill the Indian, Save the Man': Manhood at the Carlisle Indian School, 1879–1918." PhD diss., School of American Studies, University of East Anglia.

Berman, Edward H. 1983. *The Ideology of Philanthropy: The Influence of the Carnegie, Ford, and Rockefeller Foundations on American Foreign Policy*. Albany: State University of New York Press.

Bernardini, Wesley. 2005. *Hopi Oral Tradition and the Archaeology of Identity*. Tucson: University of Arizona Press.

Beyer, William. 1991. "Langston Hughes and Common Ground in the 1940s." *American Studies in Scandinavia* 23: 29–42.

Bickel, Nancy Kramer. 2000. Videotape interview with Lucy Kramer. In author's possession.

———. 2011. *Lucy Kramer Cohen: 1907–2007* [film script]. In author's possession.

———, prod. 2012. *A Twentieth Century Woman: Lucy Kramer Cohen 1907–2007* [film in DVD format]. http://lucykramercohen.com/.

Biolsi, Thomas. 1992. *Organizing the Lakota: The Political Economy of the New Deal on the Pine Ridge and Rosebud Reservations*. Tucson: University of Arizona Press.

Boas, Franz. 1911. *The Mind of Primitive Man*. New York: Macmillan.

Boorstin, Daniel J. 1941. *The Mysterious Science of the Law*. Cambridge, MA: Harvard University Press.

Bourdieu, Pierre. 1977. *Outline of a Theory of Practice*. Translated by Richard Nice. Cambridge: Cambridge University Press.

Bowen, Catherine Drinker. 1943. *Yankee from Olympus: A Biography of Oliver Wendell Holmes*. New York: Bantam.

Boyd, Colleen. 2009. "'The Indians Themselves Are Greatly Enthused': The Wheeler-Howard Act and the (Re-)Organization of Klallam Space." *Journal of Northwest Anthropology* 43(1): 3–26.

Brodkin, Karen. 1998. *How Jews Became White Folks: And What That Says About Race in America*. Piscataway, NJ: Rutgers University Press.

Bronitsky, Gordon. 1990. "Solomon Bibo: Jew and Indian at Acoma Pueblo." Albuquerque: The Link, Jewish Federation of Greater Albuquerque.

Bruyneel, Kevin. 2012. "Political Science and the Study of Indigenous Politics." Social Science Research Network, http://dx.doi.org/10.2139/ssrn.2061662.

Burnette, Robert. 1986. "Robert Burnette." In Philp 1986, 104–6.

Burt, Robert A. 1988. *Two Jewish Justices: Outcasts in the Promised Land*. Berkeley: University of California Press.

Buxbaum, Yitzchak. 1994. *The Life and Teachings of Hillel*. Northvale, NY: Jason Aronson.

Carpenter, Cari M. 2005. "Detecting Indianness: Gertrude Bonnin's Investigation of Native American Identity." *Wicazo Sa Review* 20(1): 139–59.

Cash, Joseph H., and Herbert T. Hoover. 1985. "The Indian New Deal and the Years That Followed: Three Interviews." In *The Plains Indians of the Twentieth Century*, edited by Peter Iverson, 107–32. Norman: University of Oklahoma Press.

Clark, Blue. 1994. *Lone Wolf v. Hitchcock: Treaty Rights and Indian Law at the End of the Nineteenth Century*. Lincoln: University of Nebraska Press.

Clarke, Jeanne Nienaber. 1996. *Roosevelt's Warrior: Harold L. Ickes and the New Deal*. Baltimore, MD: Johns Hopkins University Press.

Cobb, Daniel M. 2008. *Native Activism in Cold War America: The Struggle for Sovereignty*. Lawrence: University Press of Kansas.

Cohen, Felix S. 1934. "Modern Ethics and the Law." *Brooklyn Law Review* 1934. Reprinted in Cohen 1960, 17–32.

———. 1935. "Transcendental Nonsense and the Functional Approach." *Columbia Law Review* 1935. Reprinted in Cohen 1960, 33–76.

———. 1937. "Anthropology and the Problems of Indian Administration." *Southwestern Social Science Quarterly* 18: 1–10. Reprinted in Cohen 1960.

———. 1939. "How Long Will Indian Constitutions Last?" In *Indians at Work*. Reprinted in Cohen 1960, 222–29.

———. 1942. *Handbook of Federal Indian Law*. Washington, DC: Government Printing Office.

———. 1946. "The Role of Science in Government." *Social Science* 22: 195–205. Reprinted in Cohen 1960, 390–403.

———. 1949. "Indian Self-Government." In *The American Indian*. Reprinted in Cohen 1960, 305–14.

———. 1953. "The Erosion of Indian Rights, 1950–1953: A Case Study in Bureaucracy." *Yale Law Journal* 62(3): 348–90.

———. 1960. *The Legal Conscience: Selected Papers of Felix S. Cohen.* Edited by Lucy Kramer Cohen. New Haven, CT: Yale University Press.

———. n.d. Letter to Boas in Felix's handwriting, box 11, folder "Correspondence and writing related to Indian work 1930s," Lucy Kramer Cohen Papers, Beinecke Library, Yale University.

Cohen, Morris Raphael. 1927. "Property and Sovereignty." *Cornell Law Quarterly* 13: 8–30.

———. 1949. *A Dreamer's Journey: The Autobiography of Morris Raphael Cohen.* Glencoe, IL: Free Press.

Collier, John. 1922. "The Red Atlantis." *Survey* 48 (October 1922): 15–20, 63.

———. 1954. "The Genesis and Philosophy of Indian Reorganization Act Policies." In *Indian Affairs and the Indian Reorganization Act, the Twenty-Year Record,* edited by William H. Kelly, 2–8. Tucson: University of Arizona Press.

———. 1963. *From Every Zenith.* Denver: Sage.

Costo, Rupert. 1986. "Federal Indian Policy." In Philp 1986, 48–54.

Cowger, Thomas W. 1999. *The National Congress of American Indians: The Founding Years.* Lincoln: University of Nebraska Press.

Cramer, Renée Ann. 2005. *Cash, Color, and Colonialism: The Politics of Tribal Acknowledgment.* Norman: University of Oklahoma Press.

Crockett, Sam. 1961. *Frankfurter's Red Record.* Union, NJ: Christian Educational Association.

Crum, Steven J. 1994. *The Road on Which We Came: A History of the Western Shoshone.* Salt Lake City: University of Utah Press.

Culhane, Dara. 1998. *The Pleasure of the Crown: Anthropology, Law, and First Nations.* Burnaby, BC: Talonbooks.

Deloria, Vine, Jr., ed. 2002. *The Indian Reorganization Act, Congresses and Bills.* Norman: University of Oklahoma Press.

Deloria, Vine, Jr., and Clifford Lytle. 1984. *The Nations Within: The Past and Future of American Indian Sovereignty.* New York: Pantheon.

Den Ouden, Amy E., and Jean M. O'Brien, eds. 2013. *Recognition, Sovereignty Struggles, and Indigenous Rights in the United States.* Chapel Hill: University of North Carolina Press.

Dubrovsky, Gertrude Wishnick. 1992. *The Land Was Theirs: Jewish Farmers in the Garden State.* Tuscaloosa: University of Alabama Press.

Dunn, Susan. 2010. *Roosevelt's Purge: How FDR Fought to Change the Democratic Party.* Cambridge, MA: Belknap.

Dyck, Noel. 1983. "Representation and Leadership at a Provincial Indian Association." In *The Politics of Indianness,* edited by Adrain Tanner, 197–305. St. Johns, NL: Memorial University Institute of Social and Economic Research, Paper No. 12.

———. 1991. *What Is the Indian "Problem": Tutelage and Resistance in Canadian Indian Administration.* St. John's, NL: Institute of Social and Economic Research, Memorial University of Newfoundland.

Echo-Hawk, Roger. 2007a. *The Enchanted Mirror: When the Pawnees Became Indians.* Echo-hawk.com, http://www.echo-hawk.com/roger/em.

————. 2007b. "Pawnee Military Colonialism." Echo-hawk.com, http://www.echo-hawk.com/roger/pawnee_mil_colonialism.pdf.

————. 2010. *The Magic Children: Racial Identity at the End of the Age of Race*. Walnut Creek, CA: Left Coast Press.

Eisler, Kim Isaac. 2000. *Revenge of the Pequots: How a Small Native American Tribe Created the World's Most Profitable Casino*. New York: Simon and Schuster.

Ewers, John C. 2002. "Richard Sanderville, Blackfoot Indian Interpreter." In *American Indian Intellectuals of the Nineteenth and Early Twentieth Centuries*, edited by Margot Liberty, 132–43. Norman: University of Oklahoma Press.

Feldstein, Stanley. 1978. *The Land That I Show You: Three Centuries of Jewish Life in America*. Garden City, NY: Anchor.

Fischer, David Hackett, and James C. Kelly. 2000. *Bound Away: Virginia and the Westward Movement*. Charlottesville: University Press of Virginia.

Fisher, Donald. 1993. *Fundamental Development of the Social Sciences: Rockefeller Philanthropy and the United States Social Science Research Council*. Ann Arbor: University of Michigan Press.

Foley, Douglas E. 1995. *The Heartland Chronicles*. Philadelphia: University of Pennsylvania Press.

Ford, Lisa. 2010. *Settler Sovereignty: Jurisdiction and Indigenous People in America and Australia, 1788–1836*. Cambridge, MA: Harvard University Press.

Fowler, Loretta. 2002. *Tribal Sovereignty and the Historical Imagination: Cheyenne-Arapaho Politics*. Lincoln: University of Nebraska Press.

Frank, Gelya, and Carole Goldberg. 2010. *Defying the Odds: The Tule River Tribe's Struggle for Sovereignty in Three Centuries*. New Haven, CT: Yale University Press.

Frankfurter, Felix. 1960. *Felix Frankfurter Reminisces*. Recorded and edited by Harlan B. Phillips. New York: Reynal.

Freeman, Susan Tax. 2012. On Sol Tax, Some Notes. In *Action Anthropology and Sol Tax in 2012: The Final Word?*, ed. Darby C. Stapp. Journal of Northwest Anthropology, Memoir No. 8. 71–74.

French, Laurence Armand. 2007. *Legislating Indian Country: Significant Milestones in Transforming Tribalism*. New York: Peter Lang.

Fried, Frank, Harris, Shriver and Jacobson. 2012. "Company Profile, Information, Business Description, History, Background Information on Fried, Frank, Harris, Shriver and Jacobson." Reference for Business, http://www.referenceforbusiness.com/history2/24/Fried-Frank-Harris-Shriver-Jacobson.html, accessed March 7, 2012.

Fried, Morton H. 1975. *The Notion of Tribe*. Menlo Park, CA: Cummings.

Fuchs, Lawrence H. 1958. "Sources of Jewish Internationalism and Liberalism." In *The Jews: Social Patterns of an American Group*, edited by Marshall Sklare, 595–613. New York: Free Press.

Galloway, Patricia. 2006. *Practicing Ethnohistory: Mining Archives, Hearing Testimony, Constructing Narrative*. Lincoln: University of Nebraska Press.

Garry, Joseph R. 1954. "The Indian Reorganization Act and the Withdrawal Program." In *Indian Affairs and the Indian Reorganization Act: The Twenty Year Record*, edited by William H. Kelly, 35–37. Tucson: University of Arizona Press.

Gates, Paul Wallace. 1973. *Landlords and Tenants on the Prairie Frontier*. Ithaca, NY: Cornell University Press.

Getches, David H., Charles F. Wilkinson, and Robert A. Williams Jr. 1993. *Cases and Materials on Federal Indian Law*, 3rd ed. St. Paul, MN: West.

Gilman, Sander L. 1996. *Smart Jews: The Construction of the Image of Jewish Superior Intelligence*. Lincoln: University of Nebraska Press.

Gimbel, Steven. 2012. *Einstein's Jewish Science: Physics at the Intersection of Politics and Religion*. Baltimore, MD: Johns Hopkins University Press.

Glazer, Nathan. 1958. "The American Jew and the Attainment of Middle-Class Rank: Some Trends and Explanations." In *The Jews: Social Patterns of an American Group*, edited by Marshall Sklare, 138–46. New York: Free Press.

Gluckman, Max. 1961. "Ethnographic Data in British Social Anthropology." *Sociological Review* 9(1): 5–17.

———. 1964. "Introduction." In *Closed Systems and Open Minds: The Limits of Naïvety in Social Anthropology*, edited by Max Gluckman. New York: Aldine.

Golding, Martin P. 1980. "Realism and Functionalism in the Legal Thought of Felix S. Cohen." *Cornell Law Review* 66: 1032–57.

Goldman, Irving. 1937. "The Zuni Indians of New Mexico." In *Cooperation and Competition Among Primitive Peoples*, edited by Margaret Mead, 313–53. New York: McGraw-Hill.

Goldschmidt, Walter Rochs, and Theodore H. Haas. 1946. *Possessory Rights of the Natives of Southeastern Alaska; a Detailed Analysis of the Early and Present Territory Used and Occupied by the Natives of Southeastern Alaska*. Reprinted 1999 as *Haa Aani Our Land: Tlingit and Haida Land Rights and Use*, edited by Thomas F. Thornton. Seattle: University of Washington Press.

Gorman, Joshua M. 2011. *Building a Nation: Chickasaw Museums and the Construction of History and Heritage*. Tuscaloosa: University of Alabama Press.

Gregory, Brad S. 2012. *The Unintended Reformation: How a Religious Revolution Secularized Society*. Cambridge, MA: Belknap.

Gusfield, Joseph R. 1981. *The Culture of Public Problems: Drinking-Driving and the Symbolic Order*. Chicago: University of Chicago Press.

Haas, Theodore H. 1947. *Ten Years of Tribal Government Under I.R.A.* Chicago: United States Indian Service.

———. 1954. "The Indian Reorganization Act in Historical Perspective." In *Indian Affairs and the Indian Reorganization Act: The Twenty Year Record*, edited by William H. Kelly, 9–25. Tucson: University of Arizona Press.

Haley, Bruce. 1978. *The Healthy Body and Victorian Culture*. Cambridge, MA: Harvard University Press.

Halperin, Edward C. 2001. "The Jewish Problem in U.S. Medical Education, 1920–1955." *Journal of the History of Medicine and Allied Sciences* 56(2): 140–67.

Harris, LaDonna. 1986. "LaDonna Harris." In Philp 1986, 108.

Hauptman, Laurence M. 1981. *The Iroquois and the New Deal*. Syracuse, NY: Syracuse University Press.

Hauptman, Laurence M., and Jack Campisi. 1988. The Voice of Eastern Indians: The American Indian Chicago Conference and the Movement for Federal Recognition. *Proceedings of the American Philosophical Society* 132(4): 316–29.

Hietala, Thomas R. 1997. "'This Splendid Juggernaut': Westward a Nation and Its People." In *Manifest Destiny and Empire: American Antebellum Expansionism*, edited by Sam W. Haynes and Christopher Morris, 48–67. College Station: Texas A&M University Press.

Hollinger, David A. 1975. *Morris R. Cohen and the Scientific Ideal.* Cambridge, MA: MIT Press.

———. 1996. *Science, Jews, and Secular Culture.* Princeton, NJ: Princeton University Press.

———. 2002. "Why Are Jews Preeminent in Science and Scholarship? The Veblen Thesis Reconsidered." *Aleph* 2: 145–63.

Holm, Tom. 2005. *The Great Confusion in Indian Affairs: Native Americans and Whites in the Progressive Era.* Austin: University of Texas Press.

Howe, Irving. 1976. *World of Our Fathers: The Journey of the East European Jews to America and the Life They Found and Made.* New York: Simon and Schuster.

Hurtado, Albert L. 2012. *Herbert Eugene Bolton, Historian of the Borderlands.* Berkeley: University of California Press.

Ickes, Harold L. 1943. *The Autobiography of a Curmudgeon.* New York: Reynal and Hitchcock.

Jacobs, Margaret D. 1999. *Engendered Encounters: Feminism and Pueblo Cultures, 1879–1934.* Lincoln: University of Nebraska Press.

Jenkins, Philip. 2004. *Dream Catchers: How Mainstream America Discovered Native Spirituality.* New York: Oxford University Press.

Jennings, Jesse D. 1973. "The Short Useful Life of a Simple Hypothesis." *Tebiwa* 16: 1–9.

Kaplan, Jeffrey. 2000. *Encyclopedia of White Power: A Sourcebook on the Radical Racist Right.* Walnut Creek, CA: AltaMira.

Katz, Daniel. 2012. "The Multicultural Front: A Yiddish Socialist Response to Sweatshop Capitalism." In *Chosen Capital: The Jewish Encounter with American Capitalism,* edited by Rebecca Kobrin, 189–214. New Brunswick, NJ: Rutgers University Press.

Kehoe, Alice Beck. 1998. *The Land of Prehistory: A Critical History of American Archaeology.* New York: Routledge.

———. 2006a. *The Ghost Dance: Ethnohistory and Revitalization,* 2nd ed. Long Grove, IL: Waveland.

———. 2006b. *North American Indians: A Comprehensive Account,* 3rd ed. Upper Saddle River, NJ: Prentice-Hall.

———. 2012. *Militant Christianity: An Anthropological History.* New York: Palgrave Macmillan.

Kelly, Lawrence C. 1983. *The Assault on Assimilation: John Collier and the Origins of Indian Policy Reform.* Albuquerque: University of New Mexico Press.

Kelly, William H., ed. 1954. *Indian Affairs and the Indian Reorganization Act: The Twenty Year Record.* Tucson: University of Arizona Press.

Kerns, Virginia. 2003. *Scenes from the High Desert: Julian Steward's Life and Theory.* Champaign-Urbana: University of Illinois Press.

Kevelson, Roberta. 1996. *Peirce, Science, Signs.* New York: Peter Lang.

Klingenstein, Susanne. 1998. *Jews in the American Academy, 1900–1940.* Syracuse, NY: Syracuse University Press.

Kobrin, Rebecca. 2012. "The Chosen People in the Chosen Land: The Jewish Encounter with American Capitalism." In *Chosen Capital: The Jewish Encounter with*

American Capitalism, edited by Rebecca Kobrin, 1–11. New Brunswick, NJ: Rutgers University Press.

Konvitz, Milton R. 2000. *Nine American Jewish Thinkers*. New Brunswick, NJ: Transaction.

Kramer Cohen, Lucy. 1986. "Lucy Kramer Cohen" In Philp 1986, 71–72.

Krech, Shepard, III. 2012. "Thinking Big and Thinking Small: Ethnohistory in the 1970s." In *Expanding American Anthropology, 1945–1980: A Generation Reflects*, edited by Alice Beck Kehoe and Paul L. Doughty, 164–71. Tuscaloosa: University of Alabama Press.

Kroeber, Alfred L. 1955. "Nature of the Land-Holding Group." *Ethnohistory* 2: 303–14.

Laurence, Robert. 1988. "Learning to Live with the Plenary Power of Congress over the Indian Nations: An Essay in Reaction to Professor Williams' *Algebra*." *Arizona Law Review* 413: 416–19, 422–26, 435–37.

Lear, Linda J. 1981. *Harold L. Ickes: The Aggressive Progressive, 1874–1933*. New York: Garland.

Lears, T. J. Jackson. 1981. *No Place of Grace: Antimodernism and the Transformation of American Culture 1880–1920*. New York: Pantheon.

Lipset, Seymour Martin, and Everett Carll Ladd. 1974. Jewish Academics in the United States. In *The Jew in American Society*, ed. Marshall Sklare, 259–88. New York: Behrman.

Lipset, Seymour Martin, and David Riesman. 1975. *Education and Politics at Harvard*. New York: McGraw-Hill.

Locke, John. 2003. "Two Treatises of Government." In *Two Treatises of Government and A Letter Concerning Toleration*, edited by Ian Shapiro, 3–209. New Haven, CT: Yale University Press.

Lurie, Nancy O. 1956. Reply to Land Claims Cases. *Ethnohistory* 3:256–76.

———. 1961. "The Voice of the American Indian: Report on the American Indian Chicago Conference." *Current Anthropology* 2(5): 478–500.

———. 1978. "The Indian Claims Commission." *Annals of the American Academy of Political and Social Science* 436: 97–110.

Lyons, Oren. 1986. "Oren Lyons." In Philp 1986, 100.

Margold, Nathan R. 1931 (1922). "The Plight of the Pueblos." *The Nation* 132: 121–23.

Martin, Jill E. 1995. "'A Year and a Spring of My Existence': Felix S. Cohen and the Handbook of Federal Indian Law." *Western Legal History* 8: 34–60.

McLerran, Jennifer. 2009. *A New Deal for Native Art: Indian Arts and Federal Policy 1933–1943*. Tucson: University of Arizona Press.

McMillen, Christian W. 2007. *Making Indian Law: The Hualapai Land Case and the Birth of Ethnohistory*. New Haven, CT: Yale University Press.

McNickle, D'Arcy. 1973. *Native American Tribalism: Indian Survivals and Renewals*. New York: Oxford University Press.

———. 1979. "Anthropology and the Indian Reorganization Act." In *The Uses of Anthropology*, edited by Walter Goldschmidt, 51–60. Washington, DC: American Anthropological Association.

Mead, Margaret, ed. 1937. *Cooperation and Competition among Primitive Peoples*. New York: McGraw-Hill.

Medicine, Beatrice. 2001. "New Roads to Coping: Siouan Sobriety." In *Learning to Be an Anthropologist and Remaining "Native,"* 207–27. Urbana: University of Illinois Press.

———. 2006. *Drinking and Sobriety among the Lakota Sioux.* Walnut Creek, CA: AltaMira.

Mekeel, Scudder. 1944. "An Appraisal of the Indian Reorganization Act." *American Anthropologist* 46: 209–17.

Merton, Robert K. [né Meyer R. Schkolnick]. 1994. "A Life of Learning." American Council of Learned Societies Occasional Paper no. 25. Online at http://www.acls .org/Publications/OP/Haskins/1994_RobertKMerton.pdf, ISSN 1041-536X.

Metcalf, R. Warren. 2002. *Termination's Legacy: The Discarded Indians of Utah.* Lincoln: University of Nebraska Press.

Miller, Abraham H., and Euphemia V. Hall. 1984. "Jews, Radicals and Conservatives: A Review Essay." *Western Political Quarterly* 37(4): 665–77.

Miller, Robert J. 2008. *Native America, Discovered and Conquered: Thomas Jefferson, Lewis and Clark, and Manifest Destiny.* Lincoln: University of Nebraska Press.

Mitelman, Geoffrey A. 2011. "Why Can Judaism Embrace Science So Easily?" *Sinai and Synapses,* June 19. http://sinaiandsynapses.org/multimedia-archive/why-can-judaism-embrace-science-so-easily/.

Morris, Peter S. 2006. "Charles Ora Card and Mormon Settlement on the Northwestern Plains Borderlands." In *The Borderlands of the American and Canadian Wests,* edited by Sterling Evans, 172–82. Lincoln: University of Nebraska Press.

Murphy, Bruce Allen. 1982. *The Brandeis/Frankfurter Connection.* New York: Oxford University Press.

"National Affairs: Jobs and Jews." 1934. *Time,* May 21. http://www.time.com/time/magazine/article/0,9171,747415,00.html.

Newton, Nell. 2005. "Tribute to Lucy." Presentation honoring Lucy Kramer, October 28, at University of Connecticut School of Law, Hartford, upon publication of fourth edition of *Handbook of Indian Law.*

Nielsen, Waldemar A. 1972. *The Big Foundations: A Twentieth Century Fund Study.* New York: Columbia University Press.

Nye, Russel B. 1951. *Midwestern Progressive Politics.* East Lansing: Michigan State College Press.

Old Person, Earl. 1986. "Earl Old Person." In Philp 1986, 107–8.

———. 2012. "The Amskapi Pikuni from the 1950s to 2010." In *Amskapi Pikuni: The Blackfeet People,* by Clark Wissler and Alice Beck Kehoe, 177–80. Albany: State University of New York Press.

O'Neil, Floyd A. 1986. "The Indian New Deal: An Overview." In Philp 1986, 30–46.

Parker, Alex, Jerry Flute, Michael Cox, and Patricia Zell. 1976. *Report on Tribal Government, Task Force Two: Tribal Government.* Final Report to the American Indian Policy Review Commission. Washington, DC: US Government Printing Office.

Parker, Dorothy R. 1992. *Singing an Indian Song: A Biography of D'Arcy McNickle.* Lincoln: University of Nebraska Press.

Pfister, Joel. 2004. *Individuality Incorporated: Indians and the Multicultural Modern.* Durham, NC: Duke University Press.

Philp, Kenneth R. 1977. *John Collier's Crusade for Indian Reform, 1920–1954.* Tucson: University of Arizona Press.

———. ed. 1986. *Indian Self-Rule: First-Hand Accounts of Indian-White Relations from Roosevelt to Reagan.* Salt Lake City, UT: Howe Brothers.

———. 1999. *Termination Revisited: American Indians on the Trail to Self-Determination, 1933–1953*. Lincoln: University of Nebraska Press.

"Policy, Sociology, and Travels." 1861. *Westminster Review* 75: 544–57.

Pommersheim, Frank. 1995. *Braid of Feathers: American Indian Law and Contemporary Tribal Life*. Berkeley: University of California Press.

Pound, Roscoe. 1908. "Mechanical Jurisprudence." *Columbia Law Review* 8: 605–23.

Price, David H. 2004. "Tribal Communism under Fire: Archie Phinney and the FBI." *Journal of Northwest Anthropology* 38(1): 21–32.

Price, Monroe E. 1973. *Law and the American Indian: Readings, Notes and Cases*. Indianapolis, IN: Bobbs-Merrill.

Prucha, Francis Paul. 1986. *The Great Father: The United States Government and the American Indians*, abridged ed. Lincoln: University of Nebraska Press.

———. 1994. *American Indian Treaties: The History of a Political Anomaly*. Berkeley: University of California Press.

Quinton, Amelia S. 1894. "The Woman's National Indian Association." In *The Congress of Women: Held in the Woman's Building, World's Columbian Exposition, Chicago, U.S.A., 1893*, edited by Mary Kavanaugh Oldham Eagle, 71–73. Chicago: Monarch. http://digital.library.upenn.edu/women/eagle/congress/quinton.html.

Ray, Arthur J. 2006. "Anthropology, History, and Aboriginal Rights: Politics and the Rise of Ethnohistory in North America in the 1950s." In *Pedagogies of the Global: Knowledge in the Human Interest*, edited by Arif Dirlik, 89–112. Boulder, CO: Paradigm.

———. 2008. "Ethnohistory and the Development of Native Law in Canada: Advancing Aboriginal Rights or Re-inscribing Colonialism?" In *Métis-Crown Relations: Rights, Identity, Jurisdiction, and Governance*, edited by F. Wilson and M. Mallet, 1–26. Toronto: Irwin Law.

———. 2010. "From the US Indian Claims Commission Cases to Delgamuukw: Facts, Theories, and Evidence in North American Land Claims." In *Aboriginal Title and Indigenous Peoples: Canada, Australia, and New Zealand*, edited by Louis A. Knafla and Haijo Westra, 37–52. Vancouver: University of British Columbia Press.

———. 2011. *Telling It to the Judge*. Montreal and Kingston: McGill-Queen's University Press.

Reed, Stanley Forman. 1955. Opinion, *Tee-Hit-Ton Indians v. United States*, US Supreme Court, 348 US 272.

Richardson, Theresa, and Donald Fisher, eds. 1999. *The Development of the Social Sciences in the United States and Canada: The Role of Philanthropy*. Stamford, CT: Ablex.

Roback, Abraham Aron. 1935. "How Jews Think." *Time* 26(14): 39. http://www.time.com/time/magazine/article/0,9171,749142,00.html#ixzz11009WCRC.

Robertson, Lindsay G. 2005. *Conquest by Law: How the Discovery of America Dispossessed Indigenous Peoples of Their Lands*. New York: Oxford University Press.

Ronaasen, Sheree, Richard O. Clemmer, and Mary Elizabeth Rudden. 1999. "Rethinking Culture Ecology, Multilinear Evolution, and Expert Witnesses: Julian Steward and the Indian Claims Commission Proceedings." In *Julian Steward and the Great Basin: The Making of an Anthropologist*, edited by Richard O. Clemmer, L. Daniel Myers, and Mary Elizabeth Rudden, 170–202. Salt Lake City: University of Utah Press.

Rosenfield, Leonora Cohen. 1962. *Portrait of a Philosopher: Morris R. Cohen in Life and Letters*. New York: Harcourt Brace and World.

Rosenthal, Harvey D. 1990. *Their Day in Court: A History of the Indian Claims Commission*. New York: Garland.

Rosier, Paul C. 2001. *Rebirth of the Blackfeet Nation, 1912–1954*. Lincoln: University of Nebraska Press.

———. 2009. *Serving Their Country: American Indian Politics and Patriotism in the Twentieth Century*. Cambridge, MA: Harvard University Press.

Ross, Dorothy. 1991. *The Origins of American Social Science*. Cambridge: Cambridge University Press.

Roth, Cecil. (1932) 1966. *A History of the Marranos*. New York: Harper and Row.

Rusco, Elmer R. 2000. *A Fateful Time: The Background and Legislative History of the Indian Reorganization Act*. Reno: University of Nevada Press.

Seidler, Murray B. 1961. *Norman Thomas: Respectable Rebel*. Syracuse, NY: Syracuse University Press.

Sharrock, Susan R. 1974. "Crees, Cree-Assiniboines, and Assiniboines: Interethnic Social Organization on the Far Northern Plains." *Ethnohistory* 21: 95–122.

Sheehan, James J. 2006. "The Problem of Sovereignty in European History." *American Historical Review* 111(1): 1–15.

Shuldiner, David P. 1999. *Of Moses and Marx: Folk Ideology and Folk History in the Jewish Labor Movement*. Westport, CT: Bergin and Garvey.

Sklare, Marshall, ed. 1958. *The Jews: Social Patterns of an American Group*. New York: Free Press.

———. 1971. *America's Jews*. New York: Random House.

———. 1974. *The Jew in American Society*. New York: Behrman House.

Smith, Carol. 2011. "The Dress Rehearsal for McCarthyism." *Academe* 97(4): 48–51.

Smith, Jane F., and Robert M. Kvasnicka, eds. 1972. *Indian-White Relations: A Persistent Paradox*. Washington, DC: Howard University Press.

Smith, Joshua. 2010. "The Political Thought of Sol Tax: The Principles of Nonassimilation and Self-Government in Action Anthropology." *Histories of Anthropology Annual* 6: 129–70.

Soyer, Daniel. 2012. "Making Peace with Capitalism? Jewish Socialism Enters the Mainstream, 1933–1944." In *Chosen Capital: The Jewish Encounter with American Capitalism*, edited by Rebecca Kobrin, 215–33. New Brunswick, NJ: Rutgers University Press.

Spiro, Jonathan Peter. 2009. *Defending the Master Race: Conservation, Eugenics, and the Legacy of Madison Grant*. Burlington: University of Vermont Press.

Stapp, Darby C., ed. 2012. *Action Anthropology and Sol Tax in 2012: The Final Word?* Memoir No. 8. Richland, WA: Journal of Northwest Anthropology.

Steward, Julian H. 1938. *Basin-Plateau Aboriginal Sociopolitical Groups*. Bureau of American Ethnology Bulletin 120. Washington, DC: Government Printing Office.

Stocking, George W., Jr. 2000. "'Do Good, Young Man': Sol Tax and the World Mission of Liberal Democratic Anthropology." In *Excluded Ancestors, Inventible Traditions: Essays Toward a More Inclusive History of Anthropology*, edited by Richard Handler, 171–264. Madison: University of Wisconsin Press.

Strickland, Rennard, Charles F. Wilkinson, Reid Peyton Chambers, Richard B. Collins, Carole E. Goldberg-Ambrose, Robert N. Clinton, David H. Getches, and Ralph W. Johnson, eds. 1982. *Felix S. Cohen's Handbook of Federal Indian Law*. Charlottesville, VA: Michie Bobbs-Merrill.

Strong, John A. 2011. *The Unkechaug Indians of Eastern Long Island*. Norman: University of Oklahoma Press.

Sturm, Circe. 2002. *Blood Politics: Race, Culture, and Identity in the Cherokee Nation of Oklahoma*. Berkeley: University of California Press.

Synnott, Marcia Graham. 1979. *The Half-opened Door: Discrimination and Admissions at Harvard, Yale, and Princeton, 1900–1970*. Westport, CT: Greenwood.

Tax, Sol. 1964. "The Uses of Anthropology." In *Horizons of Anthropology*, edited by Sol Tax, 248–58. Chicago: Aldine.

Taylor, Graham D. 1980. *The New Deal and American Indian Tribalism*. Lincoln: University of Nebraska Press.

Taylor, M. Scott. 2007. "Buffalo Hunt: International Trade and the Virtual Extinction of the North American Bison." Working Paper 12969, National Bureau of Economic Research. http://www.nber.org/papers/w12969.

Tsuk, Dalia. 2001. "The New Deal Origins of American Legal Pluralism." *Florida State University Law Review* 29: 189–268.

Tsuk Mitchell, Dalia. 2007. *Architect of Justice: Felix S. Cohen and the Founding of American Legal Pluralism*. Ithaca, NY: Cornell University Press.

Turner, Charles C. 2005. *The Politics of Minor Concerns: American Indian Policy and Congressional Dynamics*. Lanham, MD: University Press of America.

"12 in 'Brain Trust' Called Socialists; They Are Members of Civil Liberties Union." 1934. *New York Times*, March 28, 3.

Uchmany, Eva Alexandra. 2001. "The Participation of New Christians and Crypto-Jews in the Conquest, Colonization, and Trade of Spanish America, 1521–1660." In *The Jews and the Expansion of Europe to the West, 1450 to 1800*, edited by Paolo Bernardini and Norman Fiering, 186–202. New York: Berghan.

US Supreme Court. 1955. *Tee-Hit-Ton Indians v. United States*, 348 U.S. 272 (1955). http://supreme.justia.com/cases/federal/us/348/272/case.html.

Vansina, Jan. 1985. *Oral Tradition as History*. Madison: University of Wisconsin Press.

van Willigen, John. 2002. *Applied Anthropology: An Introduction*, 3rd ed. Westport, CT: Bergin and Garvey.

Veblen, Thorstein. (1919) 1993. "The Intellectual Preeminence of Jews in Modern Europe." In *A Veblen Treasury*, edited by Rick Tilman, 285–92. Armonk, NY: M. E. Sharpe. (Original publication, *Political Science Quarterly* 34, 1919)

Wahrhaftig, Albert L. 2012. "The Carnegie Project: Action Anthropology Among the Oklahoma Cherokees." In *Action Anthropology and Sol Tax in 2012: The Final Word?*, edited by Darby C. Stapp, 23–39. Memoir No. 8. Richland, WA: Journal of Northwest Anthropology.

Wallace, Anthony F. C. 1999. *Jefferson and the Indians: The Tragic Fate of the First Americans*. Cambridge, MA: Belknap.

Warren, Dave. 1986. "Dave Warren." In Philp 1986, 60–64.

Washington, Jesse. 2012. "Who's an American Indian?" *News from Indian Country* 26(6): 1, 4–5.

Watkins, T. H. 1990. *Righteous Pilgrim: The Life and Times of Harold L. Ickes, 1874–1952*. New York: Henry Holt.

Weaver, Thomas. 2012. "From Applied to Practicing Anthropology." In *Expanding Anthropology, 1945–1980: A Generation Reflects*, edited by Alice Beck Kehoe and Paul L. Doughty, 88–93. Tuscaloosa: University of Alabama Press.

Wenger, Beth S. 1996. *New York Jews and the Great Depression: Uncertain Promise.* New Haven CT: Yale University Press.

Wenger, Tisa. 2009. *We Have a Religion: The 1920s Pueblo Indian Dance Controversy and American Religious Freedom.* Chapel Hill: University of North Carolina Press.

White, Graham, and John Maze. 1985. *Harold Ickes of the New Deal: His Private Life and Public Career.* Cambridge, MA: Harvard University Press.

White, Richard. 1983. *The Roots of Dependency: Subsistence, Environment, and Social Change among the Choctaws, Pawnees, and Navajos.* Lincoln: University of Nebraska Press.

Wiessner, Siegfried. 2008. "Indigenous Sovereignty: A Reassessment in Light of the UN Declaration on the Rights of Indigenous Peoples." *Journal of Transnational Law* 41(4): 1141–76.

Wildenthal, Bryan H. 2003. *Native American Sovereignty on Trial.* Santa Barbara, CA: ABC-Clio.

Wilkinson, Charles F. 1987. *American Indians, Time, and the Law.* New Haven, CT: Yale University Press.

———. 2005. *Blood Struggle: The Rise of Modern Indian Nations.* New York: W. W. Norton.

Willard, William, and J. Diane Pearson, eds. 2004. "Remembering Archie Phinney, a Nez Perce Scholar." *Journal of Northwest Anthropology* 38(1).

Williams, Robert A., Jr. 1986. "The Algebra of Federal Indian Law: The Hard Trail of Decolonizing and Americanizing the White Man's Indian Jurisprudence." *Wisconsin Law Review* 219: 260–65.

———. 1992. *The American Indian in Western Legal Thought: The Discourses of Conquest.* New York: Oxford University Press.

———. 1999. *Linking Arms Together: American Indian Treaty Visions of Law and Peace, 1600–1800.* New York: Routledge.

———. 2005. *Like a Loaded Weapon: The Rehnquist Court, Indian Rights, and the Legal History of Racism in America.* Minneapolis: University of Minnesota Press.

Wilson, Woodrow. 1918. "Fourteen Points." Speech to the US Congress, January 8. US Department of State, Office of the Historian. http://history.state.gov/milestones/19141920/FourteenPoints

Wissler, Clark. (1938) 1971. *Red Man Reservations.* New York: Collier. (Originally published as *Indian Cavalcade*)

Wissler, Clark, and Alice Beck Kehoe. 2012. *Amskapi Pikuni: The Montana Blackfeet.* Albany: State University of New York Press.

Woeste, Victoria Saker. 2012. *Henry Ford's War on Jews and the Legal Battle against Hate Speech.* Palo Alto, CA: Stanford University Press

Yates, Frances A. 1966. *The Art of Memory.* Chicago: University of Chicago Press.

Zeidler, Frank P. 2006. "Sewer Socialism and Labor: The Pragmatics of Running a Good City." In *Labor in Cross-Cultural Perspective*, edited by E. Paul Durrenberger and Judith E. Martí, 27–42. Lanham, MD: AltaMira.

Index

About the Author

Alice Beck Kehoe received her BA from Barnard College, and PhD from Harvard University, both degrees in anthropology. She is professor of anthropology, emeritus, at Marquette University in Milwaukee, Wisconsin.

Kehoe's first book was the college textbook *North American Indians: A Comprehensive Account*, 1981, with subsequent editions in 1992 and 2006. Other books by Kehoe on American Indians are *The Ghost Dance: Ethnohistory and Revitalization* (1989, second edition 2006), *America Before the European Invasions* (2002), and *Amskapi Pikuni: The Blackfeet People* (2012). In archaeology, she has published *The Land of Prehistory: A Critical History of American Archaeology* (1998) and *Controversies in Archaeology* (2008). She published two texts in critical thinking for Waveland Press, *Shamans and Religion: An Anthropological Exploration in Critical Thinking* (2000) and *The Kensington Runestone: Approaching a Research Question Holistically* (2005). *Militant Christianity: An Anthropological History* (2012) is Kehoe's study of the persistence of a pre-Christian worldview and ethos in the contemporary militant Christian Right.

Kehoe conducted ethnographic fieldwork with Northern Plains American Indians, particularly on the Montana Blackfeet Reservation where she continues regular visits, and in an Aymara community in Bolivia. With her late husband Thomas Kehoe, she excavated bison drives, tipi ring sites, boulder constructions, and a fur trade post, primarily in Saskatchewan (Canada), and she participated in excavations in France, the Czech Republic, Germany, and Bolivia.

Kehoe's research interests include American Indian history and contemporary circumstances, and history and theory of archaeology.